# A Telos-oriented Model of Genre Analysis
## —A Case Study of Corporate Website Genres

# 基于目的论的语类分析模式
## ——以公司网站语类为例

赖良涛 著

厦门大学出版社
XIAMEN UNIVERSITY PRESS
国家一级出版社
全国百佳图书出版单位

**图书在版编目(CIP)数据**

基于目的论的语类分析模式：以公司网站语类为例/赖良涛著.—厦门：厦门大学出版社，2012.8
ISBN 978-7-5615-4361-0

Ⅰ.①基… Ⅱ.①赖… Ⅲ.①类型学(语言学)—研究 Ⅳ.①H003

中国版本图书馆 CIP 数据核字(2012)第 195554 号

厦门大学出版社出版发行
(地址:厦门市软件园二期望海路 39 号 邮编:361008)
http://www.xmupress.com
xmup @ xmupress.com
沙县方圆印刷有限公司印刷
2012 年 8 月第 1 版 2012 年 8 月第 1 次印刷
开本:889×1240 1/32 印张:10.25
字数:305 千字 印数:1～1 500 册
定价:38.00 元

本书由浙江大学侨福建设基金资助出版

# 序

听到赖良涛博士即将出版《基于目的论的语类分析模式——以公司网站语类为例》一书，本人感到由衷的高兴，也向赖良涛博士表示祝贺。赖良涛 2007 年考入厦门大学攻读博士学位。在我的印象中，他学习刻苦用功，大量阅读语言学的有关书刊，不断提高自己的科研能力和科研水平，是一位非常勤奋的学生。2008 年，他申请国家公派研究生的博士生联合培养项目，到澳大利亚悉尼大学语言学系进行为期一年半的学习，在 James Martin 教授的指导下展开研究。

语类是系统功能语言学经常涉及的一种重要概念，因此有许多学者对其加以研究和探讨，赖良涛的著作能把系统功能语言学和社会学的理论与目的论结合起来，阐释语类的本质，提出分析语类的模型，并把它运用于公司网站语类的研究来加以验证，从而说明语类是以目的为导向的社会活动类型。该书采用级阶的概念，把语类目的分解为三个单位，并说明目的单位能决定语类的三个结构单位，目的单位和语类结构单位可构成复合体。该书并且用体现、实例化和个体化三个维度来说明语类分析的可操作性，使大家对语类能有更深刻的认识。

赖博士在回顾学者对语类研究的基础上，能够进行归纳，并指出以前研究的不足之处。与此同时，赖博士提出了自己的语类分析模型。为了说明这一模型如何应用于不同语类的分析，他选取描述性报告和公司主页语类进行了详细的对比分析，说明在不同目的的影响下不同语类的实例化过程，得出了有意义的结论。因此该书不仅提供了研究语类的另一种思路，而且丰富了语类研究的内容。

赖博士已在自己的学术生涯中迈开了可喜的一步。我期待能够看到他在功能语言学的研究上取得更多的科研成果。

杨信彰

2012 年 7 月 6 日于厦门

# Preface

For over three decades now scholars from China have pursued coursework and research in the Department of Linguistics at the University of Sydney. This has proved an invaluable exchange of scholarship, as annual international and national systemic functional linguistics (hereafter SFL) conferences bear witness. One scholar who typifies this negotiation of ideas is Lai Liangtao, who spent 18 months of his PhD program at Xiamen University working alongside us in Sydney. This book consolidates the work on genre with which he was engaged for this research.

This book, *A Telos-oriented Model of Genre Analysis*, is an important contribution to genre theory in several respects. For one thing it provides an up-to-date and very scholarly survey of relevant work on genre, including the three "grand" traditions of ESP, New Rhetoric and SFL. In addition Lai interrogates and develops the notion of purpose deployed across these traditions, inspired in part by Russian activity theory. Lai argues that a deeper engagement with telos provides a firmer grounding for work on genre staging (including phases and smaller units of meaning), and for dealing with the challenges of genres and macro-genres, synoptic and dynamic perspectives, multi-functional analysis (ideational, interpersonal and textual) and typological and topological approaches to genre agnation. In keeping with the privileging of system over structure in SFL, Lai proposes a paradigmatic telos-oriented perspective, the rewards of which he illustrates with respect to several genres which play key roles in the constitution of corporate websites.

Informing all of this discussion is Lai's careful scholarly reading of extant work and recent developments in SFL theory, including an important elucidation of the complementarity of realisation, instantiation and individuation in relation to genre theory and description. Accordingly, I would strongly recommend this book not just for scholars interested in cutting edge work on genre, but for anyone exploring the foundations of SFL theory. Lai's current research focus is on the potential applications of genre studies to language teaching in China, inspired in part by Sydney School genre-based literacy programs. It is indeed exciting to imagine what these prospective exercises in appliable linguistics have in store as our Sino-Australian conversations about language and society unfold for decades to come.

Professor J R Martin
Department of Linguistics
University of Sydney

# 前 言

语类在语言学界一直受到广泛关注，因为语类是人类语言活动的一个核心概念，语类的研究具有重大的理论意义和实践意义。从理论上来说，语类就是人类语言文化活动的基本模式，语类研究对于研究语篇结构生成、语篇动态性、文化系统、文化模式等具有重大意义。在实践上，语类研究对于课程教学、文化传承等应用领域具有重大的指导意义。近二十多年来，语类研究主要关注具体语类的语言特征，而语类基础理论和分析模式的研究进展不大。

基础理论研究很容易失之肤浅、空泛，成为好高骛远之作，语类理论研究也不例外。为了使本研究具有一定理论深度，作者从语类的核心概念“目的”出发，以哲学目的论为基本理论依据，整合社会学、社会心理学、社会符号学、系统功能语言学等相关理论，通过分析人类社会活动的目的结构来研究语类的本质、系统、结构、体现、实例化、个体化、语类关系、分析工具、分析方法等基本问题。研究的基本目的是发展悉尼学派的语类理论，提出一个相对完整可行的语类分析模式。理论深度似乎有了，但其效果是深入深出、深入浅出、还是深入不出，有待各位专家学者鉴别。

为了使新理论模式免于空泛，作者选取了 IT 业领军企业的网站语类为语料，按照体现、实例化、个体化三个维度，通过小型语料库来验证模式的可行性和应用价值。毋庸讳言，一个小型语料库对于验证新理论的实际需求来说只是杯水车薪。更大的问题在于受技术条件限制，语篇分析、特别是网站等多模态语篇分析目前基本只能靠手工，无法实现大规模计算机处理，因而分析过程中不可避免带有一些主观个人因素，分析得出的结论也必然有偏颇之处。这些问题都是今后努力的方向。

本专著是国家留学基金委资助、厦门大学外文学院和悉尼大学语言学系联合培养博士项目的结晶。首先我要感谢我的导师厦门大学杨信彰教授。数年来他一直引领着我的学术研究。博士论文的开题、框架确定、数度修改,无不凝结着他的汗水。杨教授渊博的学识、敏锐的洞察力、严谨的治学态度、宽容的学术胸怀是我一生学习的榜样。杨老师和师母无微不至的人文关怀,让我永生难忘。

其次我要感谢我在悉尼大学的导师 James R. Martin 教授。是他让我开拓了学术视野、把握了功能语言学的最前沿动态。正是他的学术宽容和批判精神让我有勇气班门弄斧,在他指导下对他一手创立的悉尼学派语类理论进行批判、整合、发展。本书中许多观点、创新,都是和他深入讨论的结果,并得到了他的首肯和鼓励。Martin 教授还数次通读论文全文并提出深入、细致的指导意见。本书将要出版之际,Martin 教授欣然作序、推介。他的帮助、指导,将让我受用终生。

还要感谢的是厦门大学连淑能教授、吴建平教授、纪玉华教授、南京师范大学辛斌教授、东北师范大学杨忠教授、浙江大学马博森教授、悉尼科技大学 Susan Hood 教授和 Theo van Leeuwen 教授以及荷兰 Tilburg 大学的 Jan Renkema 教授,他们都对本书的内容提出过中肯、独到的批评和建议。此外,我在厦门大学和悉尼大学求学期间的同学、同事、朋友等也都在论文撰写过程中提供了不少帮助、关怀。

最后还要感谢我的妻子王任华博士对书稿的校对,感谢我的家人在我多年求学期间给予的理解、支持、鼓励,感谢厦门大学出版社王扬帆女士在本书出版期间的大力协助。没有他们的支持,本书出版绝无可能。

本书是一个理论创新的尝试,其中定有许多不足甚至谬误,恳请广大读者批评指正。

# Abstract

Genre has long been treated as a subject in academic study in linguistics, literature, anthropology, ethnography and other sciences. In most genre theories, purpose has been treated as an important element. However, in most cases, it is only treated as a common sense term and taken for granted. This book presents a teleological study of genre, with purpose studied academically and treated as a pivot for the working of genres. A telos-oriented model of genre analysis is developed through an integration of the theories of teleology, sociology and SFL, and is tested through its application to a case study of corporate website genres in a small corpus consisting of 16 websites. The book thus paves a new way for the development of genre theory and genre analysis.

The necessity of a teleological perspective is entailed by the teleological nature of genres. A genre is a typification of telos-driven social actions. It is telos-driven because as realization of human activities, human actions are driven by a motive/object and directed toward a conscious purpose, and are in turn realized by specific operations subordinate to specific conditions. Purpose is the basic criterion for distinguishing one action from another. An action type will be established in a community through the recognition of similarities in terms of objectives/motives, agents, tools, and methods between individual actions, and will be routinized when it can be successfully used in new situations.

Based on the teleological ordering of human action, three teleological units are suggested: purpose, goal, and end, which are considered as underlying the three structural units of genre analysis:

genre, stage, and message. Each of the teleological/generic units can form complexes, and a higher-level unit can be embedded into a lower one. Each teleological unit is considered as consisting of representational, interactional and organizational aspects, which respectively condition the field, tenor and mode at the register stratum and the ideational, interpersonal and textual metafunctions at the discourse semantic stratum.

Based on the teleological structure of social actions, a telos-oriented genre system is developed, which includes two subsystems: simplex and complex. The simplex subsystem describes the configuration of specific goals and the complexing of the goals into the purpose of a specific simple genre. The complex subsystem describes the resources employed to organize two or more genres into a genre complex (macro-genre) based on the teleological ordering of purpose subsumption. This tentative genre system is believed as capable of capturing the underlying principle for the derivation of generic structure.

Based on the telos-oriented genre system, genre staging is considered as the result of the realization of the simplex subsystem, and may be explained teleologically by the concretization of a general and abstract purpose into several specific goals. As for genre agnation, typology is based on the difference in the values of the same system feature realized in different genres, while topology is the result of the sharing of feature values in the genre system among several genres. The theories of genre system, structure, staging and agnation are applied in the analysis of website genres.

A general and abstract genre is teleologically operationalized along three dimensions of semantic variation simultaneously: realization, instantiation, and individuation. The telos-oriented genre system is realized by a teleological structure, which is then realized by a generic structure. The three teleological aspects of a purpose are respectively realized by the corresponding register variables, which are in turned realized by the three metafunctions at the discourse semantic stratum.

Genre realization is illustrated by the exploration of the realization process of operating procedures, descriptive reports, compositional reports, and news stories.

Genre instantiation deals with the teleologically-conditioned relation between system and text. Each level along the realization dimension instantiates. Different ways of coupling and commitment instantiate the same genre into different texts. The specific instantiation process is illustrated by the analysis of the different instantiations of the descriptive report genre and the homepage genre employed on corporate websites.

Genre individuation is concerned with the achievement of the specific purpose of a genre by a user through the employment of user-specific semiotic resources. Every stratum along the realization hierarchy individuates. During the individuation process, individual users on the one hand show their respective unique identity through their unique ways of coding, and on the other negotiate their identities with each other and affiliate themselves into personality types, master identities, and finally into the system. Genre individuation is illustrated by the individuation/affiliation processes in three company profile texts of the descriptive report genre.

The specific telos-conditioned genre operationalization process preconditions semiotic resources at the register and discourse semantic strata, which are adopted as tools for the analysis of specific genres. A register is a configuration of field, tenor and mode variables, which are respectively contextual projections of ideational, interpersonal and textual metafunctions. At the discourse semantic stratum, the appraisal, involvement and negotiation systems deal with interpersonal meanings, the ideation system and the external part of the conjunction systems deal with ideational meanings, while the internal part of the conjunction system, the identification system and the periodicity system deal with textual meanings.

The specific telos-oriented genre analysis process can proceed either in a top-down or bottom-up order based on the principle of metaredundancy. The basic method is to work out the semiotic configurations at one stratum based on those of the adjacent stratum, with the pursuit of the general purpose of the specific genre as the key factor conditioning the semiotic configuration. The analysis of macro-genres should work out the logico-semantic relations among the elementary genres and show how such an organization serves the pursuit of the most general purpose of the macro-genre.

**Key Words:** genre; teleology; model of analysis; application

# CONTENTS

# Chapter 1

# Introduction

## 1.1 Rationale for the Study

The term genre comes from the Latin word "genus" and dates back to classical philosophy in Greek, where it was used in the sphere of classification. One of the earliest scholars who paid attention to the study of genre was Aristotle (cf. Section 2.1). Since then, genre has been discussed throughout the history of human civilization. Though numerous theories have been put forward, little consensus has been reached, even with regard to the definition of the term.

However, one point seems to be acceptable for all scholars of genre studies. That is, genre is concerned with human actions: literature genres, music genres, genres of fine arts, digital genres, and genres of any other everyday communication are all based on human actions. Another point seems to be accepted by most scholars since the creation of the term is that genre is concerned with typification, therefore also with classification. Thus, an acceptable view of genre is to consider it as typified ways of human actions. The study of genre is in essence the study of human actions.

Human actions are social, and teleological (Leontjev 1978, Smith 1981). They are social because human being is first and foremost social. They are teleological because they are always driven by a motive and oriented to a specific objective. Purpose as an element in the study of genre has been discussed in a variety of genre theories. For example, New Rhetoric, English for Specific Purposes (ESP), and Systemic Functional Linguistics (SFL) all discussed purpose as an integral element of genre (Miller 1984, Swales 1990, Martin 1992). Considering the teleological nature of social action, a reasonable approach to genre will be a teleological one.

However, in most cases, purpose is only treated as one of the elements of a genre, and as a common sense term without much strict academic study. In sociology and philosophy, the branch that studies the purpose of human actions is teleology. A scientific study of genre from a teleological perspective preconditions a scientific study of purposes. A teleological explanation either explains a process by the end-state towards which it is directed, or explains the existence of something by the function it fulfils (Ward 2003, Marshall 1998). Thus, a purpose-oriented approach to genre is not only teleological, but also functional. As far as the study of genre is concerned, what is most in need is the former approach. The functional approach, though also relevant, has already been followed by many scholars of genre studies (e. g. Miller 1984, Swales 1990, Martin 1992). It is out of this consideration that a teleological approach is adopted for the study of genre in this book. It is hoped that such a study will be more revealing to the nature of genre.

A teleological approach to genre presupposes a scientific study of purposes that reveals the purpose-based patterning of human actions. Among the great variety of teleological theories of human actions, Russian activity theory created by Lev Vygotsky (1978, 1997a, 1997b) and developed by A. N Leontjev (1977, 1978, 1979, 1981) provides an insightful explanation to the teleological nature of human action, while the American philosopher Quentin Smith's study of the teleological ordering of human action provides inspirations to the study of teleological structure (Smith 1981). Based on their work, a telos-oriented genre model will be developed in this book, with a view to explore the nature and the structure of genres.

A genre is a typified human action. The typification of any phenomena entails a semiotic interpretation of the phenomena concerned (Schutz & Luckmann1973: 229-241). The study of genre is thus necessarily a semiotic one. In addition, as any typification/classification is abstract, a genre as a typified human action is also abstract. In order for an abstract genre to function in our society, it has to be operationalized by specific users through the deployment of specific semiotic resources in specific instances of communication. Thus, in addition to the discussion of the abstract nature and characteristics of genre, the discussion of specific genres employed at corporate websites is necessary, as will be carried out in this book.

In summary then, a teleological approach, together with a social and semiotic perspective, is necessary and significant for genre study.

## 1.2 Aim and Research Questions

The book is a study of genre from a teleological approach based on theories of sociology (teleology in particular) and Systemic Functional Linguistics (SFL). The general aim is to develop the genre theory of SFL from a teleological perspective, establish a tentative teleological genre model, and apply it to the study of corporate website genres. Specifically, the book is intended to address the following research issues:

1) The nature of genre: what is genre from a social teleological perspective?

2) Genre system and structure: specifically, how to define the structural units of genre studies in a teleological manner and how to establish a register-neutral genre system from a teleological perspective?

3) The explanation of genre staging: how to derive a generic structure from the genre system, how to deal with the ordering and sequencing of the genre stages, and how to deal with text dynamics (register variation from stage to stage) at the genre stratum?

4) The issue of inter-genre relation: how to explain macro-genres

from a teleological perspective, and how to explain genre agnation?

5) The operationalization of genres: how to explain genre realization, instantiation and individuation from a teleological perspective, and how to deal with the relation between the three dimensions?

6) Applicability of the established genre model: what are the major corporate promotional genres on websites and how they are realized, instantiated and individuated from a teleological perspective?

## 1.3 Data Collection and Methodology

As the book is a heuristic study of genre, the data will be mainly used to prove the applicability of the new theory established in the study. For this purpose, the data will be corporate promotional texts collected from 16 websites of IT companies renowned in the world. Specifically, the websites of the following companies are covered in this study:

Microsoft (www. microsoft. com)
Linux (http: //www. linux. com/)
Apple (http: //www. apple. com/)
HP (http: //welcome. hp. com/country/us/en/welcome. html#Product)
Dell (http: //www. dell. com/)
Compaq (http: //www. compaq. com/country/index. html)
IBM (http: //www. ibm. com/us/en/)
Intel (http: //www. intel. com/)
Cisco (http: //www. cisco. com/)
Lenovo (http: //www. lenovo. com/lenovo/US/en/index. html)
Motorola (http: //www. motorola. com/us)
Acer (http: //us. acer. com/)
Siemens (www. siemens. com)
Sony (http: //www. sony. com/index. php)
Nokia (http: //www. nokia. com)
Samsung (http: //www. samsung. com/us/)

Each website contains a variety of genres. Only a few of them will be identified and discussed in the book as long as they are sufficient to illustrate the operation and applicability of the theory. The genres discussed in the book include operating procedures, descriptive reports, compositional reports, news stories, corporate homepages, and corporate content pages. For each genre, 20 texts are analyzed manually in a qualitative way to show its realization, instantiation and individuation. Due to the limit of space, only the analysis of 20 texts will be presented and discussed in detail in the book.

Each text will be analyzed on three strata: genre, register, and discourse semantics. At the genre stratum, the focus will be on the teleological structure and the generic structure (its staging and phasing). At the register stratum, the analysis will be focused on the register patterning, including the choice of specific field, tenor, and mode values and the patterning of the variable values. According to the specific requirement of the study, the analysis will be done either on the basis of the variables, or on the basis of genre staging. At the discourse semantic stratum, the analysis will be carried out mainly along the following discourse semantics systems: ideation, conjunction, appraisal, periodicity, and identification (Martin 1992, Martin & Rose 2003, 2007). Negotiation system is not discussed because it is mainly applied to the analysis of conversation and it is not very applicable to the study of website texts. In the analysis of interpersonal meanings, resources of involvement system and those for the realization of social status are also discussed when appropriate. In addition, the analysis will be carried out either in a top-down manner, proceeding from the genre and register strata to discourse semantics, or in a bottom-up manner, proceeding from the discourse semantic stratum, to the register and genre strata.

## 1.4 Organization of the Book

The book includes 7 chapters. The specific contents of each chapter are described as follows.

Chapter 1 is an introduction to the study. It first presents a brief review of the linguistic study of genre as compared with genre studies in other approaches, and then introduces the rationale of the current study and specifies the necessity of a teleological perspective to genre study. It also describes the data collection and the methodology of the study, and presents an overview of the organization of the book.

Chapter 2 is a literature review. It briefly summarizes the major academic works on genre that are directly related to this study, including the major ideas, achievements and brief assessments of the different schools and approaches concerned. The theories reviewed in the chapter include Aristotle's theory of genre, the genre theory in New Rhetoric as presented by Carolyn R. Miller, genre study in EAP as represented by John Swales, Bakhtin's theory of speech genres, the genre theory of Halliday & Hasan, and the genre theory of J. R. Martin and his colleagues.

Chapter 3 develops a telos-oriented model of genre analysis. The overall model is first presented, and then elaborated in detail in later sections. The necessity of a teleological perspective is established by exploring the teleological nature of genre, which is followed by the exploration of genre system, genre structure and inter-genre relation. The discussion then proceeds to genre realization, instantiation and individuation (the three dimensions of genre operationalization). Analytic tools at the register and discourse semantic strata are discussed. The procedures and methods for the application of this model are finally explained.

Chapters 4, 5, and 6 apply the telos-oriented genre model established in Chapter 3 to the study of corporate promotional genres on websites, with a view to operationalize the established theory and prove its applicability on the one hand, and to illustrate a genre-based approach to the study of websites in general on the other. The study in each chapter will be based on a detailed analysis at the genre, register, and discourse semantic strata.

Specifically, Chapter 4 studies the realization of genres employed on corporate websites, including the realization of four genres in particular: operating procedures, descriptive reports, compositional reports, and news stories. For each genre, a text is selected from the corporate websites, its teleological structure and generic structure are discussed, the register patterning is explored, and the discourse semantic resources are analyzed, with a view to show the metaredudancy along the realization hierarchy.

Chapter 5 studies the instantiation of genres on corporate websites. Two genres are used to illustrate the instantiation process: the descriptive report genre and the corporate homepage genre. For each genre, two texts are selected, and the instantiation processes are analyzed and compared to show the different instantiations of the same genre into different texts. As the homepage genre is always multimodal, its study also helps prove the applicability of the telos-oriented theory to multimodal genres and the modality-neutrality of the theory.

Chapter 6 studies the individuation of corporate website genres. The focus is on the descriptive report genre. Three texts of this genre are selected, each presenting a profile of the corresponding company. The different individuations of the same genre by different authors are illustrated, and the possible teleological considerings of each author that condition the respective individuation process are discussed. In addition, the affiliation of the authors' unique identities as shown in the individuations is also discussed.

Chapter 7 draws the conclusion of the study, specifies its significance, shows the limitations, and provides suggestions for future work.

# Chapter 2

# Literature Review

Genre has been the focus of academic study for a long time. Scholars from all over the world have made contributions to genre research. This chapter will present a brief review of the major schools of genre studies. Emphasis will be attached to the genre theories of Aristotle, Bakhtin, New Rhetoric, ESP, and SFL. Special attention will be paid to the principles and ideas of these approaches that are closely related to the current study.

## 2.1 Aristotle's Ideas about Genre

Aristotle is one of the earliest scholars that paid attention to the study of genre. His ideas have exerted far-reaching influence on subsequent genre theories in literary studies, linguistics, sociology, and other sciences. Aristotle's theory of genres can be roughly divided into two groups: the study of literary genres, and the study of rhetoric genres. They will be reviewed respectively in the following sections.

### 2.1.1 Literary Genre

The study of genre in Western society can be dated back to Aristotle. Aristotle discussed the issues of genre in what now can be considered as two disciplines: poetics and rhetoric. In poetics (Aristotle 1974, 1987; Warrington 1963, Garver 1994, Genette 2000), Aristotle defines poetry as the species of imitation and proposes that the domain of poetry should include not only the art in general, but also its species and their respective capacities, the structure of plot necessary for the making of a good poem, the number and nature of a poem's constituent parts, and other such relevant matters. Epic poetry, tragedy, comedy, dithyrambic poetry, and most flute-playing and lyre-playing are all modes of imitation. He distinguishes between the species of poetry in three ways: differences in their means, the object and the manner of their imitations. The means may be the language, rhythm, and harmony, used either separately or in combination. The objects represented by an imitator are actions performed. They include the agents (either "good" or "bad"), which may be human characters who have emotions (and bring moral to actions they do) or things of daily life who have no emotions (humans put emotions on things), and their actions (either "virtuous" or "vicious") which are caused by and influence the agents. Given the same means and the same kind of objects for imitation, a poet may shift between a role in a narrator and a role in an assumed character, or may remain the same throughout without any change, or his imitation may take the form of representing the whole story dramatically and his personages as actually doing the things described.

Aristotle made special efforts to elaborate on tragedy. He first presents a definition of tragedy as follows:

> A tragedy, then, is the imitation of an action (1) that is serious, has magnitude, and is complete in itself; (2) in language with pleasurable accessories, each kind introduced separately in different parts of the work; (3) in a dramatic as from a narrative form; (4) with incidents arousing pity and fear, whereby to provide an outlet for such emotions. 'By language with pleasurable accessories' I mean that with rhythm and harmony or song superadded; and by 'each kind ... separately' I mean with that in some portions verse only is employed, and in others song. (cf. *Poetics*, by Aristotle 1974: 11-12, translated by Butcher)

According to Aristotle (1942: 11-15, translated by P. H. Ebbs), tragedy is an imitation of an action that is complete, and whole, and of a certain magnitude. The poet has to employ imitation in order to produce pleasure arising from pity and fear. In addition, a tragedy must contain six (and only six) parts which determines its quality, which, in the order of their importance, are as follows: (a) the fable or plot, the combination of the incidents of things done in the story; (b) character, what makes us ascribe certain more qualities to the agents; (c) thought, which is shown in all they say when proving a particular point or expressing a general truth; (d) diction, the metric composition; (e) melody; (f) the spectacle, i. e. the stage-appearance of the actors. Melody and diction arise from the means of imitation, character, thought and plot from the objects imitated, while the spectacle from the manner.

According to Aristotle (1942: 15-22), plot is the most important part of a tragedy. A plot must be complex, and must imitate actions that arouse from pity and fear. The components of a plot include: astonishment; reversal, a change by which the action veers round to its opposite; recognition, a change from ignorance to knowledge, producing love or hatred between the persons destined by the poet for good or bad fortune; and suffering. The quantitative parts of a tragedy (the parts into which a tragedy is divided into) include prologue, episode, exode and choric song. In addition, the general structure of a plot is formulated as: outline, episodisation, complication and denouncement (resolution). In the outline part, the major agents are introduced and the setting given. Then episode is filled in, which complicates as more and more incidents are superadded until a final resolution is reached.

Aristotle (1942: 23-48) also specifies the other five elements in detail, and provides suggestions as how to write to achieve the best effect. In addition, Aristotle (1942: 36) recognizes four species of tragedy based on the prominence of one of the constituent parts in it: the complex tragedy, which is all reversal and discovery, the tragedy of suffering, the tragedy of character, and the tragedy in which the spectacle is predominant.

### 2.1.2 Rhetoric and Genre

Aristotle also discussed genres in his work on rhetoric, which is an attempt to systematically describe civic rhetoric as a human art or skill (Garver 1994, Kennedy 2007). Rhetoric is considered as the faculty of observing in any given case the available means of persuasion. It is partly a method (like dialectic) with no special subject of its own, but partly a practical art derived from ethics and politics on the basis of its conventional uses (Kennedy 2007: 16). Aristotle identifies three steps of rhetoric: invention, arrangement (taxis), and style (lexis). Invention refers to the means of persuasion available to a public by presentation of the speaker's character as trustworthy, by use of persuasive arguments, and by moving the emotions of the audience. Style (lexis) refers to the way of saying something in contrast to what is said, which can be either used in a broad sense of how thought is expressed in words, sentences, and a speech as a whole, or in the more restricted sense of word choice (diction). Arrangement (taxis) refers to the ordering of the conventional parts of an oration, especially as seen in judicial speeches (Kennedy 2007: 193). According to him, there are two necessary parts to a speech: the statement (prodissertation) which states the subject with which the speech is concerned, and the proof (pistis) which demonstrates the argument. More specifically, a forensic discourse in a court may include the parts introduction^ narration^ the proof (pistis) ^interrogation^ conclusion (Kennedy 2007).

Three (and only three) types of pisteis are identified, derived from the factors in any speech situation: ethos, presentation of the trustworthy character of the speaker, which means how the character and the credibility of a speaker can influence an audience to consider him/her to be believable; pathos, the use of the emotional effect created by the speaker and text on the audience or reader; and logos, the use of reasoning, either inductive or deductive, to construct an argument (Kennedy 2007: 21-22).

In addition, based on whether the audience is or is not a judge, in the sense of being able to take specific action as a result of being persuaded to do so, and the time with which each species is concerned, Aristotle identified three (and only three) species of civic rhetoric (cf. Kennedy 2007: 46-50): forensic, also known as judicial, which is concerned with determining truth or falsity of events that took place in the past; deliberative, also known as political, which is concerned with determining whether or not particular actions should or should not be taken in the future; and epideictic, also known as ceremonial, which is concerned with praise and blame, values, right and wrong, demonstrating beauty and skill in the present (Kennedy 2007: 20). Each species has its own end, the principal issues it is concerned. The end of forensic rhetoric is justice, that of deliberate rhetoric is the best interest of the audience, and that of epideictic rhetoric is praise or blame of the subject.

In addition, Aristotle discussed special topics and common topics for the three species of rhetoric (Kennedy 2007: 50-51). Special topics are lines of argument and specific claims especially important to one type of rhetorical species. For example, in order to argue effectively in legislature, a deliberative orator should understand finances, war and peace, national defense, imports and exports, and the framing laws. The constituents of human happiness are special topics to deliberative rhetoric. On the other hand, the special topics for epideictic rhetoric have to do with understanding virtue and vice, and the ability to prove someone to be praiseworthy or blameworthy. Similarly, the special topics of forensic rhetoric include such things as the causes of wrongdoing, the nature of human desire that drives people to do wrong, and the types of human character that lead one to commit crimes. Common topics are arguments and strategies useful in any of the three rhetorical species. Twenty-eight of such common topics are listed.

According to Aristotle, forms of persuasion are either non-artistic, involving direct evidence (e. g. facts, witnesses, documents) used but not invented by the speaker, or artistic, which are logical arguments constructed by the speaker. The latter includes two sub-types: inductive argument or paradigm which draws particular conclusion from one or more parallels, and deductive argument, called enthymeme, or rhetorical syllogism, drawing a conclusion from stated or implied premises (cf. Kennedy 2007: 21). Another interesting view is about probabilities. According to him, in rhetoric the speaker always deals with probabilities, what could happen or can happen based on what happens for the most part in such situations (Kennedy 2007: 21).

### 2.1.3 Assessment

Aristotle's ideas are very insightful when viewed from the perspective of modern genre theories. First, his definition of poetry as species of imitation of action is closely related to the definition of genre as social actions in modern genre theories, while his definition of rhetoric as the faculty of observing in any given case the available means of persuasion implies an idea of genre as potential resources for achieving a social purpose. He obviously attaches importance to the purpose of specific genres. For example, the purpose of tragedy is to produce pleasure arising from fear and pity, while forensic, deliberative and epideictic rhetoric each also have their own purposes.

Aristotle's consideration of both literary and rhetoric genres (or species in his term) indicates that the domain of his genres include both literary and civic discourses, a view which is also similar to modern genre theories in linguistics. His inclusion of language, rhythm, and harmony as means of imitation in literary genres and his discussion of delivery in rhetoric shows his awareness of the importance of multi-modalities in the realization of specific genres in addition to language.

Aristotle obviously made his contributions to the study of what is now called the schematic structure of genres. The general structure of a plot (i. e. outline ^ episodisation ^ complication ^ denouncement) can be considered as the schematic structure of the tragedy in general. Even more interestingly, his discussion of arrangement in rhetoric is actually an exploration into the general structure of civic discourse. The two general parts of a speech (statement and demonstration), and the structure of a judicial discourse (introduction ^ narration ^ the proof ^ interrogation ^ conclusion) can also be considered as a kind of schematic structure.

The three criteria (means, object and manner of imitation) for the classification of literary genres are closely related to the three situational variables of mode, field and tenor in SFL. Specifically, means is related to mode because language is a part of modality. Rhythm and harmony are factors of textual organization. Object is related to field because actions performed (including the agents, things and actions) are all ideational factors. The manner of imitation is related to tenor because the role of the poet and the dramatic or actual style of narration all are closely related to role relationship.

However, Aristotle's ideas of genre also have shortcomings. First, there is inconsistency between his theorization of literary genres and that of rhetoric genres. For example, the classification of literary genres is more based on linguistic resources (means, objects, and manner), while that of rhetoric genres more on the loose identification of the general purpose. Such inconsistency makes it difficult to integrate them into an organic theory and greatly influences the applicability of his theory. Second, though purpose has been recognized as an element, the term is taken for granted rather than academically established. This damages the basis for using purpose as a classification criterion. In addition, Aristotle's ideas about genre are heuristic rather than strictly academic, based on his intuitive contemplation rather than strict investigation and analysis. This restricts the soundness and convincibility of the ideas.

## 2.2 Bakhtin's Theory of Speech Genres

Bakhtin's theory of speech genres was established as a reaction to previous theories of genre and language as a whole. His theory is insightful and has far-reaching influence on the establishment of modern genre theories. His major ideas are distributed in such works as *Marxism and the Philosophy of Language* (1973), *The Problem of Speech Genres* (1986), *Discourse in the Novel* (1981), *Genre of the Discourse* (only a brief of sketch remained), and *The Formal Method in Literary Scholarship* (1985). In this section, the general framework of his theory will be briefly reviewed.

### 2.2.1 Utterance as the Real Unit of Speech Communication

In order to understand Bakhtin's ideas of genre, it is necessary to introduce his concept of utterance as genres are considered by him as types of utterances. According to Bakhtin,

> Any concrete utterance is a link in the chain of speech communication of a particular sphere. The very boundaries of the utterance are determined by a change of speech subjects. Utterances are not indifferent to one another, and are not self-sufficient; they are aware of and mutually reflect one another. Every utterance must be regarded as primarily a *response* to preceding utterances of the given sphere (we understand the word 'response' here in the broadest sense). Each utterance refutes, affirms, supplements, and relies upon the others, presupposes them to be known, and somehow takes them into account. Therefore, each kind of utterance is filled with various kinds of responsive reactions to other utterances of the given sphere of speech communication. (Bakhtin 1986: 91)

An utterance is considered by Bakhtin as the simplest and most classic form of speech communication. It is the real unit of speech communication, as the existence of speech lies only in the form of concrete utterance of individual speaking subjects. It has two constitutive features: change of speaking subjects and finalized wholeness of the utterance. The boundaries of utterances are determined by the change of subjects. Any utterance has an absolute beginning and an absolute end. The beginning is preceded by other utterances, while the end is followed by responsive utterances of others (Bakhtin 1986: 71).

The second constitutive feature (the specific finalization of the utterance) is closely related to the first because the change of speaking subjects takes place only "because the speaker has said everything he wishes to say at a particular moment or under particular circumstances" (Bakhtin 1986: 75-76). According to Bakhtin (1986: 76-77), the finalization of an utterance is specific and is determined by special criteria, first and foremost by the possibility of responding to it. Specifically, it is determined by three aspects: referential and semantic exhaustiveness of the theme, the speaker's plan or will, and the typical compositional and generic forms of finalization.

Bakhtin (1986: 78) argues that the speaker's plan or will determines the entire utterance, the choice of the subject, its boundaries, and the referential and semantic exhaustiveness. It also determines the choice of the generic form by relating it to a concrete individual situation of speech communication. Such a choice is determined by the specific nature of the given sphere of speech communication, semantic (thematic) considerations, the concrete situation of the speech communication, and the personal composition of the participants. When the speaker's plan is applied and adapted to a chosen genre, it is shaped and developed within a certain generic form.

According to Bakhtin (1986: 81-91), an utterance differs from a sentence in several aspects: demarcation on either side by change of speaking subject, direct contact with reality (with extra-verbal situation), direct relation to other's utterances, semantic fullness of value, and the capacity of evoking a response. Utterance is a real unit of speech communication, while sentence is a grammatical unit of language. We exchange utterances as constructed from language units such as words, phrases, and sentences.

### 2.2.2 Genre as Type of Utterances

Based on the study of utterances, speech genres are considered by Bakhtin (1986: 60) as relatively stable types of utterances in particular spheres of communications, in terms of their thematic content, linguistic style (the lexical, phraseological, and grammatical resources of language), and their overall compositional structure. As these utterances reflect the specific conditions and goals of each sphere through their content, style and structure, speech genres as stable types of utterances necessarily also reflect the conditions and goals of the relevant spheres. As Bakhtin (1986: 60) notes, the thematic content, linguistic style and compositional structure are determined by the specific nature of the particular sphere of communication.

Bakhtin (1986: 60) recognizes the boundless wealth and diversity of speech genres because each sphere of activity contains an entire repertoire of speech genres that differentiate and grow with the development of the sphere. In addition, speech genres are extremely heterogeneous, which makes their common features excessively abstract and empty.

Bakhtin (1986: 65) draws a distinction between primary (simple) and secondary (complex) genres which he considers as fundamental. Secondary genres arise in more complex and comparatively highly developed and organized cultural communication (primarily written) by absorbing and digesting various primary genres that have been taken for in unmediated speech communion. The primary genres, after absorbed in secondary genres, are altered, and lose their immediate relation to actual reality and the real utterance of others. The nature of the utterance should be revealed through the study of both types of genres.

### 2.2.3 The Dialogic Nature of Utterances and Genres

As links in the chain of speech communication of a particular sphere, utterances are not self-sufficient but mutually reflect one another. Because of these mutual reflections, each utterance is filled with echoes and reverberations of other utterances to which it is related by the communality of the sphere of speech communication (Bakhtin 1986: 91). This is the inherent dialogic nature of utterances.

The dialogism of utterances can be considered as falling into two types: retrospective dialogism and prospective dialogism. The former means that every utterance is a response to preceding utterances of the given sphere of communication. Prospective dialogism means that an utterance is also linked to subsequent utterances, directed to someone, and constructed in anticipation of an active response. This is the addressivity of utterances.

Addressivity means that any utterance is directed to someone. The addressee can take in every form, definite or indefinite, individual or collective, more or less differentiated, with high or low social status, and so on. It may or may not coincide with the actual respondent. The expected perception and response of the addressee determine the choice of genre for the utterance, the compositional devices, and the choice of language styles.

The addressivity of utterances is of great significance to the study of genres. Bakhtin (1986: 95) argues that "each speech genre in each area of speech communication has its own typical conception of the addressee and this defines it as a genre"; "the various typical forms this addressivity assumes and the various concepts of the address are constitutive, definitive features of various genres". Miller (1994) employs the concept of "addressivity" to bridge the gap between individuality and institutional nature of genre. This point will be discussed in detail again in later chapters for elaborating the individuation dimension of genre systems.

### 2.2.4 Genre and Style

According to Bakhtin (1986: 63), any style is inseparably related to individual utterances and to speech genres as typical forms of utterances. Both individual and general language styles govern speech genres. Any utterance is individual, reflects the individuality of the speaker and thus possesses an individual style. As for speech genres, the most favorable for showing individuality are those genres of artistic nature, while genres that reflect a standard form (e. g. business documents) are the least favorable in this respect. In most speech genres (except the artistic ones), the individual style does not enter into the intent of the utterance, but is only an epiphenomenon of the utterance. Various genres can reveal various layers and facets of the individual personality.

According to Bakhtin (1986: 64-65), in addition to individual style, genre is also closely related to language (or functional) styles, which are nothing other than generic styles for certain spheres of human activity and communication. The particular conditions of speech communication and a particular corresponding function (scientific, technical, etc.) give rise to particular genres, that is, certain relatively stable thematic, compositional and stylistic types of utterances. Moreover, historical changes of language styles are also inseparably linked to changes of genres.

### 2.2.5 Genre as Ideological Forms

In his work *The Formal Method of Literary Scholarship*, Bakhtin discussed the necessity of a sociological approach to genre. According to Bakhtin (1985), the formal unity of any genre is determined by its double-orientation towards social reality. Extrinsically, it is determined by its orientation towards the specific conditions of its actual realization in space and time, including the listener and perceiver, and the definite conditions of performance and perception. Intrinsically, a genre is oriented towards social reality in terms of its thematic determinateness. The formal unity of a genre is thus determined by the thematic unity of the form, which is understood as the total conception of reality produced by the generic structure as a whole, rather than by its content or simply the words used. "In any genre the intrinsic and extrinsic orientations are mutually interactive, and are simultaneously influenced by and influence other social and ideological conceptions of life" (Morris 1994: 174-175).

Every genre has developed its own unique forms and methods for conceptualizing and representing reality. Every significant genre is a complex means and methods for the conscious control and finalization of reality. A particular reality can only be understood in connection with particular generic forms of its representation, and the generic forms of expression are only applicable to certain aspects of reality. Thus, the reality of genre and the reality accessible to the genre are organically integrated. But we have seen that the reality of the genre is the social reality of its realization in the process of artistic intercourse. Therefore, genre is the aggregate of the means of collective orientation in reality, with the orientation toward finalization (Bakhtin 1985: 137). As the conceptualization of reality develops and generates in the process of ideological intercourse, a genuine poetics of genre can only be sociology of genre.

### 2.2.6 Assessment

Bakhtin's ideas of genre exert great influence on both linguistic and literary studies. His major contributions can be summarized into three points. First, the exploration of the dialogic nature of genres, especially the addressivity, helps us understand the genesis of genres. It also helps bridge the gap between the individual and institutional aspects of genres. Second, Bakhtin's exploration into the individual style and the individual personality manifested in genres foreshadows the exploration of the individuation dimension in genre studies, while his exploration of language styles (functional styles) in specific spheres of communication helps us understand the probabilistic metaredundancy between genres and a culture system in general. Third, the conceptualization of genre as ideological forms furthers our understanding of the social and ideological nature of genres and impels scholars (e. g. J. R. Martin) to adopt an interventionalist attitude in genre studies.

However, the drawbacks of Bakhtin's theory are as obvious as its merits. First, Bakhtin's definition of utterance seems more like a turn in conversation analysis rather than a unit of genre analysis and the study of utterance is inadequate. As a result, the definition of a genre as a type of utterances is also untenable. This inadequacy makes the in-depth study of genre difficult if not impossible. Second, though Bakhtin argues that the speaker's plan or will (which can be considered as another expression of purpose) determines the choice of generic forms, he has not explicitly discussed the exact way for such determination. Moreover, purpose/will/plan has not been discussed in any detail, but only used as a common-sense term. Third, Bakhtin has failed to establish a unified and operationable model for specific genre analysis, which makes his theory vague and slippery (which is partly shown in the inconsistency between his theory of speech genres and that of literary genres).

## 2.3 Genre in New Rhetoric

In New Rhetoric, genre is considered as a conventional category of discourse based on a large-scale typification of rhetorical actions. As a social action, a genre acquires meaning from situation and from the social context in which that situation arises (Miller 1984: 37). In this section, the basic doctrines and rationales of this approach will be reviewed, mainly based on the ideas of Miller (1984, 1994), though ideas of other scholars will also be taken into consideration when appropriate.

### 2.3.1 Genre as Action-Based Discourse Classification

Ever since Aristotle, rhetorical studies have been interested in the classification of discourse. In the view of New Rhetoric scholars headed by Carolyn R. Miller (1984, 1994), however, rhetorical criticism does not provide any firm principles on what constitutes a genre (a distinctive class of discourses). The problem lies in the fact that genre should not be used to refer to any kind of discourse. Rather, it should be made into a stable classifying concept that is rhetorically sound. A rhetorically sound classification should contribute to the understanding of how genre works and reflects the rhetorical experience of the people involved in the discourse, that is, should be based on the conventions of rhetorical practice. Such a classification may be based on rhetorical substance (semantics), form (syntactics), or rhetorical action the discourse performs (pragmatics). An action-based classification seems to most clearly reflect the rhetorical practice, partly because action constitutes substance and form.

Miller (1984: 25-26) identifies two general approaches to classification in modern rhetorical theories: deductive and inductive. A deductive approach is to proceed in a top-down manner by following some theoretical priori and to construct a closed system of categories. This results in a neat taxonomic system that does not reflect the rhetorical practice as the diversity and dynamism of rhetorical practice are sacrificed, and is thus a kind of reductionism. An inductive approach, on the other hand, tends to take context more into account and to stress the recurrence of similar forms in genre identification. An example is Campbell & Jamieson's conceptualization of genre as "a group of acts unified by a constellation of forms that recurs in each of its members" (Campbell & Jamieson 1978: 20). Such an approach does result in a set of genres as open class with new members evolving and old ones decaying. However, it does not ground genres in situated rhetorical actions but rather leads to formalism through its emphasis on recurrent forms. Moreover, according to Miller (1984: 27), discourse classification in other disciplines such as literature, composition, and linguistics also suffers the same problem: either the classes do not represent rhetorical action or the system is not open.

In short, Miller (1984: 27) suggests the term genre "be limited to such a type of discourse classification based on rhetorical practice and thus open and organized in situation actions (that is, pragmatic, rather than syntactic or semantic)".

### 2.3.2 Genre as Response to Recurrent Rhetorical Situations

If a genre represents an action, it necessarily involves situation and motive, as human actions are interpretable only in a situational (and also larger social) context and through the attributing of motives.

According to Miller (1984: 29-30), situations are social and semiotic constructs, which are the results of definition rather than perception. This is because human actions are based on and guided by meaning rather than material bases, and at the center of action is a process of interpretation. Before we act, we must interpret or determine the material environment, which may be subject to different interpretations. Thus, in a discourse community, a situation functions as a social construct with a well defined meaning. Genres are responses to it, and are typified rhetorical actions.

In the discourse community, successful communication requires the sharing of common types among the participants, which is possible as far as types are socially constructed. The typified situation underlies rhetorical typification. Miller draws on Alfred Schutz (cf. Schutz & Luckman 1973) for the account of typification of situations.

> Our stock of knowledge is useful only in so far as it can be brought to bear upon new experience: the new is made familiar through the recognition of relevant similarities; those similarities become constituted as a type. A new type is formed from typifications already on hand when they are not adequate to determine a new situation. If a new typification proves continually useful for mastering states of affairs, it enters into the stock of knowledge and its application becomes a routine. (Miller 1984: 29)

Through the process of typification, recurrence and similarities are created. Thus, rhetorical situations are recurrent. What recurs is our construal of situation types, rather than material configurations of objects, events, or people, as any material environment is unique, or even a perception of such configurations, as such perception is also unique both temporally and personally. This implies a rejection of the materialist interpretation of situations.

According to Miller (1984: 30), at the core of situation is exigence. Located in the social world rather than in private intention or material circumstance, it is neither a cause of rhetorical action nor private intention. "Exigence is a form of social knowledge—a mutual construing of objects, events, interests and purposes that not only links them but makes them what they are: an objectified social need" (Miller 1984: 30). It can be considered as "a set of particular social patterns and expectations that provides a socially objectified motive for addressing danger, ignorance, and separateness" (Miller 1984: 31). Thus, exigence provides the rhetor with a sense of social purpose. It also provides him with an occasion, and thus a form for making his private intentions known.

As a preponderant portion of social action in human society (especially in a settled society) lies in the form of recurrent patterns of joint actions, to base the classification of discourse on recurrent situations, on exigence as social motive in particular, is to base it upon the typical joint rhetorical actions at a given point in history and culture. Thus, the study of typical uses of rhetoric reveals much more about the character of a culture or a historical period than the individual rhetors or particular texts. Here lies the rationale of genre study as understood in New Rhetoric (Miller 1984: 31).

### 2.3.3 Meaningfulness of a Genre

According to Miller (1984: 31), the generic fusion of substantive, formal, and situational elements is the key to understating the meaningfulness of a genre.

Miller (1984: 32) follows the Aristotelian approach to substance and form. A particular fusion of the two is essential to symbolic meaning. Substance is the semantic value of discourse and constitutes the aspects of common experience that are being symbolized, while form is the ways in which substance is symbolized. Form shapes the response of the reader to substance by providing instructions about how to perceive and interpret. It consequently acquires the status of meta-information with both semantic value (as information) and syntactic (formal) value. Thus, form and substance bear a hierarchical relationship to each other.

When substance and form are fused together at one level, they acquire semantic value which is then subject to formalizing at a higher level. In other words, the fusion at one level becomes action (has meaning) at a higher level when the fusion itself acquires form. Thus, form at one level becomes a part of substance at a higher level, which makes form significant. Through this hierarchical fusion of substance and form, symbolic structures take on pragmatic force and acquire meaning (pragmatic value as action) in context. As the rhetorical forms that establish genres are formal and substantive responses to recurrent situational demands, a genre as a complex of substantive and formal features serves as the substance of forms at higher levels, and thus acquires meaning from the situation and becomes pragmatic, an aspect of social action. "As recurrent patterns of language use, genres help constitute the substance of our cultural life" (Miller 1984: 37).

As a meaningful action, a genre is rule-governed, that is, interpretable by means of convention. These rules occur at a relatively high level on a hierarchy of rules for symbolic interaction. They fall into two types. Constitutive rules stipulate the ways for fusing form and substance to make meaning, while regulative rules show how the fusion itself is to be interpreted within its contexts (Miller 1984: 34-35).

Based on the model of Frentz & Farrell (1976) and that of Pearce & Conklin (1979), Miller (1984: 35) developed a hierarchy of meaning, which, in a top-down order, includes human nature (archetype), culture, form of life, genre, episode or strategy, speech act, locution, language and experience. Each level provides context for a lower one. According to this hierarchy, genre is a level of meaning located at the level between form of life and episode/strategy. It is provided interpretive context by forms of life and is constituted by intermediate forms, i. e. strategies. At the level of locution or speech act, private motives (intention) predominate, while at the level of genre, motive becomes a conventional social purpose (exigence) within the recurrent situation. In constructing discourse, we learn to adopt social motives as ways of satisfying private intentions through rhetorical action. Thus, a genre serves as a rhetorical means for mediating private intentions with social exigence (Miller 1984: 35-36).

### 2.3.4 Cultural Basis of Genre

In her article "Rhetorical Community: the Cultural Basis of Genre", Miller (1994) further explored the relationship between culture, genre and rhetorical community. She adopts Raymond Williams's anthropological definition of culture as "a particular way of life of a time and space, in all its complexity, experienced by a group that understands itself as an identifiable group" (Miller 1994: 68). Genres are cultural artifacts, constitutive substance of a culture. A culture may be characterized by its genre set, which represents a system of actions and interactions that have specific social locations and functions as well as recurrent values or functions.

The genre set adumbrates a relationship between instantiations of a genre in individual acts and systems of value and signification. Miller draws on the structuration theory of Anthony Giddens (1984) for explaining such a relationship. According to such a theory, social relations are structured across space and time. The structure of social relations consists of rules (constitutive and normative rules) and resources (for realizing the rules). The structure is "both medium and outcome of the social practices it recursively organizes" (Giddens 1984: 25), which is called the duality of structure. The structure is virtual but must be instantiated in space and time by individual actors. Thus, actors must create structure and schematize existential situation for both themselves and others by recursively relying on already available structures (shared social classifications and interpretations). The instantiation of structure is also the reproduction of structure. "Social actors create recurrence in their actions by reproducing the structural aspects of institutions, by using available structures as the medium of their action and thereby producing those structures again as virtual order available for further memory, interpretation, and use" (Miller 1994: 71).

Thus, genre can be understood as that aspect of situated communicative structure that is capable of reproduction. "The rules and resources of a genre provide reproducible speaker and addressee roles, social typification of recurrent social needs or exigencies, topical structures (or "moves" and "steps"), and ways of indexing events to material conditions, turning them into constraints or resources" (Miller 1994: 71).

Genres belong to community. A rhetorical community is a virtual entity invoked in rhetorical discourse, which is "constituted by attributions of characteristic joint rhetorical actions, genres of interaction, ways of getting things done, including reproducing itself" (Miller 1994: 73). A rhetorical community exists in human memories and in its specific instantiations in discourses, and persists as structuring aspects of all forms of socio-rhetorical actions. It works partly through genre as the operational site of joint, reproducible social actions, mediating the private and public, singular and recurrent, micro and macro; and more generally, it operates as a site where centrifugal and centripetal forces must meet.

### 2.3.5 Methodology

In line with New Rhetoric's emphasis on the functional and

contextual aspect of genres, scholars in this approach employ enthnographic rather than linguistic methods for discourse analysis, offering thick descriptions of contexts surrounding genres and the actions texts perform within these situations (cf. Hyon 1996). For example, Miller's classification of discourse is actually ethnomethodological, and she proposes to look for ethno-categories of discourse that we have names for in everyday language (Miller 1984: 27). Schryer (1993, 1994) uses a variety of ethnographic techniques, including participant observation, interviews, and document collection to study laboratory and clinic texts. Other scholars also use ethnographic methods to study genres in academic communities (Bazerman 1988), tax accounting firms (Devitt 1991), and bank offices (Smart 1992, 1993).

### 2.3.6 Assessment

New Rhetoric has made great contributions to genre studies. First, a genre is explicitly considered as a social action, a view now accepted by many approaches of genre studies, including the ESP approach and Martin's approach. This paves the way for introducing sociological theories into genre studies, and as a result facilitates the in-depth study of the nature and working principle of genres. Second, situation acquires a very high status in genre studies, and is studied from social and semiotic perspectives rather than an individual or physical perspective. Third, genres are now studied against broad cultural backgrounds, with a culture characterized by a genre set consisting of a large number of genre instances.

However, there are also drawbacks in the genre theory of New Rhetoric. First, though genre is considered as action-based discourse classification, the criteria for such classification are heterogeneous, including substance (semantics), form (syntactics) or rhetorical action (pragmatics). The lack of an explicit unified criterion for classification greatly reduces the rigorousness of the theory. Second, the exact relationship among culture, situation and genre is not specified in the proposed hierarchy, which makes the terms vague and difficult to handle. In fact, other terms such as form of life, strategy, speech act, locution, experience are also too vague and slippery for an academic study of genre. Third, though exigence (a form of purpose) as the social motive for rhetorical actions is mentioned as the core of situations, the exploration of genres is not based on exigence, but more on semantic/syntactic features and other situational or cultural factors. This discrepancy may be partly attributed to the adoption of the anthropological approach.

## 2.4 Genre Studies in ESP

In ESP/EAP studies, genre is used as a tool for analyzing and teaching language in academic and professional settings. Major scholars in this approach include Swales (Swales 1981, 1986, 1990; Askehave & Swales 2001), Bhatia (1993, 1997a, 1997b, 1999), Thompson (1994), and some others. This section will mainly review the framework of Swales as his theory is most representative of this approach.

### 2.4.1 Definition and Characteristics of Genre

Swales provides an explicit working definition of genre. According to him:

> A genre comprises a class of communicative events, the members of which share some set of communicative purposes. These purposes are recognized by the expert members of the parent discourse community and thereby constitute the rationale for the genre. This rationale shapes the schematic structure of the discourse and influences and constrains the choice of content and style. (Swales 1990: 58)

According to this definition, some characteristics of genre can be worked out. First, a genre is a class of communicative events. A communicative event is one in which language (and/or paralanguage) plays a significant and indispensable role. It comprises the discourses, the participants, and the environment of its production and reception, including both the historical and cultural associations. In order for a class of communicative events to be recognized as a genre in a given culture, it has to gain prominence in that culture (Swales 1990: 45-46).

A set of communicative purposes shared by the members of a speech community functions as the principal criterion that turns a class of communicative events into a genre. Genres are communicative vehicles for achieving social goals. A genre may have a set of communicative goals that are consistent with each other. When the purposive elements are in conflict with each other, the effectiveness of the genre as a social-rhetorical action will be questionable, and consequently, the existence of the genre will be endangered (Swales 1990: 46-48; Askehave & Swales 2001).

According to Swales (1990: 52-53), the communicative purposes as the rationale behind a genre set constraints to allowable contributions in terms of their content, positioning and form. These communicative purposes may be fully recognized by the established members of discourse communities, partly recognized by apprentice members, either recognized or unrecognized by non-members. Recognition of these purposes provides the rationale for the members of a community to employ the genre to realize communicatively the goals of their community. This rationale gives rise to constraining conventions and exerts influence on their constantly evolving process.

Swales (1990: 49) holds that instances of a genre show varying degrees of prototypicality. Thus, a family resemblance approach is required in addition to a definition approach to genre study. Such an integrated approach "allows the genre analyst to find a course between trying to produce unassailable definitions of a particular genre and relaxing into the irresponsibility of family resemblances" (Swales 1990: 52). Thus, while the communicative purpose is the privileged property of a genre, other properties such as form, structure, style and audience expectations show varying degrees of prototypicality of the instances of a genre. If all high-probability expectations are realized, the instance will be considered as prototypical by the parent discourse community.

In addition, Swales (1990: 54-57) attaches importance to the discourse community's nomenclature for the genres as a source of insight for genre identification. According to him (Swales 1990: 55), close attention should be paid to the genre names created by the active community members who are most familiar with and most professionally involved in these genres. An appropriate approach for establishing genres would be based on investigations into actual communicative behavior, including the naming procedures of the established members and the categorizations elicited, though the value of ethnographic communication typically need further validation. Thus, Swales' methodology for genre identification is partly ethnographic.

### 2.4.2 Genre in a Discourse Community

Genres are properties of discourse communities and belong to discourse communities rather than individuals. Thus, the discourse community is an indispensable concept in Swale's model of genre study. Swales (1990: 9) holds that "discourse communities are sociorhetorical networks that form in order to work towards common goals". Six characteristics are listed as necessary and sufficient conditions for identifying a group of individuals as constituting a discourse community: (1) a broadly agreed set of common public goals; (2) participatory mechanisms of intercommunication among its members, such as meetings, telecommunications, newsletters, correspondence, and conversations, which may vary from community to community; (3) participatory mechanisms used primarily for providing information and feedback, that is, for uptake of informational opportunities, though the secondary purposes may vary according to communities:

(4) possession and use of one or more genres in the communicative furtherance of its aims, with developed and still developing discoursal expectations concerning topics, text's role in the community, as well as the form, function and positioning of discourse elements; (5) the acquisition of specific lexis, both public and professional, for realizing the genre; (6) a threshold level of members with a suitable degree of relevant content and discourse expertise, with a reasonable ratio between novices and experts as a necessary condition for the survival of the community (Swales 1990: 24-27).

### 2.4.3 Pre-genre and Genre Differences

Swales (1990: 58-61) argues that not all communicative events are instances of genres. There are pre-generic forms of verbal activity from which more specific types of interaction may have presumably either evolved or broken away. These include at least casual conversation/chat and ordinary narrative, the former being too pervasive and fundamental, while the latter operating through temporal succession and oriented towards agents of the events rather than the events themselves.

According to Swales (1990: 61-66), genres vary significantly along a number of parameters, including the complexity of rhetorical purpose, the degree of simultaneity of their instantiation, the mode of their expression (e.g. written or spoken), and the extent to which they are likely to exhibit universal or language-specific tendencies.

### 2.4.4 Schematic Structure

As shown in Swales' definition, the communicative purposes as the rationale of a genre shape the schematic structures of the discourse and constrain the choice of content and style. From the perspective of realization, it can be understood as a three-tiered model with communicative purposes realized by schematic structure, which is in turn realized by rhetorical strategies. The schematic structure of a genre is generally held as including several moves, which may in turn be realized by several steps. Rhetorical strategies (linguistic resources) are analyzed as resources for the realizations of the schematic structure (Swales 1990: 58).

Swales (1990: 84-90) turns to cognitive science for the explanation of schematic structure. He formulates the discoursal expectations and actions characteristic of a genre in terms of cognitive schemata. Two kinds of schemata are recognized, content schemata that arise from previous knowledge of the world and formal schemata that arise from previous knowledge of prior texts, both of which are considered to contribute to the recognition of genres. These schemata have associated encoding and decoding procedures, and thus shape our expectations and help us react appropriately in certain situations.

### 2.4.5 Methodology

Swales (1981, 1990) focuses on the study of research-process genres, including research articles, abstracts, research presentations, grant proposals, dissertations, and reprint requests. His methodology is an integration of anthropological and linguistic ones. In his study of research articles (Swales 1990), he first describes the evolution of research articles and the environment for its construction, and establishes the schematic structure of research articles through investigation and category elicitation. An Introduction-Method-Results-Discussion structure is identified in this way. Then a move-step analysis is applied to each of these parts. The rhetorical strategies and linguistics resources are then analyzed to show the realizations of the general structure.

### 2.4.6 Applications to ESP

Swale's interest in genre is aimed at providing an approach to ESP teaching and study. Thus, he relates genre to language-learning tasks. A task is defined as "one of a set of differentiated, sequencable goal-directed activities drawing upon a range of cognitive and communicative procedures relatable to the acquisition of pre-genre and genre skills appropriate to a foreseen or emerging sociorhetorical situation" (Swales 1990: 76). In other words, tasks can be viewed as those encoding and decoding procedures in genre-type communicative events as moderated by genre-related aspects of text-role and text-environment. Specific tasks in genre-teaching activities are primarily determined by the communicative purposes. The teaching of genre skills essentially involves the development of acquisition-promoting text-task activities.

### 2.4.7 Assessment

Swales' major contributions to genre studies can be roughly summarized into four points. First, as genre is considered as a class of communicative events, attention is drawn to the communicative function of genres, which implies a social approach to genre studies. Second, Swales realizes the critical importance of purpose in genre studies. Purpose is considered as the principal criterion for genre creation and identification, and also as the rationale for constraining the shape of the schematic structure and the choice of content and style. Third, like scholars of New Rhetoric, Swales attaches importance to the concept of community and suggests studying genre in close relation to specific communities. Fourth, the schematic structure of genre is now explicitly studied and explained based on cognitive sciences, though the explanation is a little simple and inadequate.

However, the genre theory in ESP also has its own drawbacks. First, the theory suffers the same drawback as the genre theory of New Rhetoric. Though purpose is considered as of great significance, it is used in its common sense rather than well established and studied academically. This leads to the vagueness of the theory and damages its rigorousness. Second, the social and collective nature of the genre is emphasized at the price of the neglect of the individual characteristics in the specific genre instances employed by discourse community members. Third, the exact relation among concepts such as purpose, genre, schematic structure and rhetoric strategies is not explicit enough. Particularly, how the communicative purpose constrains the schematic structure and how the schematic structure constrains the choice of rhetoric strategies have not been discussed in detail. This results in the difficulty for the operationalization of this theory.

## 2.5 Genre Theory in SFL: Halliday and Hasan

Genre is an important subject in SFL, and the genre theories of SFL hold an important position among modern genre theories. Generally speaking, SFL's approach to genre is a sociological one. However, SFL scholars hold different views concerning the theoretical status of genre, its nature, and the specific methods of research. These views can be broadly divided into two groups: the group headed by Halliday and Hasan, and the group headed by J. R. Martin. In this section, the views of the first groups will be briefly reviewed.

### 2.5.1 Halliday's Ideas of Genre

As the founder of SFL, Halliday has not dedicated any specific paper or chapter to the study of genre. However, his ideas of genre are inspiring for the genre research in SFL.

Halliday sometimes considers genre as an aspect of mode. His definition of mode includes rhetorical mode, what is being achieved by the text in terms of such categories as persuasive, expository, didactic, and the like. These categories are what have been traditionally discussed under the heading of genre, but actually are more like Gregory's functional tenor (Gregory & Carroll 1978) or Ure & Ellis's role (Ure & Ellis 1977). Halliday (1978: 62) maintains that "mode covers roughly Hyme's channel, key and genre". "The concept of genre discussed above is an aspect of what we are calling 'mode.' The various genres of discourse, including literary genres, are the specific semiotic functions of text that have social value in the culture." (Halliday 1978: 144-145)

According to Halliday's model, mode probabilistically conditions the textual metafunction of language. Genre as an aspect of mode also conditions the textual metafunction, more specifically, the symbolic organization of the text, i. e. the text structure. However, due to the interactions between mode and the other two variables (field and tenor), genre is also considered as having implications for ideational and interpersonal meanings. As a result, generic categories are held as functionally complex.

### 2. 5. 2 Hasan's Theory of Genre

Based on Halliday's ideas, Hasan has developed her own theory of genre. According to her (Hasan 1977: 229), a genre is defined as a type of discourse. The term genre is a short form of genre-specific semantic potential, determined by the meaning potential associated with a specific contextual configuration (CC). In other words, it is one calibration of the values of specific field, tenor, and mode. "Genre bears a logical relation to CC, being its verbal expression. If CC is a class of situation type, then genre is language doing the job appropriate to that class of social happenings" (Hasan 1985b: 108).

The genre-specific semantic potential is a subset of the semantic potential. The semantic potential refers only to those meanings that are formed, and which can be expressed through language; it is a manifestation of semiotic potential. The semiotic potential includes ways of doing, ways of being, and ways of saying. As culture is describable as an integrated body of the total set of meanings available to a community, the semiotic potential is culture (Hasan 1985b: 108).

As register is defined as the configuration of semantic resources that the member of a culture typically associates with a situation type (Halliday 1978: 111), then genre as a subset of semantic potential is actually placed by Hasan on the plane of register. More specifically, a genre is a text type on the register plane that is probabilistically conditioned by a situation type (i. e. contextual configurations of field, tenor and mode).

Hasan (1985a: 52-69) has developed a model of Generic Structural Potential (GSP) to deal with the text structure. According to this theory, every genre has a structural potential, i. e. a GSP. A GSP includes obligatory elements and optional elements, occurring in a certain order. Some elements are iterative, and such iteration is also optional. A genre is determined by its obligatory elements and their order of occurrence, while the optional elements determine the variation among texts that belong to the same genre. Hasan has studied service encounters and concluded that the GSP of this genre is: [(Greeting) · (Sale Initiation) ^] [(Sale Enquiry¬ · ) {Sale Request ^ Sale Compliance ^ }¬ ^ Sale ^] Purchase Purchase Closure ( ^ Finis). In this GSP, "^" indicates the order, "( )" indicates optionality; "· " means that the order of two neighboring elements are changeable, while the range of this change is indicated by "[ ]". "{ }¬ " means that the elements in "{ }" have the same number of iteration times. Hasan (1985a: 64) argues that such GSP can show the structure of many possible texts of the same genre.

Thus, genres can vary in delicacy. For some texts to belong to the same genre, however, their structure must be some possible realization of a given GSP. From another perspective, texts of the same genre can vary their structure as long as their obligatory elements and the dispositions of the GSP remain unchanged (Hasan 1985b: 108).

### 2.5.3 Assessment

There is some inconsistency in Halliday's positioning of genre. On the one hand, he considers genre as an aspect of mode and therefore is something outside language, or more precisely, something realized by language. On the other, from the perspective of rhetorical genre, he (and also Hasan) argues that "every genre has its own text structure" (Halliday & Hasan, 1976: 327), i. e. macro-structure. The macro-structure of texts turns them into a particular text-type, such as conversation, narrative, lyric, business letters (Halliday & Hasan 1976: 324). Thus a genre is classification of texts based on the organizational forms of the text, and therefore is something within language. This inconsistency is a reflection of Halliday's uncertainty concerning the status of genre in his theory, and exerts some negative influence on the development of the genre theory in SFL.

Hasan's theory of genre also has some drawbacks. First, as a genre is determined by the obligatory elements of its GSP and their order of occurrence, it seems that a genre is actually the macro semantic structure of a text type, which is in conflict with her definition of genre as a text type proper. Second, as Hasan attaches importance to the obligatory elements and their order of occurrence, her GSP is represented linearly. As linearity is the nature of syntagm rather than paradigm, what Hasan studies is structure rather than system. However, it is well known that SFL places priority on paradigm, and considers structure as derived from system. It seems that there must be systemic potentials still underlying the GSP that is not made explicit by Hasan. A penetrating study of genre should first establish a genre system comparable to systems at the lexicogrammatical stratum as shown in Matthiessen's work (Matthiessen 1995), and then derive the genre structure through the operation of realization statements. Another problem also arises from the linearity of GSP. As a genre is determined by the obligatory elements and their disposition, then texts of the same genre should faithfully realize the order of the occurrence of the elements. However, a more careful observation and analysis of actual texts will reveal that the disposition of the obligatory elements in both service encounters and fairy tales are much more flexible than that as specified in their respective GSP. For example, in a business letter, "purchase" and "purchase closure" can be stated first, and the "final event" in a fairy tale can also be presented at the beginning through the so called technique "flashback".

Hasan (1977: 229) claims that genre is the verbal expression of contextual configuration, one calibration of the values of field, tenor, and mode. In practice, the elements of the GSP of service encounters and fairy tales proposed by her mainly realize ideational metafunction and is therefore field-biased, with variations in generic structure controlled by tenor and mode. The GSP is actually the ideational macro structure of the text type, while the interpersonal and textual elements are optional (cf. Martin 1992: 504-505).

Still another problem is related to Hasan's exclusive interest in language. If a genre is considered as the verbal expression of contextual configuration (Hasan 1985b: 108), all its elements should be realized by language. However, in practice, such elements as "purchase" and "purchase closure" in service encounters are mainly realized by actions, with language only playing a secondary role. In fact, a service counter can even be realized without saying a single word. Thus, modalities other than language should be taken into account in the study of genre.

## 2.6 Genre Theory in SFL: Martin and His Colleagues

Within SFL, the genre theory of another group headed by J. R. Martin, Francis Christie, John Rothery and some others is somewhat different from that of Halliday and Hasan. In this section, the genre theory of these scholars will be reviewed.

### 2.6.1 Definition of Genre

Genre has been defined on different occasions during the development of the context theory of the group headed by Martin (cf. Martin 1984, 1992, 1997; Painter & Martin 1986; Martin & White 2005). Two of these formulations are most representative of the ideas of this group:

> ...In this model genre is a system comprising configurations of field, mode and tenor selections which unfold in recurring stages of discourse — a pattern of

register patterns in other words. In our applied work we adopted a working definition of genre as a staged, goal oriented social process. Social because we participate in genres with other people; goal oriented because we use genres to get things done and feel a sense of frustration when we don't resolve our telos; staged because it usually takes us a few steps to reach our goals. (Martin & White 2005: 32-33)

In functional linguistic terms what this means is that genres are defined as a recurrent configuration of meanings and that these recurrent configurations of meaning enact the social practices of a given culture. (Martin & Rose 2008: 6)

It can be seen from the citations that a distinction is drawn between a working definition and an academic one. Thus, while a working definition will be "a staged, goal oriented social process", an academic definition will be "patterns of register patterns", or "recurrent configurations of meaning".

### 2.6.2 The General Approach

In *Genre Relations*, Martin & Rose (2008) outlined their general approach to genre in contrast with the approaches of New Rhetoric and ESP. Five points were mentioned:

(1) social rather than cognitive (or socio-cognitive as in Berkenkotter & Huckin 1995)

(2) social semiotic rather than ethnographic, with tenor, field and mode explored as patterns of meaning configured together as the social practices we call genres

(3) integrated within a functional theory of language rather than interdisciplinary; note however that our theory is multi-perspectival (i.e. including several complementary ways of looking at text, e.g. metafunction, strata)

(4) fractal rather than eclectic, with basic concepts such as metafunction redeployed across strata, and across modalities of communication (e.g. image, sound, action and spatial design)

(5) interventionist rather than critical since following Halliday we see linguistics as an ideologically committed form of social action. (Martin & Rose 2008: 20)

### 2.6.3 Theoretical Positioning of Genre

In order to better understand what genre is for Martin and his colleagues, it is necessary to introduce Martin's context theory. Martin proposes a stratified model of context above language, which includes two strata: genre and register. Register is comparable to Halliday's context of situation (the difference is that Martin considers register as an independent stratum, while Halliday's situation is only an instance of culture), and consists of three variables, field, tenor, and mode, which are realized by the ideational, interpersonal, and textual metafunction at the stratum of discourse semantics. Above register is the stratum of genre, which means recurrent patterns of registers. Genre in this sense is comparable to Halliday's context of culture as culture can be interpreted as a system of genres. The relation between register and genre is one of meta-redundancy (Martin 1985, 1992, 1997, 1999b, 2001a).

Martin's model of context has been criticized from scholars both inside and outside SFL. The keenest criticism, which comes from Hasan (1995, 1999), focuses on Martin's use of metaredundancy in a two-tiered model of semiotic. In defense of his genre theory, he listed seven points (Martin 1999b, 2001a): (1) The need for a multi-functional characterisation of genre (since genre redounds simultaneously with field, mode and tenor); (2) the desire to strengthen field, mode, tenor and multifunction solidarity (in order to facilitate quantitive studies of register); (3) the importance of accounting for just which combinations of field, tenor and mode variables a culture recurrently exploits (as part of a more general understandings of phylogenesis—how cultures evolve; and its ontogenetic recapitulation); (4) the question of handling variation in field, tenor and mode from one stage to another within a genre (the issue of text dynamics); (5) a concern with the distinction between activity sequences (field time) and generic structure (text time) (as conditioned by mode); (6) the formalisation of trans-metafunctional valeur (the issue of agnation); (7) the problem of contextual metaphor (with one genre standing for another).

### 2.6.4 Functional Parameters for Studying Genre

Martin (1997, 2008a, 2008b, 2009) suggested some functional parameters for analyzing genres: stratification, typology and topology, synoptic and dynamic, genesis, and dimensions of semantic variation. Stratification means that context is stratified into genre and register, while language is stratified into discourse semantics, lexicogrammar, and phonology/graphology. Genesis means a framework for modeling semiotic change according to the time-depth involved. It includes phylogenesis, ontogenesis, and logogenesis, which deal with the unfolding of text, development of the individual and the expansion of the culture respectively.

In the view of Martin (and also Matthiessen), typology and topology are two complementary dimensions that are used to describe the meaning potential on any stratum (Martin & Matthiessen 1991). Typology is a kind of taxonomy based on a chosen criterion or a set of criteria; things are represented as either similar or different with respect to these criteria, with quite clear-cut boundaries in between. A topology is a set of criteria for establishing degrees of nearness or proximity among the members of some category. A topological description shows the continuum and the fuzziness of the border between things.

Synoptic and dynamic are two complementary perspectives to represent the meaning potential of genre. A synoptic system represents the meaning potential from a static perspective, while a dynamic system represents the potential actively. The actual represented statically is a text, and is a process when represented dynamically. Thus, a synoptic system generates a text, while a dynamic system generates a process.

Three dimensions of semantic variation are suggested: realization, instantiation, and individuation. Realization deals with the relationship across levels of abstraction. Specifically, genre system is realized by register, while the whole context as connotative semiotic is realized by language. Instantiation is the hierarchy of generality, which relates system to instances of use. It relates the systems of meanings as a whole to their specialization as registers and genres; at the same time, it generalizes recurring patterns of meaning across instances as text types. Individuation specializes the meaning potential according to people (for users rather than uses of language) and relates system to repertoires of use (Martin 2010a).

### 2.6.5 Genre Structure

Martin (1997) argues that a constituency representation of genre offers only a compromised image of genre phasing. He suggests that genre structure be best interpreted simultaneously from the perspectives of particulate, prosodic and periodic representations. Particulate structure organizes texts segmentally in either orbital or serial patterns. An orbital structure has one element as nuclear and other elements as satellites, while in a serial structure there are no nuclear elements and the text unfolds step by step, with each step dependent on the preceding. Prosodic structure is suprasegmental and spreads itself across the text. Periodical structure is wave-like and organizes the text into peaks and troughs based on the information flow. Particulate, prosodic, and periodical structures are related to the ideational (experiential and logical), interpersonal and textual meanings respectively.

### 2.6.6 Macro-Genre

The term macro-genre is proposed to deal with texts which combine familiar elementary genres (Martin, 1994, 1995, 1997; Martin & Rose 2008). Martin argues that the logico-semantic relations outlined by Halliday for clause complexes can also be employed to analyze the relations among the elementary genres in a macro-genre. Ideational strategies for the development of macro-genres include projection (wording and meaning) and expansion. Interpersonally macro-genres can develop through the amplification of mood, modalization, attitude and so on. Textually, macro-genres organize themselves with respect to waves of information flow. In addition, genre-embedding is also suggested, which means that a whole genre is embedded and functions as a stage in another genre.

### 2.6.7 Contextual Metaphor

In analogy with Halliday's grammatical metaphor, Martin (1997) has raised the issue contextual metaphor. Broadly speaking, contextual metaphor arises from the tension between genre and register. Every genre has some typical register patterns as its congruent realizations. However, a genre may also be realized incongruently by other registers. In this case, contextual metaphor arises. For example, a report genre can be realized metaphorically through the register configuration that typically realizes a narrative. Martin maintains that contextual metaphor, interpreted as the strata tension at the level of context, can help us gain valuable insights into one of the trajectories along which the social processes of a culture expand—by deploying register variables metaphorically to symbolize a complementary genre.

### 2.6.8 Genre and Ideology

Martin's approach to genre is interventionist, which is influenced by Bakhtin's idea of genre as ideological forms (cf. Section 2.2.5). One of the aims of his genre theory is to develop democratic pedagogies, and understand the ways that symbolic control is maintained, distributed and challenged in contemporary societies by revealing the inequalities in access to privileged genres of modern institutional field. For this purpose, Martin turns to Bernstein's code theory and maintains that it is ideology that differentially distributes control over the privileged genres of modernity, by means of differing educational outcomes. Ideology is defined by Martin (1992: 507) as a system of coding orientations and is considered as permeating every level of semiosis. Differences in coding orientations are conditioned by one's relation to power and control within the division of social labor.

In most industrial societies, the range of genres is considered as further differentiated by institutions such as science, industry, and administration. Control over these genres is conditioned by specialized pathways of education, the access to which depends on our social-economic class position. Our control over genres of power in turn conditions our status ranking in social hierarchies (related to tenor), our claim to authority in institutional fields (related to field), and our prominence in public life (related to mode) (cf. Martin 1992: 526-527; 2007a: 18-19).

### 2.6.9 Assessment

Compared with the genre theories of other approaches, the genre theory of the group headed by Martin is the most systematic and complete. The merits of this genre theory can be roughly summarized into several points. First, Martin explicitly adopts a social and semiotic approach, which is in sharp contrast with the psychological-cognitive and formal approaches. The semiotic perspective makes it possible to study genre on the basis of the study of meanings, while a social perspective enables us to draw theories of sociology for the explanation of genres. Second, Martin integrates his genre theory into his more general theory of context, and further, into the theory of SFL and Systemic Functional Semiotics. With SFL as the foundation, his theory is more operationable. Third, Martin's genre theory is based on large-scale investigations and on his long-term work on genre-based literacy (cf. Martin 1993, 1999a). The integration of theory and practice makes the theory much more convincing and appliable.

However, Martin's genre theory has its own drawbacks. The first drawback is concerned with the gap between the working definition and the academic definition. Specifically, the relationship between a staged, goal-oriented social action and recurrent configurations of meaning (patterns of register patterns) is not specified in any detail. This confusion leads to the adoption of the working definition of genre for academic studies by many scholars. The second drawback is reflected in Martin's somewhat ambivalent attitude towards purpose. On the one hand, he takes purposes the rationale for the development of his genre theory (Martin 1997: 236) and explicitly accepts the teleological nature of genre (as shown in the working definition). On the other, Martin rejects purpose as an academic term in his genre theory, partly due to his view that the purpose of social actions should be studied in sociology and philosophy rather than in linguistics. As a result, the word purpose is used in its common sense and is taken for granted, without any in-depth academic exploration. Third, while Martin's genre theory is developed as a part of SFL, the focus is on the study of structure (schematic structure in this case) rather than on system. This is inconsistent with the priority of system over structure in SFL. Fourth, Martin's theories focus on genre realization, while little attention has been paid to genre instantiation and individuation. This can be partly attributed to the underdevelopment of the instantiation and individuation theories. However, more attention needs to be paid to these two dimensions rather than simply to genre realization.

## 2.7 A Note on the Study of Web Genres

As genres collected from corporate websites will be used as the data in this study, it is necessary to present a brief review of the study of web genres. Generally speaking, web genres have not attracted much academic attention. Among the works on web genres, most are computational studies in information sciences; some are social semiotic studies. They will be reviewed respectively in this section.

### 2.7.1 Web Genre Studies in Information Sciences

The major works of this group include: *Genres on the Web: Computational Models and Empirical Studies* (Mehler, Sharo & Santini 2010), which is a collection of papers on web genres contributed by 29 authors; *Homepage usability: 50 websites deconstructed* (Nielsen & Tahir 2002); genre papers published in a series of proceedings of Annual Hawaii International Conference on System Sciences, including the work of Shepherd & Watters (1998, 1999), the work of Askehave & Nielsen (2005), and the work of Crowston & Williams (1997, 1999, 2000). These studies are heterogeneous rather than based on a unified theory. Their major features will be briefly summarized and reviewed below.

One of the most salient features of the web genre studies is the recognition of the hypertextual attribute of webpages (cf. Bateman 2008: 210). Hypertextuality is defined as the ability to link documents together and to provide technological support for following documents, and considered as the crucial new component of the new media. The emphasis on the linking ability, however, implies that the study of hypertextuality is more from a technological perspective rather than from a semiotic (semantic) perspective. As far as the study of genre is concerned, the focus should be on the semantic/semiotic relation that conditions the physical linking and navigation.

The emphasis on the linking ability leads to the emphasis on the role of medium in cyber genres. This is reflected in the distinction made between traditional genres and cyber genres by some scholars: while traditional genres are defined by the content-form pair, cyber genres are defined by the content-form-functionality triple (Shepherd & Watters 1998, 1999). This is even more clearly reflected in Askehave & Nielsen's two-dimension model of web genres, which includes both a traditional text dimension and also a medium (navigation) dimension (Askehave & Nielsen 2005). Likewise, Crowston and Williams' characterization of cyber genres based on the link types is also a manifestation of the critical role of the medium (Crowston & Williams 1997, 1999, 2000). However, medium is physical, and is only the bearer of the semiotic modality of communication. As a genre is semiotic system, the emphasis on medium rather than on modality is inappropriate.

The identification of web genres is generally based on the recognition of a list of features, which may be linguistic features in both content and form, or technological features such as types of links and medium, or a combination of content, form and functionality features, e. g. Shepherd & Watters (1999) and works by the contributors in Mehler, Sharo & Santini (2010). Purpose is discussed at times, but generally not adopted as a criterion for genre identification. This can be partly attributed to the difficulty in the computational recognition and analysis of purpose.

Last, in these studies, contextual factors and the model of language (and other modalities) are greatly simplified. This is attested by Martin (2010b: XI) when he mentioned "its relatively flat approach as far as social context and its realization in language and attendant modalities of communication is concerned". From an SFL perspective, the field, tenor, and mode factors are all conflated into text types, and the various hierarchies and complementarities of each modality (language in particular) are simply replaced by a series of features. On the one hand, this simplification may obviously facilitate computing; but on the other, it fails to reflect the complexity of the working of the genres.

### 2.7.2 Web Genre Studies in Social Semiotics

In addition to the more technological approach, another approach to web genres is a social semiotic one. The scholars of this approach include Knox (2009), Kok (2004) and Thurstun (2004). In this section, the work of Knox will be discussed as it is most representative and also most relevant to the current study.

In contrast to a more technological perspective as discussed in 2. 7. 1, Knox's unpublished PhD thesis *Multimodal Discourse on Online Newspaper Homepages: A Socio-Semiotic Perspective* (Knox 2009) is a study of web genres from a socio-semiotic perspective. More specifically, it is based on the theory of Systemic Functional Semiotics, including SFL and Systemic Functional Multimodal Discourse Analysis. The focus is on the meanings communicated on online newspaper rather than on the hypetextual linking structure. This is clearly indicated by his discussion of the ideational, interpersonal and textual meanings of homepage genres, and the semogenesis and intersemiosis of newsbites. It should be noted, however, that Knox's study of genre is based on the function-class relation similar to SFL's study of clause grammar. Purpose is not significant for him. A telos-oriented approach may be in need for an improvement of his work.

Following SFL's principle of priority of system over structure, Knox establishes a variety of systems in his study, including the basic systems of newspapers, websites, news websites, pages (including homepages and content pages), sections, news stories on online newspaper homepages, system networks of news taxonomies and newsbites, etc. Realization rules are also provided for each system. The structure is then discussed as a realization of the system. The highlighting of the paradigmatic aspect of web documents, especially that of the newsbite genre and the homepage genre, is groundbreaking. This is one of the sources of inspiration that encourages the author of this study to bring out the paradigmatic aspect of genre.

Another interesting feature of Knox's work is his application of the rank scale to the study of online newspapers (Knox 2009: 153-206). Five ranks are recognized based on the principle of constituency: newspaper, section, page, zone, and text. A function-class diagram is established for illustrating this specific rank perspective (Knox 2009: 191). This work is original and blazes a new path for the study of websites. However, there is one problem in such a rank-based study of websites. Constituency structure is based on a part-whole relationship, but the relations between the different ranks as recognized by Knox cannot be simplified as part-whole. There is at least a means-end relation holding between the different ranks (which will be discussed in more detail in Sections 3.2 and 3.3). More generally, the relation between them is macro-semantic rather than simply constituent.

In contrast to a relatively flattened theory as adopted in web genre studies in information sciences, Knox applies the complementarities (such as metafunctional diversity, axis) and hierarchies (stratification of language and context) as theorized in SFL and Systemic Functional Semiotics in general to his study. There is also inadequacy in this regard, that is, the neglect of the individuation dimension, which is in close relation to realization and instantiation. As a whole, however, the richness of the theories adopted in Knox's work helps reflect the complexity of genres as a semiotic system.

## 2.8 Summary

This chapter has presented a brief review of the major theories of genre that are relevant to the study of this book, including Aristotle's ideas of genre, Bakhtin's theory of speech genres, the genre theory of New Rhetoric, genre studies in ESP, the genre theories of Halliday and Hasan, and the genre theory of Martin and his colleagues. These theories represent the major approaches to genre studies: the literary approach developed by Aristotle and followed in literary studies through the centuries (note that theories of literary genres after Aristotle is not reviewed in detail as it is irrelevant to the current study), the rhetoric approach that can also be dated back to Aristotle and adopted in rhetoric studies, the ethnological/anthropological approach adopted in sociological theories of genre, and the linguistic approach adopted in ESP, SFL and other linguistic theories of genre. In addition, the studies of web genres are also briefly reviewed.

As a whole, through the efforts of the scholars through the ages, genre studies of different approaches have made great achievements. However, there are still some problems to be solved. First, in the theories, purpose (or intension, motive) is generally accepted as an integral element in the study genre. However, it is only used as a common-sense term without any academic exploration. Considering the teleological nature of human actions (including communicative actions), a teleological approach to genre study will help explore the nature and working principles of genres. Second, these genre studies focus on the exploration of individual genres, especially the schematic structure of the genres. The study of the underlying principles that govern the generation of a genre, especially the generation of the schematic structure of a genre is inadequate. Third, in all these theories, genre is always discussed in relation to such terms as typification, classification, or recurrent configuration, and the focus is on genre as a type, as an abstract institutional phenomenon. However, a genre as an institutional phenomenon only exists in a large number of specific instances used by specific individuals. The operationalization process should also be included in genre study.

Considering the drawbacks of existing theories, a teleological approach with the focus on the nature, working principles and the operationalization of genres is in need for genre study.

# Chapter 3

# A Teleological Perspective to Genre

In Chapter 2, the author has presented a brief review of the major schools of genre theories relevant to this study. Considering the drawbacks of these theories, Chapter 3 will develop a new model of genre analysis from a teleological perspective. In philosophy (and also sociology), the science of telos (or final causes) is called teleology. A teleological explanation either explains a process by the end-state towards which it is directed; or explains the existence of something by the function it fulfils. The former tends to be confined to theories of purposive human actions, whereas the latter is a feature of functionalism (Van Huyssteen 2003; Scott & Marshall 2005). As far as a teleological study of genre is concerned, what is most relevant is the former approach.

In the following sections, the telos-oriented model of genre analysis developed by the author will first be presented to give an overview, and will then be interpreted teleologically in detail step by step. Finally, the procedures and methods for applying this model will be discussed.

## 3.1 An Integrated Model of Genre Analysis

The telos-oriented model of genre analysis to be developed in this chapter is presented in Figure 3.1. The diagram in the figure is an extension of Martin's elaboration of the relation between stratification and semantic variation (Martin 2010a). The co-tangential circles in the figure stand for the strata involved in a semiotic (language in this case), which, in the top-down order, include genre, register, discourse semantics, lexicogrammar and phonology. The relation among the strata is one of metaredundancy. The focus will be on the genre stratum, and attention will be paid to the working of genre simplex, complex and agnation from a teleological perspective. Semiotic resources at the register and discourse semantic strata will be employed as analytic tools that help operationalize the general and abstract telos-oriented genre into specific texts of specific users. As shown in Figure 3.1, register patterning includes the configurations of field, mode and tenor of each stage, while semiotic resources at the discourse semantic stratum include systems of ideational, interpersonal and textual metafunctions respectively. The study will stop at the discourse semantic stratum as it is believed as adequate to explain the working of genre.

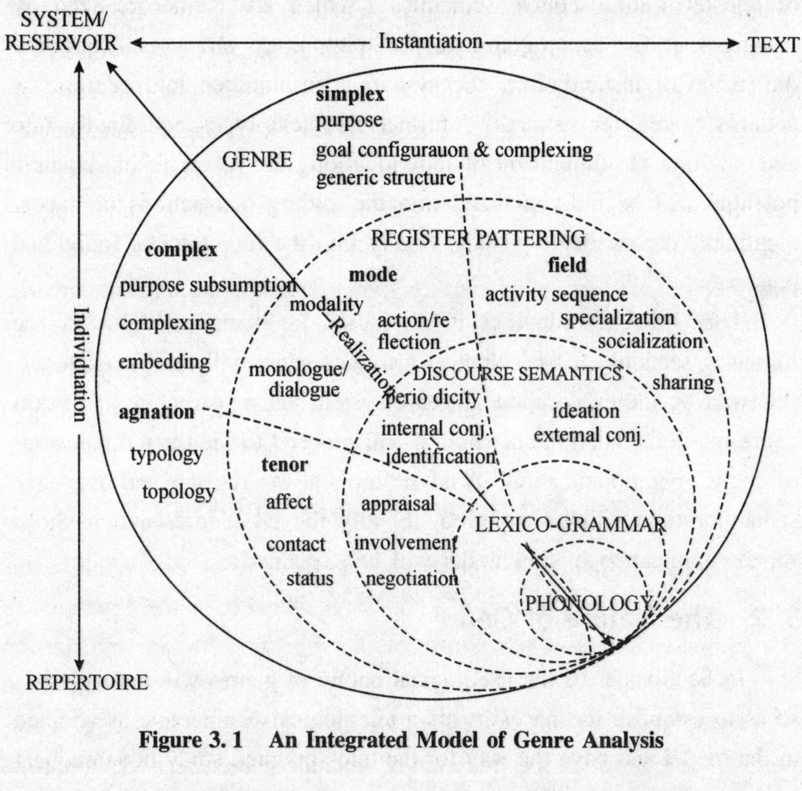


**Figure 3.1　An Integrated Model of Genre Analysis**

The two curves are used to show the metafunctional diversity of a semiotic at each stratum. That is, at the discourse semantic stratum, three metafunctions are identified: ideational, interpersonal and textual, which realize the field, tenor and mode configurations at the register stratum, and which in turn realize the representational, interactional and organizational aspects of a telos respectively at the genre stratum.

The three two-headed arrows stand for the three dimensions of genre operationalization: realization, instantiation, and individuation. The double-headedness of each arrow indicates the bidirectional nature of each dimension. At the upper left corner is the system or reservoir of all semiotic potentials of a culture, which consists of sets of genres. Along the dimension of realization, genre is realized by the realization of register into discourse semantics (which are further realized by resources at the lexicogrammar and phonology strata). Along the dimension of instantiation, the system is instantiated into genres (as patterns of register patterns), further into text types and finally into texts. Along the dimension of individuation, the reservoir of semantic potential will be individualized into the coding orientations of master identities, personality types and finally into the repertoire of individual persona.

This brief introduction is obviously far from enough. In the following sections, the teleological nature of genre will be first explored, followed by the exploration of genre system, genre structure and inter-genre relation. Then the discussion will proceed to the three dimensions of genre operationalization. Analytic tools at the register and discourse semantic strata will be explored. Finally the procedures and methods for the application of this model will be explained.

## 3.2 The Nature of Genre

In Sections 3.1, the teleological nature of genres will be explored, so as to establish the necessity of a teleological perspective as adopted in the model and pave the way for the telos-oriented study in subsequent sections. The generally accepted view of genre as human action (cf. Section 1. 1) will constitute the premise of the current study. The nature of genre will be explored largely by exploring the nature of human actions.

### 3.2.1 The Teleological Nature of Genre

The teleological perspective of this new model is entailed by the teleological nature of genre. As a genre is considered as a social action, the teleological nature of genre derives from the teleological nature of human actions, which is revealed by the activity theory as created by Lev Vygotsky (1978, 1997a, 1997b), developed by A. N Leontjev (1977, 1978, 1979, 1981) and Yrj Engestrm (1987), and popularized by Gordon Wells (1999). Russian activity theory establishes three levels of analysis: activity, action and operation. Activity is realized by action, which is in turn realized by operations.

As actions are the realizations of activities, the teleological nature of actions is derived from that of the activities. According to Leontjev (1978: 86), a basic and constituting characteristic of an activity is its objectivity. That is, human activity is directed at and driven by an object, which is twofold, in its independent existence as subordinating to itself and transforming the activity of the subject, and as a mental image, a product of its property of psychological reflection and realized as an activity of the subject.

Each activity answers a definite need of the subject. The need in itself is only a condition of the organism which serves to activate appropriate biological functions and excite the motor sphere in non-directed seeking movements. When the need meets an object that answers it, it is objectified and filled with contents derived from the surrounding world, and becomes capable of directing and regulating the activity. The activity is directed toward an object of this need, and is extinguished as a result of its satisfaction, and is produced again, perhaps in changed conditions.

Thus, the object is the true motive (motivational sphere of consciousness) of the activity, which evokes and directs the activity toward itself. As the object may be either material or ideal, the motive may also be either material or ideal, either present in perception or exclusively in the imagination or in thought. Therefore, behind an activity there should always be a need, and an activity should always answer one need or another, though the motive may be subjectively or objectively hidden (Leontjev 1978: 78-113).

Concrete types of activity may differ from one another according to various characteristics: their form, emotional intensity, temporal and special requirements, physiological mechanisms, and the method of their fulfillment. However, the major distinguishing factor is the difference of their objects. It is the object of an activity that gives it a determined direction (Leontjev, 1978: 98).

An activity is realized by an action, which is a process subordinated to a conscious purpose, that is, to the representation of the result that must be attained. Thus, while an activity is determined by an unconscious motive, an action is determined by a conscious purpose. The actions that realize activities are aroused by a motive, and are directed toward a purpose. A concrete process taking place before us appears as human activity from the point of view of its relation to motive, and appears as an action or accumulation of a chain of actions when it is subordinated to purpose. An activity usually is accomplished by a complex of actions that are subordinated to particular goals that may be isolated from the general purpose.

Purposes are not contrived by the subject arbitrarily, but are given in objective circumstances, and the isolation and perception of goals is a relatively long process of approbation by action and their objective filing. In addition, every purpose is objectively accomplished in a certain objective situation. Thus, in addition to its intentional aspect as what must be achieved, the action also has its operational aspect, that is, how and by what means it can be achieved. This is determined not by the goal in itself but by the objective conditions of its achievement. The methods for accomplishing actions are called operations. Thus, actions are related to conscious purpose, while operation to conditions. The purpose (and the specific goal) may remain the same, but the conditions in which it is assigned may change. Thus, it is specifically and only the operational content of the action that changes.

In summary, as the realization of activity, human action is driven by a motive/object, but is directed toward a conscious purpose, and is in turn realized by specific operations subordinate to specific conditions. As far as a functional study of genre is concerned, the focus will be on goal-oriented human actions. As objectivity is the basic constituting character of activities and the major distinguishing factor for recognizing different types of activity, the types of actions as the realization of activity types will be mainly identified on the basis of their different purposes. Thus, it is appropriate to adopt purpose as the major criterion for the study of genre as human action.

### 3.2.2 The Social Nature of Human Action

In addition to their teleological nature, human actions are social. The social property of human actions is the basis of the integration of sociological theories in this model. The social characteristic of actions is in part derived from the social characteristic of activities. According to Leontjev (1978: 84-85), the activity of concrete individuals takes place either in a collective, jointly with other people, or in a situation in which the subject deals directly with the surrounding world of objects. It represents a system which is included in the system of relationships of society. The activity of every individual man depends on his place in society. As the realization of activity, action is also social.

Phylogenetically, goal-directed actions in activity make its appearance as the result of transition of man to life in society, that is, of transition of man to social life. The activity of each individual is evoked by its product, which initially answers the need of each of them. However, the development of division of work leads to the isolation of intermediate partial results that are achieved by separate participators of the collective work and that in themselves cannot satisfy the workers' needs. The needs are satisfied by the sharing of the products of their collective activity, obtained by each of them through forms of the relationship binding them one to another that develop in the process of work (i. e. social relationships). The isolation of the intermediate results makes necessary the isolation of the goal, which determines the method and character of the action.

### 3.2.3 Genre as Typified Telos-oriented Social Action

Activity theory is mainly concerned with the activity and action of individuals though a social nature of action is emphasized. However, genre belongs to the collective, that is, an institution. Thus, there is a gap between particular actions of individuals and the actions of the institution that the individuals belong to. This gap is bridged through the typification of teleological social actions.

The typification of social actions presupposes a semiotic view. Human actions are based on and guided by meaning and at the centre of actions is a process of interpretation. This is because the isolation of purpose and specific goals, choice of tools, and the determination of the subjects are all based on the interpretation of the situations. Thus, though each of individual actions is unique in terms of their material configuration of objects, tools and agents, they can be interpreted as comparable, similar, or analogous to other actions. These similar actions can be interpreted semiotically as recurrent actions (cf. Miller 1984).

The specific typification process is well explained by Schutz & Luckmann (1973: 229-241). According to their theory, a type is a uniform relation of determination sedimented in prior experiences. It arises from a situationally adequate solution to a problematic situation through the new determination of an experience which could not be mastered with the aid of old determination relations (Schutz & Luckmann 1973: 231). Determination as used here is synonymous with interpretation. Thus, new experience is made familiar through the interpretation and recognition of relevant similarities, and these similarities become constituted as a type (Miller 1984). When old typifications on hand are inadequate to determine a new experience, a new type is formed from these old typifications. If the new typification proves continually useful for mastering new experiences, its application then becomes a routine. Applied to the typification of social actions, the recognition of similarities in terms of agents, tools, objects/motives and methods between different individual actions leads to the establishment of an action type. When the type can be used successfully in new situations, it becomes routinized. However, if the action type is inadequate to deal with new experiences, a new type will be established based on ready-made types.

Genre as typified social action, however, is both medium and outcome of the recursive social practices. This is supported by what is called the duality of structure by Anthony Giddens in his structuration theory (Giddens 1984). A genre is only an abstraction. It has to be instantiated through the operations that realize the social actions in specific space and time. As a medium and resource, the specific social action of any individual is based on the routines of a genre that have been previously established in the society. In order to act appropriately in a society, each individual recursively relies on already available genres (types of social actions), including their purposes and routinized schematic structures, and possibly even the specific methods. On the other hand, the instantiation of a genre in space and time necessarily reproduces the genre of the collective. That is, the social actors reproduce the purpose, structure, and possibly the tools (operational methods) of the specific genre, and therefore make the genre recur. The genre as produced in the action is further available for use in future.

Interestingly, this aspect of genre is also captured by Bakhtin who emphasizes the addressivity as a constitutive feature of utterances and speech genres (Bakhtin 1986: 94-100; also cf. Section 2.2.3). Every utterance is a response to previous utterances and necessarily draws on them. In addition, it also anticipates a response, and is addressed to some specific or indefinite potential audience. The utterance of each individual thus necessarily reproduces patterned notions of institutional or social others, and the society or culture must provide utterance types by which the individuals can do this. Thus, this addressivity provides a mechanism by which individual actions/utterances and genres as routinized action types of a society can interact with each other. This explains the phrase "recurrent configurations of meaning" used in Martin's definition of the nature of genre (Martin & Rose 2008: 6).

In summary, genre is a typification of telos-oriented social actions. As telos-orientedness is the nature of social actions and therefore the nature of genre, a telos-oriented approach to genre study is necessary and tenable.

### 3.2.4 Teleological Structure of Social Action

In order to carry out a penetrating exploration of genres, it is necessary to carry out an academic study of the telos of social actions (this forms a sharp contrast to those approaches where purpose/telos is taken for granted and used in its common sense). The teleological nature of human actions has been already discussed in the previous sections by drawing on the activity theory. In this section, the teleological structure of human actions will be explored based on Quentin Smith's study of the teleological orders of human actions. Slight adaptation will be made to suit the purpose of this study.

According to Smith (1981), there are three types of aims in human voluntary actions: ends, goals and purposes, which are interconnected through four teleological orders: parts-of, means-to, concretization, and subsumption. Ends refer to the aims that are directly pursued in voluntary actions. They include ends-in-themselves and subordinate ends, while the latter are "means to" achieve the former, and maybe prior to, contemporaneous with or interspersed with the former. The complete subordinate end of a voluntary action and the complete end-in-itself of a voluntary action together form (i. e. are parts of) the complete "actional end". The complete actional end of each voluntary action constitutes a different and separate whole end, such that the different actional ends are not related to each other as "parts of" some larger ends.

Where ends are immediate aims of voluntary actions, immediately and directly attained by a voluntary action, goals are mediate ends of these actions, and must be attained by a series of voluntary actions, such that they become attained only through the attainment of a series of complete actional ends. Goals are differentiated from complete actional ends in terms of positing and pursuing continuity; but they do not necessarily differ in their contents (although they usually do). Formally goals can be defined as aims that are constituted by two or more ends, which are ordered to goals as "parts of" them. Goals are ordered to each other by the two relations of "part of" and "means to". Most goals are "parts of" larger goals, and some goals can also be "means to" other goals. The "means to" order between goals culminates in goals-in-themselves, which are goals that are pursued for their own sake, and are not "means to" any further goals.

Goals are concretion/concretization of purposes, that is, the concrete determinations of undetermined instances of universals, in the sense that they are aims involving particular and concrete phenomena in the world. A purpose by itself is abstract: it is not an aim that relates to some particular phenomenon in the world. For this reason it cannot be pursued in terms of itself. It can only be pursued in terms of concretization of itself, that is, in terms of aims involving particular phenomena. One or more purposes are "subsumed" under another purpose if the latter purpose is more general in its nature than the former purposes. The "most general" purpose is the supreme purpose in the order of purposes. All other purposes are subsumed under this purpose, and it is subsumed under no further purpose.

Whereas ends and goals constitute the unique individuality of our actions, purposes are the unconditioned meanings of our actions. They are the ultimate "reason" of our actions. While goals are the meaning of ends, in that ends are pursued for the reason that they realize goals, purposes are the meaning of goals, for purposes are the "reason why" we pursue goals. Smith (1981) contends that the "meaningfulness" of purposes is not conditioned by any further type of aim, as they are not "ordered to" a higher level of aims. Purposes orient our choice and pursuit of actions. The pursuit of particular ends and goals is determined by which purposes we wish to attain.

Smith (1981) concludes that we have three types of aims, interconnected through four teleological orders, which forms a five-leveled teleological structure of human action, each level being an interrelationship between some of these aims. The structure includes an inter-ends level, ends-goals level, inter-goals level, goals-purposes level, and inter-purposes level.

What also deserves attention is Smith's classification of ends into physical, mental and interpersonal types. Physical ends are either to alter the physical structure of my surroundings (such as to saw a branch in half), or to alter and move my body for its own sake (as is the case when I engage in exercise); mental aims are to "bring to my mind" ideas, images or memories; interpersonal ends are to influence or affect the consciousness of another person. Influencing his consciousness may consist of informing him of some ideas, giving him some practical directives, inducing some emotional response in him (such as to make him "feel at home" or to "feel intimidated"), and altering his awareness in other ways.

Smith (1981: 312) points out that "this classification of ends, actions and feelings of striving is not, and cannot be, a rigid one, as many of the concrete instances of these phenomena are mixtures of physical, mental or interpersonal aspects".

Considered from a metafunctional (and also semiotic) perspective, the combination of physical and mental ends match the ideational metafunction, whereas the interpersonal ends match the interpersonal metafunction. In addition, we can add an organizational type of ends, which deals with the ways for organizing and enabling the physical/mental and interpersonal ends during the process of their pursuit. Naturally, these organizational ends match the textual metafunction. Since the types of ends are always mixed together in concrete instances, it is tenable to treat them as three aspects of the same end. That is, each end has three aspects: representational, interactional and organizational. As a goal consists of different ends, it will also be tenable to identify representational, interactional and organizational aspects of a goal.

## 3. 3 A Telos-Oriented Genre System

After the teleological nature of genre is explored, Section 3. 3 will proceed to interpret the teleological configuration (that is, purpose configuration, goal configuration and goal complexing) of genre simplex as shown in Figure 3. 1. For this purpose, according to SFL's principle of priority of system over structure, this section will develop a tentative genre system based on the study of the teleological structure of social actions (which is an effort to overcome Hasan and Martin's neglect of the paradigmatic aspect of genre, cf. Sections 2. 5. 3 and 2. 6. 9). The system will form the basis for the derivation of genre structure (generic structure), and also the basis for the exploration of inter-genre relation and genre operationalization. Theories of system and structure in SFL are discussed in Halliday (1961, 1966a), Halliday & Matthiessen (2004), and Kress (1976), and will not be introduced here.

### 3.3.1 Mutual Compatibility Between Smith and Leontjev's Theories

Before the application of Smith's work to genre study, it should be noted that Smith's theory seems to be consistent with and complementary to Leontjev's activity theory. In Smith's theory, purpose, goal, and end are all based on volitional, conscious actions. They belong to actions in Leontjev's activity theory as an action is subject to a conscious purpose. More exactly, Smith's study can be considered as an insightful analysis of the teleological structure of the action in Leontjev's framework. As far as the use of terms is concerned, Leontjev's purpose is conscious, and his goal is something subordinate to purpose, which seems to be compatible with Smith's use of purpose and goal. Smith has an additional level, that is, end, which is not discussed by Leontjev. As a social psychologist, Leontjev will naturally focus on the psychological aspect as shown by his close attention to activity (which simply lacks in Smith's work). In addition, Leontjev's operation is related to specific conditions in instantiation, which is also absent in Smith's study. However, Leontjev lays emphasis on the social aspect of both activities and actions, and this is also consistent with Smith's focus on social action. More important, Leontjev's exploration of the teleological nature of activity and action can provide a psychological support to Smith's teleological approach to human action, and to any teleological approach in general. In Summary, Smith's work can be seen as an insightful discussion of Leontjev's action and thus be integrated with the general framework of the activity theory.

### 3.3.2 Structural Units of Genre Analysis

In order to establish a genre system, it is necessary to determine the hierarchy of the basic structural units for genre analysis, so that the level where the system features are to be located can be determined.

If genre is to be regarded as a separate stratum as shown in Figure 3.1, one challenge is to set up a hierarchy of structural units at this stratum comparable to the units at the lexicogrammar stratum. To date, no satisfactory unit hierarchy at the genre stratum has been set up in spite of the attempts witnessed in this regard. It seems that the problem can be solved through the application of the teleological structure with only slight adaptation.

Smith (1981) has set up five teleological levels of social actions, with a level considered as a kind of relation between different types of aims. However, if a teleological level is defined as any of the results of the application of the inter-aim relations, six teleological levels can be obtained: end (a complete actional end consisting of an end-in-itself), end complex (a complete actional end consisting of an end-in-itself and one or more subordinate ends), goal (consisting of a goal-in-itself), goal complex (consisting of a goal-in-itself and one or more subordinate goals), purpose, and purpose complex (consisting of two or more purposes subsumed under it).

When the types of aims are applied to the genre stratum, it seems that a purpose matches a genre, as both are abstract and need be concretized; a goal matches a phase, as both are mediate and need be realized by immediate social actions; an end matches a message, which is realized by a ranking clause in language or by any other kind of volitional actions in the case of other modalities. End complexes are pursued by message complexes, goal complexes by phase complexes (which are called stages), purpose complexes by genre complexes (which are called macro-genres, directed at an ultimate purpose). As far as the establishment of a simple genre system is concerned, the system features will be located at the level of goals pursued by phases, because it is the subsumption of different specific goals pursued by corresponding phases that leads to the achievement of the purpose of a genre.

### 3.3.3 A Teleological Genre System

Based on the discussions above, a tentative telos-based genre system is developed in this section, as shown in Figure 3.2 (on p. 67). In this genre system, the start point is necessarily genre. It can be divided into two types: simplex and complex (the two terms are more appropriate than the corresponding teleological terms such as purpose and purpose subsumption because what is presented here is a genre system rather than a teleological system). "Complex" refers to genre complexes created through the recursive use of interdependence types (cf. Matthiessen 1995: 126, 139). The teleological process underlying a genre complex is purpose subsumption, which creates a purpose complex. The "logico-semantic relation" system includes two disjunctive features: expansion and projection. Expansion includes three sub-features: elaboration, extension, and enhancement, whereas the projection feature includes locution and idea. The "recursion" system includes two choices: "recur", which leads to a re-selection of the entry condition of complex, and "stop", which means that no recursion occurs. However, taxis (parataxis and hypotaxis) does not form an option in genre complex, as there is no paratactic idea or hypotactic wording in genre complex (cf. Martin 1994: 34-36). Instances of genre complexes (macro-genres) include all kinds of hyper-texts on websites, such as the hyper-texts of Cisco, Siemens, Lenovo websites as included in this study.

Simplex refers to a simple genre, underlying which is a single purpose. It includes two conjunctive systems: a goal configuration system, and a goal complexing system. A goal is configured with three simultaneous aspects (representational, interactional, and organizational), which redound with the field, tenor, and mode configurations respectively on the register stratum. The goal configuration process can recur. The number of times of recursion determines the number of phases in a genre.

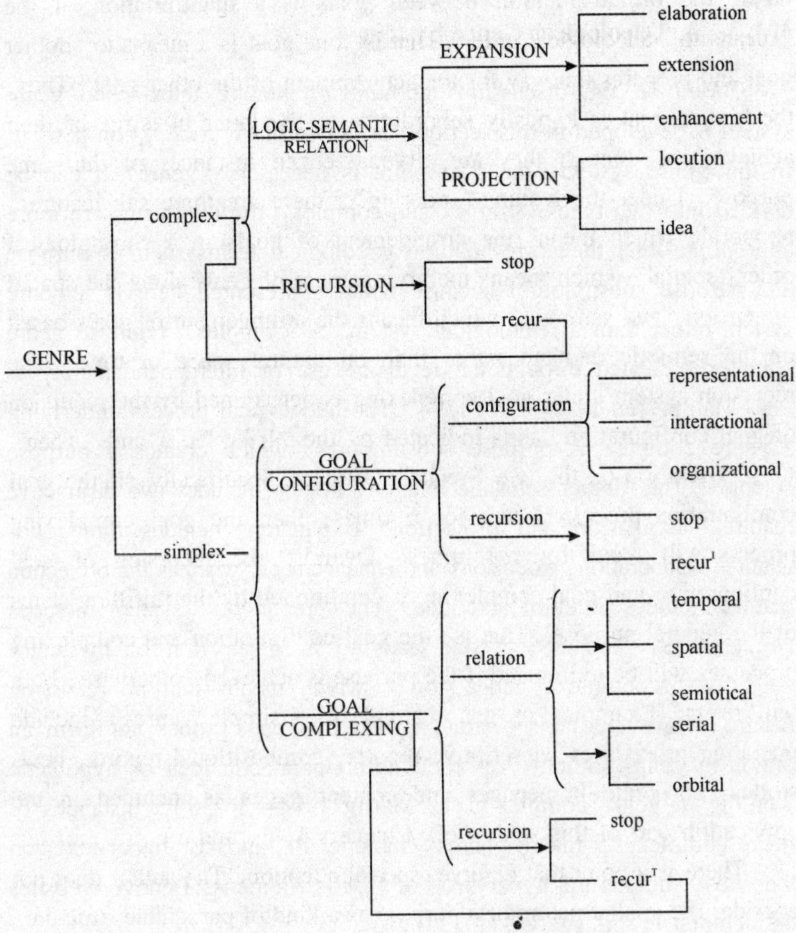


**Figure 3.2 A Telos-Oriented Genre System**

The goal complexing system deals with the relations between different goals. It includes two sub-systems: relation and recursion. The goal relation system includes two features: nuclearity and ordering. The former includes two sub-features: serial and orbital. Serial relation means that two or more goals are on an equal status with each other and are equally concretized instances of a purpose/genre. On the other hand, the orbital relation between goals is a manifestation of the "means to" teleological order. That is, one goal is a means to another goal and prepares the way for the achievement of the other goal. Thus, the former goal is logically subordinate to the latter in terms of their achievement, though they are all concretized instances of the same purpose. Under the feature "ordering", there are three sub-features, temporal, which means the arrangement of goals in a chronological order, spatial, which means the arrangement of goals along the spatial dimension, and semiotic, which means the arrangement of goals based on the semiotic demand rather than on natural space or time. The recursion system under goal complexing is determined by the recursion of goal configuration, as is indicated by the "If" ("I") and "Then" ("T") relation on the two "recur" features. Specifically, if the goal configuration process recurs for n times, then the goal complexing process will recur for n-1 times. Overall, the recursion of goal configuration and goal complexing is conditioned by the fulfilling status of the general purpose. That is, the goal configuration and complexing processes will be terminated if the purpose is achieved; otherwise, both will recur. Examples of genre simplexes (simple genres) include operating procedures, descriptive reports, compositional reports, news stories, corporate homepages and content pages as included in the application part of this study (cf. Chapters 4, 5, and 6).

There is a point that deserves special attention. The author does not consider the goal structure of a purpose as a kind of particulate structure. A particulate structure means constituency; that is, a superordinate structure consists of some subordinate constituent structures. The teleological order between a purpose and goals is concretization. As Smith (1981: 322) contends, "it is the nature of purposes to be undetermined instances of universals, and it is the nature of goals to be the particular determinations of these instances." This means that a purpose-oriented genre is an abstraction, and needs to be concretized and realized by the goal-oriented stages. Thus, the serial/orbital structure of the goal-driven stages does not belong to particulate structure, but is rather a kind of metafunctionally neutral teleological structure.

## 3.4 Genre Staging: The Derivation of Schematic Structure

In Section 3.3, the teleological configuration of both genre simplex and complex are interpreted through the establishment of a teleological genre system. Section 3.4 will proceed to explain the derivation of genre structure (generic structure) from the genre system, which is called genre staging. Martin's seven points in defense of his genre theory will also be discussed when appropriate (cf. Section 2.6.3).

### 3.4.1 Staging as a Result of System Realization

Genre staging is a very important concept in genre theory. It is often discussed in the form of generic structure, also called schematic structure. Genre staging is generally seen as caused by the need to take several steps to achieve the purpose of our routinized actions (Martin & White 2005: 33), while the staging structure is considered as the major reflex of differences in purpose among different texts (Eggins & Martin 1997).

From the teleological perspective of the current model, genre staging can be explained by the concretization of a general and abstract purpose into several specific goals. That is, each stage in the genre is determined by the corresponding goal. The specific contents of a stage are determined by the specific goal configuration, which is an organic integration of the representational, interactional and organizational aspects of the goal. The relations among the different goals determine the specific relations among different stages. Broadly speaking, these relations fall into two types: serial and orbital. The number of stages in a genre is determined by the number of specific goals in the concretization of the purpose, which is in turn determined by the necessity of the achievement of the purpose. In the genre system, this is dealt with by the recursion subsystem under the goal complexing system: if the purpose is achieved, then goal complexing will be terminated; otherwise, it will recur until the purpose is achieved.

As a whole, the schematic structure of each genre (genre staging) is the result of the choices made in the goal configuration and goal complexing systems. In other words, it is the result of the realization of the genre simplex system into a genre structure. This is consistent with SFL's principle of the priority of system over structure, with structure as the realization of system. This approach avoids the discussion of the generic structure without the discussion of the underlying system, which, in the author's view, is a major defect in the previous work on generic structure in SFL (cf. Sections 2.5.3 and 2.6.9).

### 3.4.2 Order vs. Sequence

The goal complexing process as shown in the genre system (also in the integrated model in Figure 3.1) generates the ordering rather than sequencing of the goals and therefore also the ordering of the stages of a specific genre. The distinction between order and sequence is of great significance to the understanding of this model. This is related to another defect in the representation of generic structure in the current genre theories of SFL, that is, the implication of linearity of the generic structure. More specifically, a genre as represented in these theories seems to unfold linearly from one stage to the next, though with recursion in some cases. This is witnessed in Hasan's work on Generic Structure Potential (GSP). For example, according to Hasan, the GSP of shopping transaction is [(Greeting) (Sale Initiation) ^ ] [(Sale Enquiry¬ · ) {Sale Request ^ Sale Compliance ^ } ¬ ^ Sale ^ ] Purchase ^ Purchase Closure ( ^ Finis). In this GSP, the round brackets indicate optionality of enclosed elements, the dot " · " indicates more than one option in sequence; the square brackets indicates the range of options, "¬" shows iteration, "{ } ¬" indicates that the degree of iteration of the elements within the braces is the same; "^" means "followed by" (Halliday & Hasan 1985: 64; Hasan 1996b: 54-56). The linearity of the GSP is clearly shown by the use of the term "sequence" and the symbol "^". Actually, Hasan (and other scholars) realized such a defect and tried to overcome it by making a distinction between order and sequence. Specifically, order is considered as something deeper, and the same order is considered as able to generate different sequences. However, due to the lack of a system for generating the GSP, such a distinction still does not help much to avoid the implication of linearity.

The linearity inherent in the GSP and other models of generic structure makes it unable to explain the flexible structure of actual texts in our life. Even in a text of shopping transaction, Purchase Closure can be stated before the Purchase stage. As for texts on websites (and other media), the different stages of a genre can be distributed circularly or hyper-textually, without any implication of linearity. The generic structure of such texts cannot be explained by a linear model of genre structure.

Linearity, as an inherent feature of sequence, is derived from the instantiation process. Instantiation includes two aspects, encoding (including writing/speaking in language and the composing of text in other modalities) and decoding (including reading/hearing and interpretation in the case of other modalities). Both encoding and decoding need to take place along certain special and temporal dimensions, hence the linearity. In other words, instantiation is related to logogenesis, which refers to the unfolding of the text, and is necessarily a sequence, and hence the linearity.

Genre staging dealt with by the system network as developed in the new model avoids such implication of linearity. Generic structure here is a result of the realization of the genre system. As system is paradigmatic and abstract, it has nothing to do with specific time and space. Specifically, the goal configuration processes which determine the stages in a genre can take place simultaneously rather than one after another; they can take place in different spaces without any implication of time; they can even take place just along a semiotic dimension, neither spatially nor temporarily. The specific ordering of the stages is conditioned by the choice of relation under the goal complexing system.

It should be noted, however, that what the goal complexing system conditions is the order of the stages rather than a specific sequence. What underlies the order is the relation between different stages (concretized goals) and between each stage (goal) and the whole genre (the general purpose). As a result, the stages in a genre can be organized temporally, spatially, or simply semiotically. In the case of temporal ordering, a stage that occurs first in terms of physical time can be placed after another stage that occurs later in physical time. In the case of spatial ordering, the stages of a genre can be instantiated in a specific text either vertically in a top-down way, horizontally in a left-right way, obliquely or circularly, as can be seen in texts in new media such as websites. In the case of semiotic ordering, the distribution of the stages is determined by the internal semiotic relation between the stages, e. g. the degree of newsworthiness, significance, etc. Thus, the ordering of genre stages has no direct relation with any specific sequence. A specific sequence of the stages in a text is the result of the instantiation of the genre ordering. In short, genre staging (schematic structure) shows the internal ordering of the stages rather than the specific sequencing. The non-linearity of genre staging is very important for the understanding of website texts, as will be shown in the study of websites in Chapters 5 and 6.

### 3.4.3 Text Dynamics

The recursion of the goal configuration processes in the model also helps explain the problem of text dynamics, i. e. the variation of register from stage to stage ( cf. Martin 1999b: 32; Martin 2001a: 289 ). This is related to a defect in the traditional analysis of context in SFL, that is, to state the field, tenor, and mode features of a text in a single step, as if the values of the three variables remain consistent throughout the whole text. However, in practice, it is quite possible for the values of field, tenor, and mode to vary from stage to stage in a single text. For example, as far as tenor is concerned, affect may be first unmarked, and then become marked. As for field, a text may begin by shortly introducing the function of a product, and then proceed to an explanation of its working mechanism. In addition, the modality can change from language in the first stage to both language and image in the next stage. This is the problem of text dynamics, which has neither been appropriately explained theoretically nor adequately explored in text analysis.

Genre staging as presented in the new model can help explain the variation in field, tenor and mode from one stage to another within a genre. In the model as developed here, a goal has three aspects: representational, interactional and organizational. They are respectively realized by the field, tenor and mode choices at the register stratum. As genre staging is caused by the concretization of purpose into a series of goals and each stage is driven by the corresponding goal, the specific configuration of representational, interactional and organization aspects of a goal conditions the configuration of field, mode and tenor in the corresponding stage. In the process of goal complexing, underlying each stage is a process of goal configuration. As the specific goal configuration process varies from stage to stage, naturally the configuration of field, mode and tenor will also vary from stage to stage. As it is natural to have different goals in different stages of genre, so is the register variation among different stages. In fact, textual dynamics is caused by the concretization of purpose into different specific goals. Without such goal variation, every stage of genre ( and a text ) will look the same. This helps further our understanding of the dynamic aspect of genre and text.

In addition to register variation from stage to stage, the relations between adjacent stages can also vary from one to another, which is another aspect of text dynamics. The relation between Stages 1 and 2 may be chronological, while that between Stages 2 and 3 may be spatial or purely semiotic. In other words, the development of staging in a genre may be based on varying types of relations, rather than on a simple type of relation. "Text-time" and "field-time" may be employed simultaneously in a simple genre.

## 3.5 Inter-Genre Relations

After genre simplex is explored, attention will be paid to the exploration of inter-genre relations, that is, to the exploration of the ways for a simple genre system to expand into larger systems. Inter-genre relations will be discussed along two dimensions: genre complexing (including embedding) and genre agnation, as shown in the model in Figure 3.1.

### 3.5.1 Genre Complexing and Embedding: Macro-Genres

Martin (1994, 1995, 1997) proposes the term macro-genre for texts which combine familiar elementary genres such as recounts, report, explanations, expositions and so on. Macro-genres are actually genre complexes. From a teleological point of view, genre complexes are determined by purpose subsumption, with some purposes subsumed under a more general purpose. Martin (1997) also suggests employing logico-semantic relations as outlined by Halliday (1994) for clause complexes for the analysis of genre complexing. They include two conjunctive types: expansion, which is sub-classified into elaboration, extension, and enhancement, and projection, which includes idea and locution. In addition, there is a recursion system, which deals with recursive complexing. According to Martin (1994), taxis (including parataxis and hypotaxis) is not a resource for genre complexing.

In addition to genre complexing, another way to form a macro-genre is embedding. That is, a genre is made to function as one multivariate stage in the development of another (Martin 1994). This is analogous to downward rankshift at the lexicogrammar stratum. From a teleological perspective, what happens in this case is that a specific goal of a concretized purpose is achieved through the achievement of another purpose. Genre complexing and genre embedding are basic ways for the development of long and complicated texts.

### 3.5.2 Genre Agnation

The issue of genre agnation was put forward by Martin (1999b: 33) as a formalization of trans-metafunctional valeur, and as part of the ambition to map a culture as a system of genres. According to him, as patterns of field, mode, and tenor variables, genres are obviously related in terms of field agnation, tenor agnation and mode agnation. However, the focus of genre agnation is on the relationship among genres as combinations of the register variables, rather than on the relation between each of the field, mode, tenor values of one text and that of another. The significance of genre agnation lies in that it is through agnate relation that separate genres form systems, which is what is defined as culture by Martin.

Genre agnation has been explored in two complementary dimensions by Martin (2001a): typology and topology. Typological analysis deals with genre agnation categorically, classifying text as one generic type or another. In practice, Martin's genre typology focuses on the interdependencies across metafunctions, with genre systems established by the simultaneous application of ideational (rhetorically organized vs. activity organized), interpersonal (persuade that vs. persuade to) and textual (generalized vs. instantial) criteria (cf. Martin 2001a: 302-303). Based on the telos-oriented genre system as developed in Section 3.3, genre typology should be based on the difference between the general purposes of different genres. Specifically, each feature of the goal configuration and the goal complexing subsystems can function as a criterion for sub-classifying a genre family. Therefore, genre typology focuses on the different values of the same system feature realized in different genres. For example, both analytical exposition and hortatory exposition have a generic structure [Dissertation ^ Augmentation ^ Reiteration], and the interactional aspect of the general purpose of both is to persuade the reader. The major difference, however, lies in the representational aspect of their general purposes. For an analytical exposition, it is the proper formulation of some proposition; while for a hortatory exposition, it is the need to take some action.

While typological analysis focuses on differences between genres, topological analysis approaches genre agnation as a matter of degree, arranging genres on clines with respect to their similarities and differences. Based on six parameters selected respectively from the ideational, interpersonal and textual metafunctions, Martin has worked out an ontogenetic topology for a range of secondary school history genres (see Martin 2001a: 304-318 for more details). From a teleological perspective, genre topology can be considered as the result of the sharing of feature values in the genre system. The degree of feature sharing determines the degree of similarity and difference between two genres. Such degree is conditioned, on the one hand, by the number of shared features of the genres, on the other, by the adjacency of the values of the shared features as realized in the different genres. For example, in the recount genre family, autobiographical recounts, biographical recounts, and personal recounts all have a generic structure [Orientation ^ Record]. An autobiographical recount and a biographical recount share many features: tell the reader (interactional) the story of an individual's life (representational) in a temporal (episodic time), serial way (organizational). A personal recount shares less features with the other two: tell the reader (interactional) the story of the happenings to an individual (representational) in a temporal (following serial time), serial way (organizational). In addition, in autobiographical and biographical recounts, the representational value is "the story of an individual's life", while in a personal recount, it is "the story of the happenings to an individual". Thus, the former two are more alike, while the latter is a little distant from the other two.

## 3.6 Genre Realization

The above sections have presented a teleological analysis of the genre system and genre structure. In one word, genre system is represented as a telos-oriented system, and genre structure is considered as a teleological structure derived from the telos-oriented system. However, both genre system and genre structure are highly abstract and the telos of a genre need be achieved by employing specific resources at lower strata. In other words, a genre need be operationalized through the employment of semiotic resources conditioned by the telos. In Sections 3.5, 3.6 and 3.7, the three dimensions of genre operationalization as shown by the three two-headed arrows in Figure 3.1 will be interpreted.

The study of genre operationalization will be based on the stratification of language and of social semiotics in general, as shown by the co-tangential circles in Figure 3.1. Stratification is one of the ways in which a simple system can be expanded into a complex one (Halliday 2003), an ordering in symbolic abstraction of the subsystems of a semiotic, and thus can be considered as the defining organizational characteristic of all semiotic systems (Matthiessen 2007). As far as this study is concerned, the context will be considered as stratified into two layers: genre and register, while language into three strata: discourse semantics, lexicogrammar, phonology/graphology (Martin 1985, 1992, 1997, 1999, 2001a). Stratification can be formalized by metaredundancy (Lemke 1984, 1995; Halliday 1992; Martin 1992; Matthiessen 1995). Redundancy is a formal way of describing the probablistically predicable co-occurrence of two things within a context (Lemke 1984, 1995). It is symmetrical (bidirectional) and can be recursive. As far as this study is concerned, it suffices to say that genre is metaredundant with register, while register is in turn metaredundant with discourse semantics. Based on the stratification and metaredundancy theory, the three dimensions of genre operationalization will be interpreted respectively.

Realization refers to "the stratal organization of the system (and therefore also of the process) whereby the expression is said to realize the content" (Halliday 2003). It indicates the inter-strata relationship, with the lower stratum realizing the upper one. This is a kind of meredundancy relation (Halliday 1992), as the choice of features in one stratum is probablistically predictable with the choice of features in another stratum. According to Martin's model of context (Martin 1985, 1992, 1997, 1999b, 2001a; cf. Section 2. 6. 3), genre is realized by register. As the relationship of inter-stratum realization can be formally explained by the notion of metaredundancy (Halliday 1992; Martin 1992, 2010a), it can be said that genre metaredounds with register. Specifically, genre can function as the environment for the partly predicable combinations of different registers. That is, there is a first-order redundancy relation between different specific registers as some combinations of the registers are more likely than others. Then the pattern of combinations of the registers is redundant with the genre as a larger "context". This is the second-order redundancy, hence the metaredundancy. In the author's view, this may be what is meant by Martin & White (2005: 32-33) when they suggest that genres are patterns of register patterns. In other words, the field, tenor, and mode variables in a culture will combine in partly predicable patterns, and these register patterns will also occur in partly predicable ways conditioned by the corresponding genres.

It should be noted, however, that in the discussion of genre realization, it is necessarily to take discourse semantics (texts) into consideration as texts (including multimodal texts) are what we really encounter in our daily life, and the existence of genre and register depends on their realization by discourse semantics in specific texts. As register redounds with discourse semantics, a relation of metaredundancy also exists among the three strata. That is, genre redounds with the redundancy of register with discourse semantics. In other words, genre is realized by the realization of register in discourse semantics.

From the teleological approach to genre as developed in this study, at the core of genre is purpose, which is concretized into a series of goals in corresponding stages. As goal configuration takes place in each stage of the genre, the representational, interactional and organizational aspects of the goal configured in each stage will condition the field, tenor and mode configurations in the corresponding stage. That is, based on the goal configuration of a specific stage, we can partly predict the corresponding configurations of field, tenor, and mode choices at the same stage. On the other hand, if we know the field, tenor, mode choices made in a stage, we can also partly predict the corresponding goal of that stage.

It should be noted that, while there is redundancy relation between the representational aspect of a goal and the field, the interactional and organizational aspects can also exert influence on the choice of field values indirectly through the goal configuration process. Likewise, tenor values may be indirectly conditioned by the representational and organizational aspects of the corresponding goal, and mode values may be indirectly conditioned by the representational and interactional aspects of the goal. This is also true for the redundancy relation between register variables and the three metafunctions at the discourse semantic stratum.

The patterning of the field, tenor and mode configurations of different stages is conditioned by the goal complexing process, that is, conditioned by the ways the general purpose of genre is concretized into the goals. In this way, the patterning of register configurations realizes the schematic structure of the genre, and is in turn realized by the structure of the text. The specific field, tenor and mode configurations are respectively realized by the ideational, interpersonal and textual meanings on the discourse semantic stratum. Taken as a whole, the goal-oriented genre is realized by register patterns, which are in turn realized by discourse semantics. As the ultimate conditioning factor is the telos of the genre, such a genre realization process is teleological.

Realization relation also exists between discourse semantics and lexicogrammar, and between lexicogrammar and phonology. As the focus of this study is genre and the discussion up to discourse semantic resources is enough to show the genre realization process, the exploration will generally stop at the discourse semantic stratum. Lexicogrammar will be dealt with only when it is necessarily. This practice will be followed in the discussion of genre instantiation and individuation.

## 3.7 Genre/Register Instantiation

Realization is a principle through which the resources at the register and discourse semantics strata are employed to achieve the general purpose of a genre. That is, realization deals with the way through which resources at lower strata can be employed to achieve the telos of a genre. However, this is still too abstract. In order to achieve a specific purpose of a specific genre, specific instances of semiotic resources need be employed at each stratum of a social semiotic. This aspect will be dealt with along the dimension of instantiation.

Instantiation refers to the relation between an instance and the system that lies behind it. Instance and system are of the same phenomenal order. They are the same phenomenon differing in observer perspectives. A text instantiates a system, while an act of meaning instantiates the meaning potential. Instantiation is a cline rather than a dichotomy, with meaning potential and acts of meaning defined as the two poles (Halliday 1999, 2005). Like realization, instantiation is also telos-conditioned as instances of genres (texts) are employed to achieve specific purposes. As instantiation is a dimension of semantic variation according to instances of use, from a teleological perspective, it can be said that genre instantiation deals with the achievement of a specific purpose of a genre by deploying specific instances of semiotic resources.

Instantiation is a hierarchy of generalization, a cline between system and text (as shown in Figure 3.1). The system (as generalized meaning potential) is instantiated into genres (patterns of register patterns as semantic sub-potential), further into text types (as generalized semantic actual), and finally into texts (as affording instances) and readings (as subjectified meanings) (Martin 2007a, 2007b, 2009).

Following Martin's model of instantiation (Martin 2008a, 2008b, 2010a), every stratum of realization instantiates. As far as context is concerned, genre and register are considered as at the same level of generality. That is, they are treated at the same level in the instantiation hierarchy. This can be explained by the fact that situation (register) is nothing but social action. The difference between genre and situation is that genre is typified, routinized social action of a community oriented to a social purpose, while situation (register) is a specific social action of some individuals. As at the center of social action is meaning, both genre and register are semiotic constructs rather than physical or material phenomena.

Instantiation shows how far specific texts both confirm realizational predictions and uniquify meaning. It can be studied along two basic dimensions: coupling and commitment (Martin 2008a). Both coupling and commitment are conditioned by the general purpose of a specific genre. In the following two sections, the specific ways of coupling and commitment that are available for genre instantiation will be explored.

### 3.7.1 Coupling

Coupling refers to the way in which meanings combine. "Since the realization hierarchy deals with combinations of meaning by and large within strata, metafunctions, ranks and simultaneous systems, an indefinitely large set of possible combinations is left open. Since texts specify combinations from this set, the concept of coupling is required to focus attention on how this unfolds" (Martin 2010a: 24). In contrast with the realization hierarchy which allows a large space of freedom of combination, the instantiation hierarchy constrains the possible combinations in order for the meaning potential of the culture to be manifested in a specific act of communication. "While all couplings the system allows are possible, from the perspective of register and genre, each culture relies on relatively routine combinations which can be generalized up the instantiation cline; innovation involves couplings which can't be generalized so" (Martin 2008b).

Coupling can be inter-stratum, cross-metafunctional, inter-modality, or inter-system. As far as inter-stratum coupling is concerned, a specific genre can be coupled with different register patterns. Basically, there will be congruent genre-register coupling, that is, a specific genre is typically associated with a specific type of registers; or the coupling may be incongruent, which means that a genre is coupled with a register pattern that is typically used for the realization of another genre. The latter case is called contextual metaphor (Martin 1997), which is analogous to grammatical metaphor. While grammatical metaphor arises due to the tension between semantics and grammar, contextual metaphor arises due to the tension between genre and register. From a teleological point of view, as the core of genre is purpose, the same purpose is achieved by operational methods that are typically employed to achieve other purposes. However, as the purpose remains the same, the genre can remain unchanged in this specific case. An example of contextual metaphor is given by Martin (1997), which is a report instantiated in a register typically associated with a recount. That is, the field, tenor and mode choices as predicted on the basis of the general ideational, interpersonal and textual features of the text makes the text look like a narration of the author's personal experience, but certain features of the text are intended to instantiate a report genre.

Cross-metafunctional coupling refers to the coupling between meaning features of different metafunctions. At the genre stratum, different representational, interactional and organizational aspects can be selected and configured in the goals of the different stages, which also make the general purpose have different teleological couplings. At the register stratum, different field, tenor and mode values can be selected and combined together from register to register. For example, the monologue/action mode can be coupled with a specialized field with high degree of sharing among the interactants of equal status, frequent contact and positive affect, or the dialogue/reflection mode can be coupled with a non-specialized field with low degree of sharing among the interactants of unequal status, low degree of contact and negative affect. At the discourse semantic stratum, different features can be selected from different discourse semantic systems and combined in different ways.

Inter-modality coupling often appears in multi-modal texts. For example, in daily face-to-face communication, gesture and facial expressions will be coupled with language. On websites pages, language will be coupled with image, music, and video. It should be noted that a genre may be instantiated by any one or more modalities when appropriate. The modalities may be employed alternately in different stages, which will be shown in the study of corporate homepage and content page genres in the application part.

### 3.7.2 Commitment

According to Martin (2008b), commitment is concerned with the amount of meaning potential activated in a particular process of instantiation, i. e. the relative semantic weight of a text. It has to do with the degree to which meanings in optional systems are taken up, and within systems, the degree of delicacy selected (Martin 2010a).

At the genre stratum, as far as optionality is concerned, some stages of a genre are obligatory and some are optional. A text where an optional stage of the genre is instantiated is more committed than one where only obligatory stages are instantiated. The choice of an optional system is conditioned by the general purpose of the genre. For example, the "coda" stage of the anecdote genre (with a generic structure orientation ^ remarkable event ^ reaction ^ coda; cf. Martin & Rose 2008: 56-61) is optional. A specific anecdote with a coda is more committed in this respect than one without the coda. As far as the degree of delicacy is concerned, the stages of a genre may be instantiated either simply by one or more messages, or by some phases each of which includes a certain number of messages. A stage of genre instantiated in a text by a series of phases is more committed than the same stage of the same genre instantiated in another text by just one or more messages. In the case of orbital structure, a text of the structure with both nucleus and satellites is more committed than a text of the same genre with only the nucleus.

At the register stratum, as far as field is concerned, the degree of commitment is closely related to the degree of sharing among the interactants of a culture. That is, the higher the degree of field sharing, the less committed will be the text as many shared information can be taken as shared background information and omitted. As for tenor, the degree of affect is most obviously related to commitment. Depending on the specific purpose of the author, there can be more or less of affect instantiated in the text. For example, academic genres and administrative/legal genres will have the least amount of affect, while promotion genres will have a great amount of affect.

At the discourse semantic stratum, the ideational meanings are oriented to a particulate structure. In an orbital type of the particulate structure, a text with both the nucleus and peripheral parts instantiated will be more committed compared with another text with only the nucleus instantiated. The degree of commitment varies in direct ratio with the number of peripheral elements. This is analogous to transitivity/ergativity structure in a clause at the grammatical stratum. In terms of transitivity analysis, a clause with the process, obligatory and optional participants and other circumstances is much more ideationally committed than a clause with only the process and obligatory participants. In terms of ergativity analysis, a clause with only the process and medium instantiated is less committed than one with also the agent and range instantiated in addition to the process and medium. At the rank of word group, a group (nominal, verbal, or adverbial) with both head and modifiers are more committed than a group with only the head and the necessarily deictic element. In summary, as far as ideational meaning is concerned, the nucleus is the obligatory element, while the peripheral elements are optional. Thus, different degrees of commitment can first be caused by the choice or non-choice of peripheral elements. When peripheral elements are chosen, then the degree of commitment is conditioned by the number and complexity of the peripheral elements instantiated.

In the case of a serial structure, there are multiple nucleus organized in an interdependent way. As all nucleus must be instantiated, the degree of commitment is conditioned by the degree of specification of each nuclear. From the perspective of logico-semantic relations as discussed by Halliday, serial structure can be said to be established mainly by extension, while the specification of each nuclear may be developed either through elaboration or enhancement. As far as lexis is concerned, commitment can be explored on the basis of hyponymy and meronomy. That is, a superordinate is less committed than its subordinate terms. In addition, abstract words are generally less committed than their corresponding concrete words/phrases (cf. Hood 2008).

As interpersonal meanings are realized by prosodic structures, the commitment of interpersonal meanings is closely related to the prosodic structure. According to Martin & White (2005: 19 - 21), prosodies of interpersonal meaning can be established in a text through three ways: saturation, intensification, and domination. Saturation is opportunistic, with the prosody manifested wherever it can. For example, in order to emphasize the ability of a person, resources for the positive judgment of the person's capacity will be employed whenever appropriate through the texts (Martin & White 2005: 19). In this case, other things being equal, the degree of commitment of interpersonal meanings is determined by the amount of opportunistic manifestations of the prosody in the text; the more manifestations of the prosody, the more committed is the text in this aspect of the interpersonal meaning.

Intensification involves amplification, with the volume gradually tuned up so that the prosody makes a bigger splash that reverberates through the surrounding discourse. This can be achieved by repetition of various kinds, submodification, exclamative structure or superlative morphology (Martin & While 2005: 20). In this case, other things being equal, the degree of commitment is determined by the volume of the prosody; the higher the volume, the more committed is the text in this aspect of the interpersonal meaning.

Domination means that the prosody associates itself with meanings that have other meanings under their scope, thus dominating the other meanings. Grammatically, domination can be achieved either by mood structure where the Mood function establishes the mood, modality and polarity of the clause; or it can be achieved by associating the dominating prosody with interpersonal Themes, which will be followed in the Rheme (Martin & White 2005: 21). When the prosody is realized by domination, the degree of commitment of the specific prosody is determined by the range of its domination scope. As a large scope implies that the prosody is resonated in a longer stretch of text, the text is more committed in this aspect of the interpersonal meaning. For example, in a questionnaire, the interrogative mood will dominate a great range of the text; while in an answer sheet, the declarative mood will dominate the text. Thus, a questionnaire is more committed in the demand of information, whereas an answer sheet is more committed in the providing of information.

Textual meaning is realized by periodical structures. Texts organize themselves with pulses of informational prominence, with the beginning functions as a hyper/macro-Theme, and the end a hyper/macro-New (cf. Section 3.10). Thus, levels of periodic structure imply a culminative form of realization, with the beginning and end of each layer in the organization of the text especially significant from the perspective of textual meaning. As far as commitment is concerned, the ideational and interpersonal meanings instantiated in one text by a phase or stage may be instantiated in another text by a highly condensed clause, thus functioning as it were a kind of hyper/macro Theme of that stage, as is demonstrated by summary writing texts provided by Hood (2008). Thus, the condensed clause is much less committed than the original clause, and the summary text is also less committed than the original text.

### 3.7.3 Iconization and Dual Instantiation

In addition to the basic two dimensions (i. e. coupling and commitment), there are other two aspects of instantiation that deserve special attention: iconization and dual instantiation. According to Martin (2009), iconization refers to the process of instantiation whereby ideational meaning is discharged and interpersonal meaning charged. It can be considered as a special type of coupling of ideational and interpersonal meanings whereby interpersonal meaning is foregrounded and the ideational meaning is backgrounded to the extent that it can be ignored. In a sense, it can be seen as a process opposite to the instantiation in some academic texts whereby the ideational meaning is charged and the interpersonal meaning discharged to the extent possible. Martin (2009) suggests that iconization is the basic instantiation principle behind the genesis of playful headlines, metaphors and idioms as well, and is the easiest to bring to consciousness in the context of images, artifacts and people (peace symbols, flags, statues, team colors, famous leaders and so on).

Dual instantiation refers to the instantiation of the meaning potential simultaneously in two or more modalities, e.g. language and image, language and music/sound, language and gesture, etc. It is the basic principle that underlies multimodal texts. Examples include some children's picture books, with the event of each story instantiated by words and images simultaneously on every page of the book. Dual instantiation should be distinguished from complementary instantiation of meaning potentials in multimodal texts. In the latter case, one part of the meaning potential is instantiated in one modality, while another part instantiated in another modality. In contrast, dual instantiation is the instantiation of the same part of the meaning potential in different modalities.

## 3.8 Genre Individuation

While instantiation is concerned with the specialization of the meaning potential according to the instances of language use, individuation deals with the specialization of the meaning potential according to the users (Martin 2006, 2008a, 2010a). As far as the teleological study of genre is concerned, while genre instantiation deals with the ways to achieve the specific purpose of genre by employing specific instances of semiotic resources, genre individuation is concerned with the achievement of the specific purpose of a genre by employing user-specific semiotic resources (resources available at each strata of a semiotic that is conducive to the pursuit of the purpose).

The key variable here is user(s). User is critical in the study of genre because genres are social actions performed by human beings. When we talk about genre as an abstract system of semiotic potential, it seems that user as a factor is dispensable. However, genre is not simply an abstraction. Every genre must be employed by users in actual social life to serve their own purposes. Thus, when actualized in social life, every genre will be imbued with the unique purpose of each user. In other words, every user employs the semiotic potential of each specific genre to achieve their own purpose and serve their own interests. Likewise, the employment of semiotic resources at the strata of register and discourse semantics is also conditioned by the purpose of each individual. This is the individual aspect of the telos of each genre.

On the other hand, like language system, genre as system only exists in the social life of collectivity. The telos of each genre necessarily reflects the collective goal and interests of the genre community. As such, there is tension between the individual and collective aspects of the telos in a genre. During the actualization process of a genre, each user will necessarily make his own choices and employ appropriate semiotic resources at each stratum to achieve his own purpose, thus foregrounding his unique identity. On the other, in order to pursue his purpose by employing a specific genre, the individual aspect of the purpose of each user should be consistent with the collective purpose of the genre community. Each user should employ resources to negotiate his identity with other users of the same genre, and affiliate himself to the genre community.

Thus, genre individuation can be explored along two trajectories: individuation and affiliation. This is consistent with Martin's general framework of linguistic theory (Martin 2008a, 2010a). Individuation is related to Bernstein's recognition rules and classification, i. e. it is concerned with the recognition of different identities regulated by the classification principle that relays power, while affiliation is related to realization rules (realization in Bernstein's sense) and framing, i. e. concerned with the negotiation among and across identities (Martin 2010a; Bernstein 1999, 2000). From a teleological perspective, individuation is concerned with the achievement of the unique purpose of the user by employing user-specific resources that show his unique identity in a community, while affiliation is concerned with the negotiation of the specific purposes of different users into a general purpose of a genre community.

Individuation can only be studied in relation to instantiation and realization. This is because a user can only achieve his unique purpose and construe his unique identity by instantiating the purpose and identity in a text, while a text can only be formed by drawing on the realization resources that members of a culture share (Martin 2008a).

According to Martin (2010a), all levels of the realization hierarchy individuate, just as all of these levels instantiate. At the stratum of genre, a specific user will have his unique aspect of purpose in addition to the collective aspect, and resultantly his unique way of goal configuration. This will be necessarily reflected in some form of variation in the generic structure, for example, addition or deletion of optional phases, and different sequences of the structure deriving from the same structure order. At the stratum of register, the user will make appropriate register configurations that are suitable for realizing his individualized genres. Similarly, at the discourse semantic stratum, the choices of the ideational, interpersonal and textual meanings, the ways of coupling, and the degree of commitment will help construe his unique identity and serve his own interests. In fact, the instances employed by a user in a text will all necessarily help the user achieve his own purpose, and show his unique identity. In this sense, it is the unique ways of coupling and commitment of a specific user at all levels of a semiotic that helps establish the unique identity of the user, and serve his interests. On the contrary, as far as affiliation is concerned, it is the shared ways of coupling and commitment at different strata of a semiotic that helps generalize personalities (persona) into personality types (subculture), personality types into master identities (coding orientation), and master identities into a culture system. These shared meanings are what are called bonds, and the network of bonds affiliate individual members to a community.

The trajectory of affiliation is well described by Knight's work (Knight 2010). As shown in Figure 3. 3 (on p. 92), the minimal social unit on the cline of affiliation is a bond, which is realized by a coupling in affiliative negotiations in text. Bonds can be clustered into a bond network, i. e. a particular community, as indicated by the broken line. Solid lines between bonds in the bond networks indicate the clustering of shared bonds into community value sets. The bonds can be further clustered into more generalized ideological divisions of community (master ideological networks), which are less than the overall communing potential of the system of bonds in the culture. According to Knight (2010), the affiliative negotiation of identity should be interpreted logogenetically, instance by instance and bond by bond. In other words, affiliation can be viewed as an ongoing process through logogenesis in couplings within a text, and communities are construed as social persons that build up shared bonds within these instances. Also, culture is considered as functioning to presumably constrain possible open choices from the semiotic system into a system of bonds in affiliation, while participants affiliate a communing potential around these bonds (Knight 2010).

Knight's model basically reveals the process of affiliation. The only need for adjustment is the definition of bond. That is, in addition to shared ways of coupling, shared ways of commitment can also form the basis of bonding. Moreover, coupling as the basis of bond may not necessarily be only restricted to the coupling between interpersonal and ideational meanings. It can include all forms of coupling between semiotic resources at all strata along the hierarchy of realization.

In a sense, individuation in the narrow sense can be considered as the reverse of affiliation. Where affiliation is based on the sharing of meanings among the members of a community, individuation is a process of foregrounding unique ways of meaning making of individual members. Thus, within a culture, in order to construe its master identity, a class (or a generation, an ethnic group, etc.) will employ

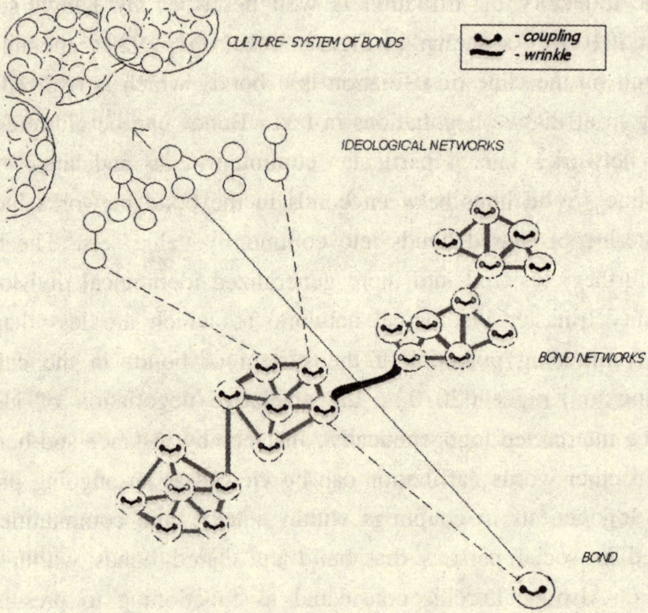


**Figure 3.3 Affiliation as Conceptualized by Knight (2010)**

its unique ways of meaning making that is not shared by other classes within the same culture. Members of a subculture will also have distinctive ways of meaning making unshared by other subcultures. Likewise, each individual member of a subculture will have to show his unique identity by showing his unique ways of action.

## 3.9 Register Patterning

In order to show the specific process of telos-conditioned genre operationalization, it is necessary to analyze the realization, instantiation and individuation of specific genres based on the stratification of language (and of a semiotic system in general) and the metaredundancy relation among the different strata. For this purpose, discussion on the genre stratum alone is insufficient. Rather, resources at the register and discourse semantic strata that are available for genre operationalization should also be analyzed. In SFL, the most viable theories of register and discourse semantics are developed by Martin (1992) and Martin & Rose (2003, 2007). They are adopted as analytic tools in this model, as shown in Figure 3.1. The register stratum will be first interpreted. A register is a configuration of three variables: field, tenor and mode. They are discussed respectively below.

### 3.9.1 Mode

Mode (Martin 1992: 508-523) refers to the role of language in realizing social action. It can be studied along two dimensions: interpersonally along the dimension of monologue/dialogue, and ideationally along the dimension of action/reflection. As far as the interpersonal semiotic space is concerned, what is critical is the ways in which channels of communication affect the possible interaction between the speaker and listener, which is conditioned by the kind of feedback that is possible. Two kinds of contact are possible: visual and aural.

However, unlike Martin's emphasis on physical contact between the interactants, in this study, contact will be used to indicate the interactants' semiotic contact with the message communicated. Both visual and aural contact may be unidirectional or bidirectional. When the modality is language, writing can be defined as visual contact, which may be unidirectional (such as books) or bidirectional (such as letters); speaking can be defined as aural contact, which may also be unidirectional (such as radio) or bidirectional (chatting). Both bidirectional speaking and writing can be further classified according to the speed of feedback (instant or delayed). For writing, further distinctions can be made either based on the degree of reply expectation (e.g. public texts vs. private texts), or on the degree of self-consciousness involved (visual and aural objectification). For speaking, further distinctions can be made according to the degree of turn-taking.

Ideationally, mode mediates the degree to which language is part of or constitutive of what is going on. Texts can be scaled along the action/reflection dimension according to the extent to which texts are structured with respect of the activity sequence aspect of field. Thus, a distinction can be made between iconic texts, which are organized with respect to the activity sequence, and non-iconic texts, which are not. In iconic texts, language may either be ancillary with the activity sequence mainly realized by social actions, or constitutive with activity sequence mainly realized by linguistic texts. Within the latter type, language may either monitor, reconstruct, or generalize what is going on. Non-iconic (genre-structured) texts may be further divided into those which review field-structured texts, and those which are not organized around activity sequence in any respect. In addition, a distinction can be made between activity-oriented texts and thing-oriented texts. Activity-oriented texts are organized around time as the key variable. However, for thing-oriented texts, the same principles may also be applied, with place (including composition and setting) rather than time as the critical parameter. People, places and things can be monitored by commenting on them; objects can be reconstructed through description and generalized as generic species in reports.

Modality as a part of mode refers to the modality of communication, such as language, image, color, music, and gesture. In most cases, communication is carried out simultaneously through two or more modalities, i. e. through multi-modal texts. Among all the modalities, language is the most exhaustively studied. In SFL, images has been well studied by O'Toole (1994) and Kress & van Leeuwen (1996/2006), music and sound have been well studied by van Leeuwen (1999), space is accounted for by Martin & Stenglin (2007), action by Martinec (1998, 2000a, 2000b), and color by Kress & Leeuwen (2000). As for the study of inter-modality relations, Martin's approach is to deal with it on the basis of the logico-semantic relations in SFL (Martin & Rose 2007, 2008; Halliday 1994; Halliday & Matthessien

2004).

### 3.9.2 Tenor

Tenor is the negotiation of social relationships among participants (Martin 1992: 523). It mediates social relationships along three dimensions: status, contact, and affect (cf. Poynton: 1984, 1985, 1990a, 1990b). Status refers to the relative position of interlocutors in a culture's social hierarchy (Martin 1992: 525). The basic opposition is between equal and unequal, depending on the comparability of the social ranking of the participants. The key principle of its realization is the reciprocity of choice, with equality of status realized through the same kinds of choices by the interlocutors, and inequality of status realized through different kinds of choices. For inequality, a further distinction is made between dominance and deference. In addition, some selections are typically associated with speakers of high status, and other kinds of choices with speakers of lower status (cf. Martin 1992: 528-529). It should be noted that it is the patterns of interpersonal choices across wholes texts rather than individual choices that is meaningful. This also applies to the realization of contact and affect, that is, to the realization of the whole tenor system.

Contact is concerned with the degree of involvement of interlocutors, which is determined by the nature of fields the interlocutors participate in—how much contact they involve, how regularly, and the nature of the activities (Martin 1992: 528). A basic distinction can be first made between involved and uninvolved contact. Involved contact is cross-classified according to two features: the nature of social activity and the regularity of contact. Social activity is further subclassified into three types, family, work, and recreation, while regularity of contact includes two features, regular and occasional. The realization of the contact need be considered from the perspective of both system and process. The system-oriented principle is proliferation, which means that the degree of contact determines the predictability of the meanings at risk: less contact implies fewer choices available, while more contact more choices available. The process-oriented principle is of contraction: less contact requires more explicit realization of the meanings, while more contact requires less degree of explicitness of the realization. Specific linguistic resources are typically associated with the realization of the distinctions with the contact systems (cf. Martin 1992: 532). It should be noted that contact as a factor of tenor refers to social (interpersonal) contact between the participants, while contact discussed as a factor of mode refers to the semiotic contact to the messages. The two should not be confused.

Affect refers to the degree of emotional charge in the relationship between participants. It is not manifested in all texts (Poynton 1985: 78), but is more likely to be realized in involved than uninvolved contact situations, and with equal status than with unequal ones. Affect can be positive or negative. Positive affect can be sub-classified into satisfaction, security and fulfillment, while negative affect into discord, insecurity, and frustration. It can also be oriented to oneself, or to someone else. In addition, it can either be permanent, which is kind of disposition, or transient, which can be interpreted as a surge of affect. Affect is realized according to the principle of amplification. It can be turned off, or turned on and balanced between speakers. In addition, the volume can be normal (which is called disposition) or very loud (which is a surge). Martin (1992: 533-535) studied both the content form and expression form of affect. As far as the content form is concerned, affect is realized through the iteration of affect meanings; as for the expression form, parameters of pitch, rate, loudness, vowel length, aspiration and other paralinguistic features are stretched, thus functioning as additional resources for amplification.

### 3.9.3 Field

Field refers to the sets of potential activity sequences oriented to some global institutional purpose and is the contextual projection of experiential meaning (Martin 1992: 536). Martin's study of activity sequences is partly based on the work of R. Barthes (1966, 1977). Field can be studied along three dimensions: the degree of sharing among the members of culture, the degree of specialization, and the nature of socialization. As far as the degree of sharing is concerned, some fields may be shared by most members of a culture, while others may be participated more selectively. Fields may be more or less specialized. In addition, they may be socialized through oral transmission or written transmission. Martin (1992: 544) provided a provisional network of field based on a scale of common/uncommon sense. In the network, a distinction is first made between oral transmission and written transmission based on the nature of socialization. Orally transmitted fields are subclassified into domestic and specialized ones (which includes recreation and trading fields), while fields transmitted through writing into administration and exploration ones.

In addition, field has also been studied from a sociological perspective based on knowledge structures inspired by Bernstein (2000) and developed by Muller (2000) (cf. Martin 2007a, 2007b). The basic method is to classify fields based on sociological criteria. For example, Bernstein (1990, 1999, 2000) makes a distinction between everyday horizontal discourse and the vertical discourse of the humanities, social science and natural science. Within vertical discourse, a further distinction is made between the hierarchical knowledge structures characteristic of science and the horizontal knowledge structures of the humanities. The former is a coherent, explicit and systematically principled structure, hierarchically organized, which attempts to create very general propositions and theories that integrate knowledge at lower levels, and in this way shows underlying uniformities across an expanding range of apparently different phenomena. The latter is "a series of specialized languages with specialized modes of interrogation and criteria for the construction and circulation of texts" (Bernstein 1999: 161-162).

## 3.10 Discourse Semantic Systems

After the register stratum is interpreted, the author will proceed to interpret the discourse semantic stratum of the new model. Martin (1992) and Martin & Rose (2003, 2007) propose several discourse semantic systems to deal with meanings at the discourse stratum: the appraisal, involvement and negotiation systems deal with interpersonal meanings, the ideation system and the external part of the conjunction system deal with ideational meanings, while the internal part of the conjunction system, the identification system and the periodicity system deal with textual meanings.

The ideation system focuses on the content of the discourse, that is, what kinds of activities are undertaken and how the participants undertaking the activities are described and classified. Three subsystems are identified: taxonomic relations, nuclear relations and (actual) activity sequences. Taxonomic relations deal with the chains of relations between lexical elements in a text, and include repetition, synonymy, contrast (opposition and series), class (class-member and co-class), and meronymy. Nuclear relation describes the relations between elements in clauses. A clause includes a center (the process, or range), nucleus (the medium or the range), margin (the agent and beneficiary) and periphery (the circumstance). The (actual) activity sequence deals with relations between activities as they unfold in a text. Basically, a distinction can be made between expectance sequence and implication sequence. It should be noted that activity sequence is actual as a part of the ideation system but is potential as a part of the field. Thus, there is no conflict when it is discussed at both the register and discourse semantic strata.

The conjunction system deals with the inter-connections between activities, that is, the logical meanings of the discourse. It is concerned with resources for connecting messages, via addition, comparison, temporality, and causality. A distinction can be made between external conjunction and internal conjunction. The former construes a field beyond the text and is a part of the ideational metafunction, while the latter is used for the internal organization of the text and is a part of the textual metafunction. For both external and internal conjunctions, four types can be recognized: addition (either additive or alternative), comparison (either similar or different), time (either successive or simultaneous) and consequence (either concluding or countering, including cause, means, condition, and purpose).

The appraisal system (cf. Martin 1992; Martin & Rose 2003, 2007; Martin & White 2005) is concerned with evaluation, the attitudinal meanings negotiated in the text, the strength of the feelings involved, and the ways of value sourcing and reader alignment. It includes three subsystems: attitude, engagement and graduation. Three types of attitude are identified: affect (expressing people's feelings), judgment (of people's characters) and appreciation (of the value of things). In addition, attitude may be positive or negative, and may be explicitly inscribed or invoked (expressed indirectly). Engagement is concerned with the source of the attitude. A choice can first be made between monogloss (without recognition of dialogistic alternatives) and heterogloss (with recognition of dialogistic alternatives). Under heterogloss, entertain and attribute contribute to dialogic expansion, while proclaim and disclaim to dialogic contraction. The resources of modality in Halliday's grammar (Halliday 1994) are re-interpreted and covered under the engagement system. Graduation is concerned with attitude amplification. It includes two choices: force, which is concerned with assessment of the intensity of the attitude and can be achieved either through intensification or quantification, and focus, which is concerned with the prototypicality and preciseness of categories. Force can either rise or fall, while focus can either be sharpened or softened.

The negotiation system deals with interactions as exchanges between the speakers, specifically, the ways of role adoption and assignment, and the organization of moves in dialogue. It is concerned with resources for exchanging information and goods & services in dialogue and is based on the mood analysis in Halliday's grammar (Halliday 1994). As the data of this study is based on written language, the negotiation system will not be discussed.

The identification system deals with the tracking of participants, i. e. how the peoples, places, and things are introduced into the discourse and kept track. The reference of peoples or things may either be presented if their identity is unknown, or presumed if their identity is recoverable. Presuming can be achieved through anaphora, cataphora, esphora, homophora, endophora and exophora.

The periodicity system focuses on the rhythm of the discourse, the layers of prediction that flag for the readers what to come, and the layers of consolidation that accumulate the meanings that are made. A distinction can first be made between serial development through which the parts of a text are added on to one another loosely without waves of information flow, and hierarchical/periodical development through which a text is organized through waves of information flow. In hierarchical development, the peak of prominence at the beginning of a clause is the Theme, while the peak of prominence at the end of the clause is the New. At the level of discourse, the part at the beginning that predicts the subsequent content of each phase is the hyper-Theme, while the part that functions as an accumulation of new information is the hyper-New. Likewise, Themes at higher level are macro-Themes, while higher-level News distilling hyper-news are macro-News.

The involvement system for realizing contact relation is still underdeveloped. Resources for realizing this system can be recognized. For example, a low degree of involvement may be realized by the use of major clauses without ellipsis, contraction or vocation, the use of full names, the use of standard, non-technical, specific and core words, the use of monologue and endophoric forms, and the use of experiential congruence (Martin 1992: 532). In addition, resources for realizing status relation are also briefly discussed, but no in-depth exploration is carried out (cf. Martin 1992: 529). The involvement system and the system for realization social status will be discussed only briefly in the application chapters.

## 3.11 Application of the Model

In the previous sections, the telos-oriented model of genre analysis as shown in Figure 3.1 is interpreted part by part. In this section, the procedures for the application of the model will be stated.

The analysis of a simple genre can proceed either in the top-down order or in the bottom-up order. This is because the metaredundancy relation is bidirectional. That is, we can not only partly predict the semiotic resources of an upper stratum based on the analysis of those at a lower stratum, but also partly predict the semiotic resources of a lower stratum based on those at an upper stratum. As far as the application of this model is concerned, we can either proceed from the genre stratum downward to the register and discourse semantic strata, or proceed from the semantic stratum and upward to the register or discourse semantic stratum. The basic principle is to work out the semiotic configurations at one stratum based on that of the adjacent stratum.

In the top-down order, the start point is the genre stratum (the procedures of a bottom-up analysis are just the reversal of those of a top-down analysis). The general purpose of the genre should be first identified, the goal configuration and complexing (as concretization of the general purpose) should be explored so as to show the teleological structure of the genre. As the realization of the teleological structure, the generic structure can be worked out, which conditions the macro structure of the specific text instances of the genre.

The teleological and generic structures are realized through register patterning. Based on the configuration at the genre stratum, the register configuration (the configuration of field, tenor and mode variables) and patterning of a specific genre should be worked out stage by stage. The analysis of field should focus on the activity sequence concerned, with the degree of specialization, the degree of sharing and the nature of socialization taken into consideration. For the analysis of mode, the variables include modality, action/reflection orientation and monologue/dialogue orientation. As for tenor analysis, the variables to be considered include affect, contact and status. In addition, the patterning of the field, tenor and mode values at each stage and between different stages should be explored.

Register configuration is realized by discourse semantic resources. For the analysis of ideational meaning, the ideation system and the external conjunction resources can be explored. The analysis of interpersonal meaning should focus on the resources of the appraisal system, involvement system, power relation, and the negotiation system in the case of conversation study. The study of the textual meaning should focus on the resources of the periodicity system, identification system and internal conjunction system. The resources can be analyzed stage by stage to show the macro structure of the genre instance (text). In the case of a multimodal genre, the analysis of discourse semantic stratum should be based on the semantic systems of the specific modalities (for example, the meaning-oriented visual grammar of Kress & Leeuwen 2006).

A macro-genre (genre complex) is the result of the subsumption of several purposes into an even more general purpose. In the study of a macro-genre, the focus should be on the logico-semantic relations among the simple genres, which can be either expansion (including elaboration, extension, and enhancement) or projection (including idea and locution). Embedding should also be taken into consideration when a genre functions as a stage (or a part of stage) of another genre. In addition to genre complexing, genre agnation is another aspect of inter-genre relation. Agnation can be studied either typologically or topologically. A typological analysis should classify genres into different types by employing one feature of the genre simplex system as the criterion, and thus foreground the different values of the feature realized by different genres. Topological analysis arranges genres on clines with respect to their similarities and differences.

In addition to realization, genre can also be studied along the dimensions of instantiation and individuation. Both dimensions can be studied either in a top-down or bottom-up manner. The study of genre instantiation should focus on how the same abstract genre is instantiated into different specific texts through different ways of coupling of semiotic resources and different degrees of semiotic commitment at each stratum, so as to pursue the specific purpose of each text. In a bottom-up manner, the focus should be on how the different individual texts can be generalized (de-instantiated) into different text types, further into different register types and finally into specific genres. The study of genre individuation should focus on how the same abstract genre is employed by different users to achieve their different specific purposes and show their unique identities through their unique ways of semiotic configurations at different strata. In a bottom-up manner, the focus should be on how the users' shared ways of semiotic configurations at each stratum help them pursue the shared teleological aspects and negotiate their individual identities (persona) into personality types (a subculture), coding orientation (master identities) and finally into the system (culture). The three dimensions of operationalization are different aspects of the same process, and should always be considered together even the emphasis can be on any one of them. The study of genre along any dimension should be based on the analysis of the semiotic configurations at each stratum of a semiotic.

The model is teleological, because at the core of genre is its teleological configuration, including the configuration of the general purpose and its concretization into specific goals. Therefore, during genre analysis at any stratum, telos should always be kept in mind as the guiding principle, and attention should always be paid to how the configurations of semiotic resources at different strata are ultimately conditioned by the teleological configuration of the genre, and how they in return serve the pursuit of the general purpose of the genre.

## 3.12 Summary

Chapter 3 has developed a telos-oriented model of genre analysis. The model is first presented in a diagram to give an overview and then interpreted in detail part by part. The necessity of a teleological perspective to genre study is first discussed by exploring the teleological nature of genre, with genre considered as a typification of telos-oriented social actions. The teleological structure of social actions is analyzed, and adopted as the basis for the development of a telos-oriented genre system. Genre structure (staging) is then explored as a derivation from the genre system. Inter-genre relations are explored teleologically along the dimensions of complexing (including embedding) and agnation. In addition, the operationalization of an abstract genre is discussed teleologically along the dimensions of realization, instantiation, and individuation. Analytic tools at the register and discourse semantic stratum are discussed. At last, the procedures and methods for the application of the model are explained. In Chapters 4, 5, and 6, the telos-oriented genre model developed by the author will be tested through its application to the study of a series of genres on corporate promotional websites.

# Chapter 4

## Corporate Website Genres and Their Realization

In Chapter 3, a telos-oriented model of genre analysis has been established. However, the feasibility and applicability of the model for practical genre analysis still needs testing. In the following three chapters, the model will be tested by applying it to the analysis of genres on corporate promotional websites. As the application of the genre model requires the operationalization of specific genres, the study in the subsequent chapters will be carried out along the three dimensions of operationalization, i. e. genre realization, instantiation and individuation respectively.

The tools and the methodology of analysis will be based on those developed in Chapter 3 (cf. Sections 3. 9 and 3. 10; refer to Martin 1992; Martin & Rose 2003, 2007, 2008; Martin 2008a, 2008b for more details). The analysis will stop at the discourse semantic stratum because analysis of discourse semantic resources at the level of texts (as instances of genre) will better show the working of genre. Naturally, the analysis of discourse semantic resources and that at higher strata are based on lexicogrammatical analysis, but the specific lexicogrammatical analysis will only be mentioned when it is conducive to analysis at higher strata.

Chapter 4 is intended to test the model along the dimension of genre realization. Four genres will be discussed respectively: an operating procedure, a descriptive report, a compositional report and a news story. The focus will be on the telos-oriented realization of each genre through the configuration of semiotic resources at the genre, register and discourse semantic strata based on the metaredundancy relation.

## 4.1 Operating Procedures

Procedures teach the reader how to perform a specialized sequence of activities that has a specialized function (e. g. instrumental or ritual function) in a culture in relation to certain objects and locations (Martin & Rose 2008: 182). Five procedural genres are recognized by Martin & Rose among the procedure family: everyday procedures, operating procedures, cooperative procedures, conditional procedures, and technical procedures. They are used in many contexts, such as domestic, recreational, educational, scientific and industrial contexts (Martin & Rose 2008: 181-229). What will be discussed here is the operating procedure, which describes the steps in a specialized activity. The schematic structure of an operating procedure is described as Objective ^ Steps (Martin & Rose 2008: 187).

Operating procedures are frequently adopted on all the websites in the corpus of this study. In fact, almost each user manual of each product (both hardware and software) and service (e. g. download and customer support services) has adopted this genre. Text 1, an extract from Microsoft's website, is an example of the operating procedure genre. The messages realized by ranking clauses are numbered in brackets for convenience of analysis.

Text 1 Delete Files Using Disk Cleanup

(1) If you want to reduce the number of unnecessary files on your hard disk to free up disk space and help your computer run faster, use Disk Cleanup. (2) It removes temporary files, (3) empties the Recycle Bin, (4) and removes a variety of system files and other items that you no longer need.

1. (5) Open Disk Cleanup by clicking the Start button, clicking All Programs, clicking Accessories, clicking System Tools, and then clicking Disk

Cleanup.

2. (6) In the Disk Cleanup Options dialog box, choose whether you want to clean up your own files only or all of the files on the computer. (7) If you are prompted for an administrator password or confirmation, type the password or (8) provide confirmation.

3. (9) If the Disk Cleanup: Drive Selection dialog box appears, select the hard disk drive that you want to clean up, (10) and then click OK.

4. (11) Click the Disk Cleanup tab, (12) and then select the check boxes for the files you want to delete.

5. (13) When you finish selecting the files you want to delete, click OK, (14) and then click Delete files to confirm the operation. (15) Disk Cleanup proceeds to remove all unnecessary files from your computer.

(http://windows. microsoft. com/en-US/windows-vista/Delete-files-using-Disk-Cleanup, accessed on March 3, 2010)

In the following sections, the realization process of the operating procedure genre will be explored based on the analysis of Text 1. The teleological and generic structures of the genre will be explored first. Then the realization at the genre, register, and discourse semantics strata will be analyzed step by step to show the metaredundancy relation as conditioned by the pursuit of the general purpose of the genre.

### 4.1.1 Teleological and Generic Structures

Based on the teleological genre system as developed in Chapter 3, the realization of the genre system can be analyzed as follows (the realization rules are greatly loosened as long as they are adequate to show the realization process because at present it is impossible to state the realization of the goal system by a goal structure strictly according to the realization rules due to the lack of systematic analysis of the goals of our social actions):

Purpose of the simplex: to teach the learner/or learners the operating steps in a specialized activity, which is concretized into:

Goal 1: to teach the learner the objective of the operation

Goal 2: to teach the leaner the steps of the operation
Goal complexing: relation: orbital, semiotical; recursion: stop

According to the analysis above, an operating procedure genre is a genre simplex, whose purpose is to teach the reader or readers the operating steps in a specialized activity. This purpose is concretized into two goals. Goal 1 is to tell the reader the objective of the operation in one phase, with the messages organized semiotically. Goal 2 is to teach the reader the specific steps for performing the operation with the messages organized temporally and serially. The relation between the two goals is orbital, with Goal 1 as the nucleus, Goal 2 as the satellite. In addition, they are organized semiotically rather than spatially or temporally. As there are only two goals configured, which only requires one complexing process, the goal complexing process does not recur. The realization of the system results in an operating genre with a generic structure Objective ^ Steps.

### 4.1.2 Realization at the Genre and Register Strata

The macro structure of Text 1 as generated at the genre stratum can be roughly analyzed as follows:

Purpose: teach the leaner (learners) the way to delete files using disk cleanup, which is concretized into:
Goal 1: tell the learner the objective of the operation (to delete files using disk cleanup)
Goal 2: tell the learner the means (specific steps) of the operation (temporal)
Relation between Goal 1 and Goal 2: semiotical (purposive)
Realized by the macro structure: Objective ^ Steps

This macro structure is clearly indicated by the organization of Text 1. Specifically, Messages (1) - (4) (the first paragraph) state the general objective of Text 1, while the numbered paragraphs state the steps for achieving the objective. Each step in Stage 2 constitutes a phase. This staging will be further supported by the analysis at the register and discourse semantic strata in later sections.

As for inter-stratum realization, from a teleological perspective, the teleological system and structure of the genre conditions the choices at the register stratum. Each goal configuration process conditions the register configuration at the corresponding stage, while the goal complexing process conditions the patterning of the registers at different stages. In order to illustrate the telos-conditioned metaredundancy relation between register and genre, the register patterning of Text 1 is analyzed in detail below.

**Table 4.1 Field Configuration of Text 1**

| | Activity Sequence/ Taxonomy | Degree of sharing | Degree of Specialization | Nature of Socialization |
|---|---|---|---|---|
| Stage 1 | Stating the objective | Low | High | Institutionalized |
| Stage 2 | Operating Activity | Low | High | Institutionalized |

According to the analysis in Table 4.1, the activity sequence of Stage 1 is concerned with stating the purpose of the operation to be implemented, while that of Stage 2 is to describe the steps of the operating activity. This is redundant with (mutually predictable with) the representational aspect of Goal 1 and Goal 2 respectively. The taxonomies are conditioned by the activities, and will be analyzed in detail during the discussion of the discourse semantics of the genre. As operating procedures are discourses of specialized activities, the field is specialized, and institutionalized, with low degree of sharing between the expert and the learner.

The tenor configuration of Text 1 is analyzed in Table 4.2.

**Table 4.2 Tenor Configuration of Text 1**

| | Social Relation | Status | Contact | Affect |
|---|---|---|---|---|
| Stage 1 | Corporate expert-learner | Unequal: dominance | Uninvolved | Unmarked |
| Stage 2 | Corporate expert-Learner | Unequal: dominance | Uninvolved | Unmarked |

According to the tenor analysis in Table 4.2, in both stages, the social relation is that between an expert and a leaner (or learners); they are of unequal social status, i.e. the learner is expected to follow the instructions of the expert. The contact between them is distant. The affect is unmarked, which is typical of specialized technological activities. The tenor of the two stages and the text as a whole redounds with the interactional aspect of the purpose. Specifically, as the purpose is to teach the learner the specialized activity of deleting files using a special tool, the social relation is naturally between an expert and the learner, with the learner expected to follow the instructions, and with distant contact between them. In addition, typically activities between an expert and a learner will show little affect.

The mode configuration of Text 1 is analyzed in Table 4.3.

**Table 4.3 Mode Configuration of Text 1**

| | Aural/Visual Contact | Modality | Monologue/Dialogue | Action/ Reflection |
|---|---|---|---|---|
| Stage 1 | Unidirectional Visual | Language | Monologue; publicly-addre-ssed, reply less likely; visually solidified, high degree of self-consciousness | + Reflection; semiotically structured; |
| Stage 2 | Unidirectional Visual | Language(major); image(auxiliary) | Monologue; reply less likely; high degree of self-consciousness | + Action; temporally structured; generalizing |

As shown in the analysis in Table 4.3, in both Stages 1 and 2, there is only one-way visual contact between the interactants. In Stage 1, language is the only modality, while in Stage 2, language is the major modality with image as the auxiliary modality. In both stages, the text is a monologue, addressed to public readers, and is unlikely to be replied by readers. The text is visually solidified as it is typed and published on a webpage, with high degree of self-consciousness during the composing process. Stage 1 is a reflection of the purpose of the activity as language is constitutive of the on-going process, and correspondingly is semiotically structured (rather than structured temporally or spatially). Stage 2 is more towards the action end as it is highly likely for language only to play an auxiliary role and accompany the real operating process, while the text section is temporally structured based on the order of the operating steps. In addition, Stage 2 is a generalization of the operating steps rather than a recording of the details of an actual operating process. Based on this analysis, it can be seen that the mode of the text is redundant with the organizational aspect of the purpose of the genre. More specifically, Stage 1 is subject to a semiotic organization, while stage 2 is temporally organized. Some aspects of the mode are indirectly conditioned by the field. Specifically, Stage 1 is towards the reflection end, which is conditioned by the semiotic nature of the objective, while the + Action orientation of Stage 2 is redundant with the actional nature of the operating steps.

It should be noted, however, that redundancy implies only partial predictability. This means that only some of the register choices can be predicted from the choices of genre values, while others can not. In Text 1, the specific degree of field sharing, specialization and institutionalization, the specific degree of low involvement and unmarkedness of affect, the choice of modality, monologue/dialogue, the specific degree of contact and inequality cannot be predicted from the choices at the genre stratum. These choices are subject to factors during the instantiation and individuation processes, and reflect the other facet of redundancy relation between register and genre. This principle applies to redundancy-based analysis in subsequent analysis.

### 4.1.3 Realization at the Discourse Semantic Stratum

At the discourse semantic stratum, the resources will be analyzed mainly in terms of the following discourse semantic systems: the ideation system, conjunction system, identification system, periodicity system, and appraisal system. Negotiation system will not be discussed as all the texts in this corpus are written. Resources for encoding involvement and social status will also be discussed briefly when appropriate.

The ideational resources of Text 1 are analyzed in Table 4.4 below.

**Table 4.4 Ideational Resources of Text 1**

| Message | Nuclear | Center | Nuclear | Peripheral |
|---|---|---|---|---|
| Stage 1:<br>(1) | | use | Disk Cleanup | If you want to reduce the number of unnecessary files on your hard disk to free up disk space and help your computer run faster |
| (2) | It (Disk Cleanup) | removes | temporary files | |
| (3) | | empties | the Recycle Bin | |
| (4) | | removes | a variety of system files and other items that you no longer need | |

Table 4.4 continued

| Message | Nuclear | Center | Nuclear | Peripheral |
|---|---|---|---|---|
| Stage 2 Phase 1: (5) | | Open | Disk Cleanup | by clicking the Start button ●, clicking All Programs, clicking Accessories, clicking System Tools, and then clicking Disk Cleanup. |
| Phase 2: (6) | | choose | whether you want to clean up your own files only or all of the files on the computer | in the Disk Cleanup Options dialog box |
| (7) | | type | the password | If you are prompted for an administrator password or confirmation |
| (8) | | provide | confirmation | |
| Phase 3: (9) | | select | the hard disk drive that you want to clean up | If the Disk Cleanup: Drive Selection dialog box appears |
| (10) | | click | OK | |
| Phase 4: (11) | | Click | the Disk Cleanup tab | |
| (12) | | select | the check boxes for the files you want to delete | |
| Phase 5: (13) | | click | OK | When you finish selecting the files you want to delete |
| (14) | | click | Delete files to confirm the operation | |
| (15) | Disk Cleanup | proceeds to remove | all unnecessary files from your computer | |

From the above analysis, it can be seen that Stage 1 consists of two activity sequence, one stating the activity of the user (users) and its purpose (as a peripheral element), and the other the functions of the Disk Cleanup. The two sequences realize the field of Stage 1 (stating the objective). Stage 2 consists of a sequence stating the operating steps that the user is expected to follow, and a simple clause stating the operation of the Disk Cleanup. The boundary between the two stages is clearly shown by the taxonomic relations between the processes. Specifically, Stage 1 ends with a taxonomy stating the functioning of the Disk Cleanup (remove-empty-remove), while Stage 2 mainly consists of a taxonomy stating the operating of the user. As for the taxonomy of entities, the nuclear elements to the left of the table include two types: the tool (Disc Cleanup) and the user ("you"). Nuclear elements to the right form two taxonomies: files to be reduced (temporary files, the recycle bin, a variety of system files and other items, all unnecessary files) and the range of user's operations. The peripheral elements respectively state the purpose, manner, condition, time and location of the operation. Most of the entities and the process verbs in the taxonomies are concrete and specialized, appropriately realizing the field of a specialized operation.

The conjunction resources of Text 1 are analyzed in Table 4.5.

**Table 4.5 Conjunction Resources of Text 1**

| Staging | Internal Conjunction | Message | External Conjunction |
|---|---|---|---|
| Stage 1 | | (1) | |
| | (2), (3), (4) additive to (1) | (2) | |
| | additive to (2) | (3) | |
| | Additive to (3) | (4) and | |
| Stage 2: Phase 1 | | (5) | 1. |

Table 4.5 continued

| Staging | Internal Conjunction | Message | External Conjunction |
|---|---|---|---|
| Phase 2 | | (6) | 2. successive to Phase 1 |
| | | (7) | (7) and (8) successive to 6 |
| | | (8) | (8) additive to (7) |
| Phase 3 | | (9) | 3. successive to Phase 2 |
| | | (10) (and then) | (10) successive to (9) |
| Phase 4 | | (11) | 4. successive to Phase 3 |
| | | (12) and then | (12) successive to (11) |
| Phase 5 | | (13) | 5. successive to Phase 4 |
| | | (14) and then | (14) successive to (13) |
| | | (15) | (15) successive to (14) |

The identification resources of Text 1 are analyzed in Table 4.6. (on p. 116) As shown in the analysis, only three types of participants are tracked throughout the whole texts: "you", "unnecessary files", and "Disk Cleanup". They respectively refer to the Agent, Range (Goal) and Peripheral (Means) of the operations. The user (leaner) is presumed through the second person pronoun "you", which can be identified by exophoric reference based on the context, and then tracked either by anaphora through repetition and implicitness (as indicated by the symbol "ø"). The types of unnecessary files are fist presented in Stage 1, and then tracked by anaphora. The tool Disk Cleanup is first presented, and then tracked either through repetition or by anaphoric reference through the use of the determiner "the". In addition, the participants involved in the operating process (including options and buttons, and tabs, e. g. All Programs, Accessories, System Tools, OK, Delete files) that are not related to participants already presented are presented. Those related to participants that are already presented are presumed through the use of deictic elements or qualifiers, or both (e. g. the Disk Cleanup Options dialog box, the Disk Cleanup: Drive Selection dialog box, the hard disk drive that you want to clean up, the Disk Cleanup tab, the check boxes for the files you want to delete).

**Table 4.6 Identification System of Text 1**

| | The learner | Unnecessary files | Disk Cleanup |
|---|---|---|---|
| Stage 1 | You, your, your; ø, you | the number of unnecessary files, temporary files, a variety of system files and other items that you no longer need | Disk Cleanup, it |
| Stage 2 (phase 1) | ø | | Disk Cleanup |
| Phase 2 | ∅, you, your; you, ø | your own files; all of the files on the computer | Disk Cleanup (options) |
| Phase 3 | ∅; ø | | Disk Cleanup (: drive selection) |
| Phase 4 | ∅; ø, you | | Disk Cleanup (tab) |
| Phase 5 | You, you, ø; ø | the files you want to delete; all unnecessary files | Disk Cleanup |

As for the resources of the periodicity system, the text is mainly organized serially rather than hierarchically. Stage 1 functions as the macro-Theme of the text, as a kind of introduction that is to be developed in the next stage. However, there is no macro-New, as Stage 2 is developed serially through explicit numbering of the steps concerned. Thus, one step is followed by another, and the text is ended when all the steps are taken. Serial organization is typically used in operating procedures, though in some cases in combination with small hierarchies of periodicity.

As far as the analysis of appraisal resources is concerned, there is little appraisal meaning in this text. Specifically, there is no inscribed attitude. A few words can be said to invoke some kind of appreciation meanings. In Stage 1, the listing of the functions of Disk Cleanup can be considered as a sort of positive appreciation of the tool. Such a positive appreciation is invoked by the use of such words as "free up disk space and help your computer run faster" and "removes a variety of system files and other items that you no longer need". In Stage 2, the last message "Disk Cleanup proceeds to remove all unnecessary files from your computer" can also invoke such positive valuation of Disk Cleanup. As a whole, little affect is involved in the text, which faithfully realizes the unmarked affect in the tenor configuration.

The unequal social status in the tenor, more specifically, the dominance of the expert is realized by various resources. For example, the expert functions as the primary knower, teaching the learner the techniques for using Disk Cleanup, while congruent forms of imperatives are used to realize the instructions that the learner are expected to follow. As for involvement resources that realize the social contact, the text shows a low degree of involvement. This is reflected by the employment of monologue, endophoric reference of presumed participants (as discussed in the analysis of identification resources), explicit conjunctions as realized by step numbering, and experiential congruence at the discourse semantic stratum, as well as the use of major clauses without any ellipsis and contraction, and the use of full names for all the options, buttons, and tabs at the lexicogrammar stratum (cf. Martin 1992: 532).

When all the analysis at each stratum is considered together, it can be seen that the teleological configuration of the operating procedure genre conditions the generic/macro structure of Text 1, which in turn partially conditions the configuration of register resources of the text, and ultimately redounds with the semiotic configurations at the discourse semantic stratum of Text 1. As a result, the semiotic configuration at each stratum of Text 1 is governed by the teleological configuration of the genre (in particular the purpose to teach the learners the way to delete files using disk cleanup), and cannot but serve the pursuit of the purpose of the genre.

## 4.2 Descriptive Reports

Reports are genres that classify and describe entities, focusing on their description, classification, and composition. Three types of report genres are recognized by Martin & Rose (2008: 141-142): descriptive reports, classifying reports and compositional reports. The first type classifies a phenomenon and then describe its features, the second subclassifies a number of phenomena with respect to a given set of criteria, and the third describes the components of an entity. It should be noted that though reports are discussed by Martin & Rose against the background of scientific discourses, they are used in a much wider range of discourses in our life. For example, in corporate promotional websites, it is quite common to describe a company, classify its products, and describe the components of an organization or a product. In the analysis of corporate websites in this study, two report genres are identified: a descriptive report and a compositional report. The descriptive report will be studied first in this section.

Descriptive reports are extensively employed on corporate websites, especially in the part providing information about the company concerned. Columns with frequent use of this genre include company profiles and descriptions of its social responsibility, etc. From the perspective of the corporation concerned, what are described in these columns are the characteristic features of the different aspects of the corporation. Thus, what is employed is the descriptive report genre rather than the description genre. In this section, the company profile of Linux (Text 2) will be used as an example and analyzed to show the realization of the descriptive report genre.

Text 2 Linux Profile

About Us

(1) Within two years, the Linux ecosystem is projected to reach $50 billion, spanning the enterprise computing, desktop/net books and embedded markets. (2) The Linux Foundation is the nonprofit consortium dedicated to fostering the growth of Linux. (3) Founded in 2007, the Linux Foundation sponsors the work of Linux creator Linus Torvalds and (4) is supported by leading Linux and open source companies and developers from around the world.

(5) The Linux Foundation promotes, protects and standardizes Linux by providing unified resources and services needed for open source to successfully compete with closed platforms.

(6) Promoting Linux and Providing Neutral Collaboration and Education

(7) The Linux Foundation serves as a neutral spokesperson for Linux and (8) generates original content that advances the understanding of the Linux platform. (9) Its web properties, including Linux. com, reach approximately two million people per month. (10) It also fosters innovation by hosting collaboration events—including LinuxCon—among the Linux technical community, application developers, industry and end users to solve pressing issues facing the Linux ecosystem. (11) Through the Linux Foundation's community programs, end users, developers and industry collaborate on technical, legal and promotional issues.

(12) Protecting and Supporting Linux Development

(13) It's vitally important that Linux creator Linus Torvalds and other key kernel developers remain independent. (14) The Linux Foundation sponsors them so they can work full time on improving Linux. (15) The Linux Foundation also manages the Linux trademark, (16) offers developers legal intellectual property protection and a legal defense fund and (17) coordinates industry and community legal collaboration and education.

(18) Improving Linux as a Technical Platform

(19) The Linux Foundation offers application developers standardization services and support that makes Linux an attractive target for their development efforts. (20) These include: the Linux Standard Base (LSB) and the Linux Developer Network. (21) The Linux Foundation also provides services to the Linux development community, including an open source developer travel fund, legal support and other administrative assistance. (22) Through its workgroups, members and developers can collaborate on key technical areas which can include everything from Cloud Computing to Printing in Linux. (23) Finally, users can access Linux training through its technical training program.

(http://www.linuxfoundation.org/about, accessed on March 3, 2010)

The teleological and generic structures of the descriptive report genre will be first analyzed. Then the analysis will be carried out at the discourse semantic stratum before it proceeds to the register stratum and finally to the genre stratum. It should be noted that the specific order of analysis among the three strata can vary with the purpose of the analysis as along as the metaredundancy relation is clearly shown. The order adopted in this section (which is different from that in Section 4.1) is intended to show the metaredundancy relation between the three strata in a bottom-up way.

### 4.2.1 Teleological and Generic Structures

The purpose of a descriptive report is to classify and describe a phenomenon. Its stages are generally Classification followed by Description (Martin & Rose 2008: 142). On the basis of Martin & Rose' work, the teleological structure of a descriptive report can be analyzed as follows:

Purpose: to classify and describe a phenomenon to a reader (readers), which is concretized into:

Goal 1: to describe the classificatory attribute of the phenomenon to the reader (readers) (semiotic)

Goal 2: to describe the specific features/aspects of the phenomenon to the reader (readers) (semiotic)

Relation between Goal 1 and Goal 2: semiotic

Realized by the generic structure: Classification ^ Description

Possible phasing: the description of each feature or aspect constituting a phase

### 4.2.2 Realization at the Discourse Semantic Strata

In order to provide a better analysis, a vague macro structure of the text can first be identified. This is clearly indicated by the type setting of the text. As the three icons interact with the following three sub-headings respectively, it can be seen that the text consists of two stages, with the first paragraph as the first stage, where those following the icons (including the three icons) as the second. The three sub-headings indicate the three phases within Stage 2.

The ideation resources of Text 2 are analyzed in Table 4.7. It can be seen that the major activity sequence in the text is about the functioning of the Linux Foundation, which includes such main processes as "sponsor", "promote", "protect", "standardize", "serve", "generate", "foster", "protect", "support", "manage", and "offer". Other process verbs are concerned either with the attributes of the products or services provided by Linux Foundation, or with the operations that the community members can carry out via the services provided by Linux Foundation.

**Table 4.7 Ideational Resources of Text 2**

| Staging | Nuclear | Center | Nuclear | Peripheral |
|---|---|---|---|---|
| Stage 1 (1) | the Linux ecosystem | is projected to reach | $ 50 billion | Within two years |
| | (the Linux ecosystem) | spanning | the enterprise computing, desktop/net books and embedded markets | |

Table 4.7 continued

| Staging | Nuclear | Center | Nuclear | Peripheral |
|---|---|---|---|---|
| (2) | The Linux Foundation | is | the nonprofit consortium dedicated to fostering the growth of Linux | |
| (3) | the Linux Foundation | sponsors | the work of Linux creator Linus Torvalds | |
| (4) | (the Linux Foundation) | is supported | by leading Linux and open source companies and developers from around the world | Founded in 2007 |
| Stage 2 (5) | The Linux Foundation | promotes, protects and standardizes | Linux | by providing uni-fied resources and services needed for open source to successfully compete with closed platforms |
| Phase 1 (6) | | Promoting providing | Linux Neutral Collaboration and Education | |
| (7) | The Linux Foundation | serves | as a neutral spokesperson | for Linux |
| (8) | (the Linux Foundation) | generates | original content that advances the understanding of the Linux platform | |
| (9) | Its web properties, including Linux.com | reach | approximately two million people per month | |

Table 4.7 continued

| Staging | Nuclear | Center | Nuclear | Peripheral |
|---|---|---|---|---|
| (10) | It (the Linux Foundation) | fosters | innovation | by hosting collaboration events-including Linux Con-among the Linux technical community, application developers, industry and end users to solve pressing issues facing the Linux ecosystem |
| (11) | end users, developers and industry | collaborate | on technical, legal and promotional issues | through the Linux Foundation's community programs |
| Phase 2 (12) | | Protecting and Supporting | Linux Development | |
| (13) | Linux creator Linus Torvalds and other key kernel developers remain independent | is | vitally important | |
| (14) | The Linux Foundation | Sponsors | them (Linux creator Linus Torvalds and other key kernel developers) | so they can work full time on improving Linux |

Table 4.7 continued

| Staging | Nuclear | Center | Nuclear | Peripheral |
|---|---|---|---|---|
| (15) | The Linux Foundation | manages | the Linux trademark | |
| (16) | (The Linux Foundation) | offers | developers legal intellectual property protection and a legal defense fund | |
| (17) | (The Linux Foundation) | coordinates | industry and community legal collaboration and education | |
| Phase 3 (18) | | improving | Linux | as a Technical Platform |
| (19) | The Linux Foundation | offers | application developers standardization services and support that makes Linux an attractive target for their development efforts | |
| (20) | These (standardization services and support) | include | the Linux Standard Base (LSB) and the Linux Developer Network | |

Table 4.7 continued

| Staging | Nuclear | Center | Nuclear | Peripheral |
| --- | --- | --- | --- | --- |
| (21) | The Linux Foundation | provides | services to the Linux development community, including an open source developer travel fund, legal support and other administrative assistance | |
| (22) | members and developers | can collaborate | on key technical areas which can include everything from Cloud Computing to Printing in Linux | through its workgroups |
| (23) | users | can access | Linux training | through its technical training program |

Several taxonomies can be identified in the text. The taxonomy of Linux technical/development community (based on meronymy) includes such items as Linux Foundation, Linux creator Linus Torvalds, developers, industry, end users, and collaborating companies. The taxonomy of Linux system includes Linux ecosystem and the Linux platform. Another taxonomy is concerned with the services/support provided by Linux Foundation. It includes such items as collaboration and education service (neutral collaboration and education), service related to Linux development (including sponsorship, trademark management, legal intellectual property protection and legal defense fund), platform improvement service (including standardization service and support), and services related to Linux development community (an open source developer travel fund, legal support and other administrative assistance, and technical training program).

As a whole, it can be seen that the ideation resources of Text 2 are concerned with the functioning and property of Linux Foundation.

The conjunction resources of Text 2 are analyzed in Table 4.8. It can be seen that all of the conjunction resources of Text 2 are of the internal type, and are used to organize the text rather than relating to the specific activities. This forms a sharp contrast with the external conjunctions typically employed in operating procedures (cf. Section 4.1.3). Another feature is the frequent use of reworking conjunctions, which is used to elaborate the details of a general feature. For example, in stage 2, the author first presents an overview of the general functions of Linux, and then elaborates on each of the functions in a separate phase. The different functions in the three phases are organized through additive conjunctions. Within each phase, the text is basically organized in the same way. Specifically, the heading functions as a summary of the phase, which is followed by a description of the specific features of that function, with the specific features connected with each other through additive conjunctions.

**Table 4.8 Conjunction Resources of Text 2**

| Staging | Internal | Message | External |
|---|---|---|---|
| Stage 1 | | (1) | |
| | Additive to (1) | (2) | |
| | Additive to (2) | (3) | |
| | Additive to (3) | (4) | |
| Stage 2 | | (5) | |
| Phase 1 | Phases 1-3 reworking (5) | (6) | |
| | (7) -11 reworking (6) | (7) | |
| | Additive to (7) | (8) | |
| | Additive to (8) | (9) | |

Table 4.8 continued

| Staging | Internal | Message | External |
|---|---|---|---|
| | Additive to (9) | (10) | |
| | Additive to (10) | (11) | |
| Phase 2 | Additive to Phase 1 | (12) | |
| | (13) – (17) reworking (12) | (13) | |
| | Consequence to (13) | (14) | |
| | (15) – (17) Additive to (13)/(14) | (15) | |
| | Additive to (15) | (16) | |
| | Additive to (16) | (17) | |
| Phase 3 | Additive to Phase 2 | (18) | |
| | (19) – (23) Reworking (18) | (19) | |
| | Reworking (19) | (20) | |
| | (21) – (22) additive to (19)/20 | (21) | |
| | Additive to (21) | (22) | |
| | Additive to (21) – (22) | (23) | |

The identification resources of Text 2 are analyzed in Table 4.9 (on p. 128). As shown by the analysis, two groups of entities are tracked throughout the text, the Linux Foundation, and the Linux system, as shown in Table 4.9. They represent the critical concepts for an introduction in the "about" part. The entities are presented repeatedly and must be identified through endophoric reference, even in cases where they can be presumed through anaphoric reference. Specifically, "the Linux Foundation" is presented 10 times, but presumed only 4 times, while "Linux" system is presented repeatedly throughout the text. The frequent presenting of a key concept is conducive to its popularization among the publicity.

**Table 4.9 Identification Resources of Text 2**

| Staging | The Linux Foundation | Linux |
|---|---|---|
| Stage 1 (1) | | Linux ecosystem |
| (2) | The Linux Foundation | Linux |
| (3) | the Linux Foundation | |
| (4) | the Linux Foundation | (Leading) Linux |
| Stage 2: (5) | The Linux Foundation | Linux |
| Phase 1 (6) | | Linux |
| (7) | The Linux Foundation | Linux |
| (8) | | the Linux platform |
| (9) | Its | |
| (10) | It | the Linux ecosystem |
| (11) | (Through) the Linux Foundation's | |
| Phase 2 (12) | | Linux (Development) |
| (13) | | |
| (14) | The Linux Foundation | Linux |
| (13) | The Linux Foundation | the Linux (trademark) |
| Phase 3 (14) | | Linux |
| (15) | The Linux Foundation | Linux (trademark) |
| (16) | | |
| (17) | | |
| (18) | | |
| (19) | The Linux Foundation | Linux |
| (20) | | Linux Standard Base, Linux Developer Network |
| (21) | The Linux Foundation | |
| (22) | its | |
| (23) | its | |

As for the periodicity system, Text 2 is organized serially rather than through hierarchies of periodicities. Several layers of macro-

Themes and hyper-Themes can be identified, but there is no corresponding hyper-New or macro-New. Specifically, the title of the text "about us" can be considered as the first level macro-Theme of the whole text. Stage 1 then can be considered as the second Level macro-Theme, Paragraph 1 of Stage 2 functions as the hyper-Theme of Stage 2, while the subheading of each phase functions as the hyper-Theme of the corresponding phase. For each macro-Theme or hyper-Theme, there is no corresponding Macro/hyper-New functioning as a summary of the previous text sections. The lack of macro/hyper-New is typical of serially organized texts, and is a characteristic feature of corporate promotion texts on websites.

The appraisal resources of Text 2 are analyzed in Table 4. 10.

**Table 4. 10 Appraisal Resources of Text 2**

| Attitude | Affect | Affect unmarked |
|---|---|---|
| | Judgment | social esteem-normality: invoked: standardization service |
| | | Social esteem-capacity: inscribed: successfully (compete with closed platforms); independent invoked: promotes, protects, standardizes by providing unified resources and services needed for open source to successfully compete with closed platforms; makes Linux an attractive target; foster innovation by hosting collaboration events to solve pressing issues facing the Linux ecosystem; promoting and providing collaboration and education; protecting and supporting Linux development, improving Linux as a Technical platform; provide services, support and other assistance |
| | | Social sanction: propriety: non-profit consortium |
| | Appreciation | Reaction: attractive (target); pressing (issues) |
| | | Valuation: original; innovation; collaboration; vitally important, successfully |
| | | Composition: unified (resources and services) |

Table 4.10 continued

| Engagement | | Monologue |
|---|---|---|
| Graduation | Force | vitally |
| | Focus | (Reach) approximately (two million people per month) |

According to Table 4.10, it can be seen that throughout the text, affect is unmarked. That is, the author has not expressed any explicit affect to the Linux Foundation. However, there are some judgment resources in both stages. Most of these judgment resources are invoked, and most are concerned with the capacity of the Foundation. Specifically, by describing the various functions, capacities, and significance of the Foundation, the author is intended to invoke a powerful image among the audience. There are also a few resources for inscribed positive appreciation, such as "attractive", "original", "innovation" and "important", which are used to positively evaluate the result or significance of the actions taken by the Linux Foundation or its members. These evaluation resources, however, are combined with other resources concerning the functions or actions of Linux Foundation, and they together serve as implicit (invoked) positive judgment of the capacity of Linux Foundation. The employment of judgment resources implies that the Linux Foundation, though an institution, is treated like a person, whose behavior can be judged according to social standards. In addition, the description of the various services and support that can be provided by the Foundation helps foreground the significance of the Foundation. This is another kind of invoked appreciation. As far as engagement is concerned, the whole text is developed in a form of monogloss. There is only one voice, i.e. the voice of the author. In addition, there are only two words for graduation in the whole text. The lack of graduation resources makes the text precise and relatively objective.

Resources of the involvement system as a part of the interpersonal resources will only be briefly discussed as the study of involvement resources is still at its infant stage. In Text 2, resources in both stages indicate a low degree of involvement between the promoter and readers. The markers include experiential congruence throughout the text, monologue, frequent employment of endophoric reference rather than anaphoric or cataphoric reference for the identification of entities, extensive use of standard and specific words, the use of major clauses with no ellipsis or contraction, as well as the use of full names of the Linux Foundation, the System, and the creator, etc. As for the realization of social status, the whole texts show no trace of either domination or deference. This indicates a relative equal relation between the promoter and readers.

### 4.2.3 Realization at the Register and Genre Strata

According to the analysis of the ideational resources in Section 4.2.2, it can be seen that the activity sequence/taxonomy of Stage 1 is concerned with introducing the Linux Foundation to be described and Linux's general attributes, while that of Stage 2 is a description of the specific features (functions) of the Linux Foundation. In both stages, the information about Linux Foundation is not shared by the reading public, and is not specialized. In addition, it also requires institutionalized social education.

**Table 4.11 Field Configuration of Text 2**

| | Activity Sequence/Taxonomy | Degree of sharing | Degree of Specialization | Nature of Socialization |
|---|---|---|---|---|
| Stage 1 | Introducing the Linux Foundation to be described and its general attributes | low | low | Institutionalized |
| Stage 2 | Describing the specific features (functions) of the Linux Foundation | low | low | Institutionalized |

The analysis of the interpersonal resources indicates that the text is an interaction between the describer/promoter and the reading public, with equal social status between them. However, there is little contact and the degree of involvement is low. In addition, the affect is unmarked. Thus, the tenor configuration of Text 2 can be analyzed in Table 4.12.

**Table 4.12 Tenor Configuration of Text 2**

| | Social Relation | Status | Contact | Affect |
|---|---|---|---|---|
| Stage 1 | Describer-the public | Equal | Low | Unmarked |
| Stage 2 | Describer-the public | Equal | Low | Unmarked |

The analysis of the textual resources shows that the text is presented visually through language. It is presented in monologue and publicly addressed, with reply less likely, and with high degree of consciousness as it is prepared beforehand. As language plays a major role, the text is a reflection of the phenomenon. It is semiotically structured, and developed in a serial manner. The mode configuration of Text is shown in Table 4.13.

**Table 4.13 Mode Configuration of Text 2**

| | Aural/Visual Contact | Modality | Monologue/Dialogue | Action/Reflection |
|---|---|---|---|---|
| Stage 1 | Visual-Uni dire ctional | Language | Monologue: publicly addressed, reply less likely; visually solidified, with high degree of consciousness | Reflection; Semiotically structured; serially developed |
| Stage 2 | Visual Unidirectional | Language | Monologue: publicly addressed, reply less likely, with high degree of consciousness | Reflection; Semiotically structured; serially developed |

Based on the analysis of the register patterning of Text 2, the specific macro structure of the text can now be worked out:

Stage 1: classifying the phenomenon to be described as Linux Foundation and providing its general attributes to the reading public

Stage 2: describing the specific features of Linux Foundation to the reading public

When the macro structure of the text is compared with the teleological structure of a descriptive report, it can be seen that the register patterning of Text 2 is a realization of the descriptive report genre. As a whole, the configuration of the semiotic resources at the discourse semantic stratum of Text 2 redounds (or realizes) with its register configuration, which in turn realizes the generic and teleological configuration of the descriptive report genre and serves the pursuit of the purpose of the genre to classify and describe a phenomenon (Linux Foundation in this case). As the whole realization process is ultimately conditioned by the purpose of the genre, it is teleological.

## 4.3 Compositional Reports

Unlike a descriptive report that classifies a phenomenon and describes its features, a compositional report classifies a phenomenon and describes its different parts. It is concerned with the part-whole organization of the phenomenon (cf. Martin & Rose 2008: 146-147).

Composition reports are frequently employed on corporate websites, either to describe the composition of products, or to introduce the organization of an executive team. Text 3 is an instance of this genre extracted from Cisco's website, describing the composition of Cisco's Board of Directors. What is presented here is only a part of the original text (see http://investor.cisco.com/directors.cfm for the whole text). The biographies of only 2 members of the Board of Directors are provided here, with the remaining biographies of other 13 members omitted, as they are very similar to the provided ones. It is believed that such treatment will not be detrimental to the illustration of the compositional report genre and its realization.

Text 3　Cisco's Board of Directors

(1) Board of Directors

(2) The following biographies reflect the 2009 Proxy Statement.

(3) Carol Bartz

Chief Executive Officer, Yahoo! Inc.

(4) M. Michele Burns

Chairman and Chief Executive Officer, Mercer LLC

(5) Michael D. Capellas

Chairman and Chief Executive Officer, First Data Corporation

(6) Larry Carter

Former Senior Vice President, Office of the Chairman and CEO, Cisco Systems, Inc.

(7) John T. Chambers

Chairman and Chief Executive Officer, Cisco Systems, Inc.

(8) Brian L. Halla

Chairman and Chief Executive Officer, National Semiconductor Corporation

(9) John L. Hennessy Ph. D.

President, Stanford University

(10) Richard Kovacevich

Former Chairman, Wells Fargo & Company

(11) Roderick C. McGeary

Chairman of the Board, BearingPoint, Inc

(12) Michael K. Powell

Senior Advisor of Providence Equity Partners and Chairman of the MK Powell Group

(13) Arun Sarin, KBE

Former Chief Executive Officer, Vodafone Group Plc

(14) Steven M. West

Founder and Partner, Emerging Company Partners

(15) Jerry Yang

Co-Founder and Chief Yahoo, Yahoo! Inc.

(16) Carol Bartz

(17) Chief Executive Officer, Yahoo! Inc. Ms. Bartz, 61, has been a member of the Board of Directors since November 1996 and (18) has served as Lead Independent Director since November 2005. (19) She has served as Chief Executive Officer and as a member of the board of directors of Yahoo! Inc. since January 2009 and (20) as President of Yahoo! since April 2009. (21) From May 2006 to February 2009, she was Executive Chairman of the Board of

Autodesk, Inc. (22) From April 1992 to April 2006, she served as Chairman of the Board and Chief Executive Officer of Autodesk. (23) Prior to that, she was employed by Sun Microsystems, Inc. from 1983 to April 1992.

(24) M. Michele Burns

(25) Chairman and Chief Executive Officer, Mercer LLC Ms. Burns, 51, has been a member of the Board of Directors since November 2003. (26) She is the Chairman and Chief Executive Officer of Mercer LLC. (27) She began her career in 1981 at Arthur Andersen, LLP and (28) became a partner in 1989. (29) In 1999, Ms. Burns joined Delta Air Lines, Inc. assuming the role of Executive Vice President and Chief Financial Officer in 2000 and holding that position through April 2004. (30) Delta filed for protection under Chapter 11 of the United States Bankruptcy Code in September 2005. (31) From May 2004 to January 2006, Ms. Burns served as Executive Vice President, Chief Financial Officer and Chief Restructuring Officer of Mirant Corporation, taking on the company's bankruptcy restructuring. (32) Upon successful restructuring and emergence of the company from bankruptcy, Ms. Burns joined Marsh & McLennan Companies, Inc. as Chief Financial Officer in March 2006. (33) She assumed the role of Chairman and Chief Executive Officer of Mercer six months later. (34) Ms. Burns also serves on the board of directors of Wal-Mart Stores, Inc.

....

(http://investor.cisco.com/directors.cfm, accessed on Martin 3, 2010)

### 4.3.1 Teleological and Generic Structures

The general purpose of a compositional report is to describe the composition of a phenomenon, while the schematic structure of a compositional report is considered as Classification ^ Composition (Martin & Rose 2008: 146-147). The teleological structure of the compositional report genre can be analyzed as follows:

Purpose: to describe the composition of a phenomenon to the reading public, which is concretized into:

Goal 1: to classify the phenomenon to be described to the reading public; semiotic, orbital

Goal 2: to describe the composition of the phenomenon to the reading public; semiotic or spatial, serial

Relation between Goal 1 and Goal 2: semiotic, orbital

Realized by the generic structure: Classification ^ Composition

### 4.3.2 Realization at the Genre and Register Strata

As an instance of the compositional report genre, the teleological structure of Text 3 can be analyzed as follows:

Purpose: to describe the composition of Cisco's Board of Directors to the reading public, which is concretized into:

Goal 1: to classify the phenomenon to be described as Cisco's Board of Directors

Goal 2: to describe the composition of the Board of Directors

The teleological structure is realized by the following macro structure:

Stage 1: (1) – (2), presenting Cisco's Board of Directors to be described

Stage 2: (3) – (33) (and the omitted biographies) describing the composition of the Board of Directors,

Phase 1 of Stage 2: (3) – (15) general information of the members of the Board of Directors

Phase 2 of Stage 2: (4) – (33) (and the omitted biographies) bibliographical information of each of the members

The register configurations of Text 3 are analyzed in Tables 4.14, 4.15 and 4.16. Table 4.14 (on p. 137) shows the field configuration. It can be seen that the activity sequence and taxonomic relations of Stage 1 are concerned with the presentation of the Cisco's Board of Directors to be described, while those of Stage 2 are concerned with the presentation of the composition of the Board. As the text is intended to introduce the composition to the reading public, the field is not well shared between the interactants. In addition, though the composition of the Board is not a specialized field, its interpretation requires institutionalized social education.

**Table 4.14 Field Configuration of Text 3**

| | Activity Sequence/ Taxonomy | Degree of sharing | Degree of Specialization | Nature of Socialization |
|---|---|---|---|---|
| Stage 1 | Presenting Cisco's Board of Directors to be described | low | low | Institutionalized |
| Stage 2 | Composition of the Board of Directors | low | low | Institutionalized |

Table 4.15 presents the tenor configuration of Text 3. In terms of tenor configuration, the text is an interaction between the promoter and the reading public with an equal status between them. In addition, as there is little contact between them, the degree of involvement is low. The text is presented in a relatively objective tone and the affect/ attitude is not marked.

**Table 4.15 Tenor Configuration of Text 3**

| | Social Relation | Status | Contact | Affect |
|---|---|---|---|---|
| Stage 1 | Promoter-reading public | Equal | Uninvolved | Unmarked |
| Stage 2 | Promoter-reading public | Equal | Uninvolved | Unmarked |

Table 4.16 shows the mode configuration of Text 3. As shown by the analysis, the text is presented visually through language (in writing) in a form of monologue. It is addressed to the reading public with reply less likely, and with high degree of consciousness as it is most likely prepared beforehand. In addition, as language plays the major role, the text is a reflection. It is structured semiotically rather than structured spatially or temporally, and is serially developed rather than through periodical hierarchies.

**Table 4.16 Mode Configuration of Text 3**

| | Aural/Visual Contact | Modality | Monologue/Dialogue | Action/ Reflection |
|---|---|---|---|---|
| Stage 1 | Visual | Language | Monologue: publicly addressed, reply less likely; visually solidified, with high degree of consciousness | + Reflection; Semiotically structured; serially organized |
| Stage 2 | Visual | Language | Monologue: publicly addressed, reply less likely, with high degree of consciousness | + Reflection; Semiotically structured; serially developed |

When the register configurations are viewed stage by stage in relation to the configuration at the genre stratum, it can be seen that the configurations of field, tenor and mode resources in Stages 1 and 2 faithfully realize the macro structure and the teleological structure of the text, and serve the pursuit of the purpose.

### 4.3.3 Realization at the Discourse Semantic Stratum

As the realization of a composition report, Text 3 is entity-focused rather than event-focused. Its ideational meanings are mainly realized by taxonomies. Several taxonomies can be identified. First, the composition of the Board of Directors constitutes a taxonomy based on class-member relationship. Specifically, the Board includes 15 members, Carol Bartz, M. Michele Burns, Michael D. Capellas, Larry Carter, John T. Chambers, Brian L. Halla, Richard Kovacevich, Roderick C. McGeary, Michael K. Powell, Arun Sarin, KBE, Steven M. West, and Jerry Yang. Another taxonomy consists of different job positions based on co-class relation, including such items as chairman, chief executive office, president, senior vice president, senior advisor, executive chairman, member of the Board of Directors, executive vice president, chief financial officer, and chief restructuring officer, etc. The third taxonomy consists of a series of periods, as shown in the peripheral column in the activity sequence and nuclear relation analysis in the Table 4. 17.

The analysis of activity sequence and nuclear relations are carried out only in Phase 2 of Stage 2, as shown in Table 4. 17 below.

**Table 4. 17 Activity Sequence and Nuclear Relations of Phase 2, Stage 2 of Text 3**

| Staging | Nuclear | Center | Nuclear | Peripheral |
|---|---|---|---|---|
| Phase 2 (16) | Carol Bartz | | | |
| (17) | Chief Executive Officer, Yahoo! Inc. Ms. Bartz, 61 | has been | a member of the Board of Directors | since November 1996 |
| (18) | | has served | as Lead Independent Director | since November 2005 |
| (19) | She | has served | as Chief Executive Officer and as a member of the board of directors of Yahoo! Inc. | since January 2009 |
| (20) | | | as President of Yahoo! | since April 2009 |
| (21) | she | was | Executive Chairman of the Board of Autodesk, Inc. | From May 2006 to February 2009 |
| (22) | she | served | as Chairman of the Board and Chief Executive Officer of Autodesk | From April 1992 to April 2006 |

Table 4. 17 continued

| Staging | Nuclear | Center | Nuclear | Peripheral |
|---|---|---|---|---|
| (23) | she | was employed | by Sun Microsystems, Inc. | prior to that, from 1983 to April 1992 |
| (24) | M. Michele Burns | | | |
| (25) | Chairman and Chief Executive Officer, Mercer LLC Ms. Burns, 51 | has been | a member of the Board of Directors | since November 2003 |
| (26) | She | is | the Chairman and Chief Executive Officer of Mercer LLC. | |
| (27) | She | began | her career | in 1981 at Arthur Andersen, LLP |
| (28) | | became | a partner | in 1989 |
| (29) | Ms. Burns | joined | Delta Air Lines, Inc. | in 1999 |
| | | assu-ming | the role of Executive Vice President and Chief Financial Officer | in 2000 |
| | | holding | that position | through April 2004 |
| (30) | Delta | filed | | for protection, under Chapter 11 of the United States Bankruptcy Code in September 2005 |

Table 4.17 continued

| Staging | Nuclear | Center | Nuclear | Peripheral |
|---|---|---|---|---|
| (31) | Ms. Burns | served | as Executive Vice President, Chief Financial Officer and Chief Restructuring Officer of Mirant Corporation | From May 2004 to January 2006 |
| | | taking on | the company's bankruptcy restructuring | |
| (32) | Ms. Burns | joined | Marsh & McLennan Companies, Inc. as Chief Financial Officer | Upon successful restructuring and emergence of the company from bankruptcy, in March 2006 |
| (33) | She | assumed | the role of Chairman and Chief Executive Officer of Mercer | six months later |
| (34) | Ms. Burns | serves | on the board of directors of Wal-Mart Stores, Inc. | |

Based on the analysis in Table 4.17, it can be seen that the sub-phases of the text are indicated by the sub-headings. The nuclear column to the left of the center mainly includes Identified, Carrier, and Medium functions, while the nuclear column to the right includes Identifier, Attribute, and Agent functions. The center column mainly includes processes of relation (including both attributive and identifying ones) and only four material processes (employed, began, filed, taking on), which indicates that the text is mainly entity-focused rather than activity-focused. The peripheral column mainly includes circumstances of time and duration, and only a few circumstances of purpose, reason and place. Thus, within each sub-phase, the text is organized according to the temporal sequence, more specifically, according to the periods of the career life of the members concerned. As a whole, the configurations of taxonomic relations, activity sequences and nuclear relations of the text center around and serve the description of the composition of the Board.

As for conjunction resources, the overall text is organized through internal conjunctions. Specifically, Stage 1 and Stage 2 are related to each other through internal part-whole relation. Within Stage 1, Message 2 is an internal rework to Message 1. Within Stage 2, the two phases are related to each other through internal rework relation. In Phase 1, the names (and their positions) are related to each other through internal additive relation. In Phase 2, the sub-phases are clearly signaled by the subheadings, and are related to each other through internal additive relation. Each subheading (the name) is elaborated by corresponding messages in the sub-phase through internal rework conjunctions, while the messages within each subphase are related to each other through external temporal successive conjunctions. In addition, each subphase is related to the corresponding message in Stage 1 through internal rework (elaboration) conjunctions. The large proportion of internal conjunction resources faithfully realizes the semiotical structuring in the mode analysis.

As far as the periodicity system is concerned, Stage 1 can be considered as the macro-Theme of the whole text, providing overview information for the succeeding sections. Within Stage 2, Phase 1 functions as the hyper-Theme of the whole stage, providing an outline for the information to be presented in Phase 2. In addition, each title (the name of the member to be described) is also a hyper-Theme for the corresponding section. However, there is no macro-New or hyper-New in the text. As a result, the development of the text is not achieved through hierarchies of periodicity, but through serial organization, which is consistent with the mode analysis.

The identification system of the text is relatively simple. Each member of the Board of Directors is presented in the first stage, and then tracked in the corresponding phase in Stage 2. For example, Carol Bartz is first presented in Stage 1, represented again in the heading and the first message of the corresponding phase in Stage 2, and then tracked throughout the phase through pronouns. M. Michele Burns is presented and tracked basically in the same way, except that she is presented more frequently in the corresponding phase (refer to Table 5.17).

In the text, except a piece of appreciation resources (the word "successful"), attitude as a whole is unmarked. However, the description of the rich professional experience of the members of the Board can help invoke a positive judgment of the capacity of the members, and also a positive appreciation of the composition of the Board. As for engagement resources, in Stage 1, the biographies of the members of the Board are attributed to Cisco's 2009 Proxy Statement. In addition, another source of the information is Cisco Corporation. Except these, however, there are no other engagement resources involved in Stage 2 and the details of each biography are presented in the form of bare assertions. Moreover, there are no graduation resources in the text. The relative lack of appraisal resources is a faithful realization of the tenor configuration of unmarked affect, and serves to present a detached description of the Board.

The text shows a low degree of involvement between the interactants. This is indicated by the use of major clauses without contraction, full names of the members of the Board, standard and specific words, and endophoric reference. In addition, the social status between the interactants is intended to be equal, though the promoter functions as the primary knower and controls the interaction process. The low degree of involvement is conducive to an impartial official description of the Board to the reading public.

In summary, the configurations of the ideational, interpersonal and textual resources in Text 3 faithfully realize its register configuration, which in turn appropriately realizes the teleological configuration of the text (in particular the purpose to describe the composition of Cisco's Board of Directors to the reading public), which is an instance of the general purpose of the compositional report genre, and thus realizes the genre in general. Such a realization process is telos-oriented as the configurations of semiotic resources of Text 3 at each stratum is ultimately conditioned by the general purpose of the compositional report genre, and serves the pursuit of this purpose.

## 4.4 News Stories

News stories are a relatively new genre that made its appearance around the turn of the 19th century (Iedema, Feez & White 1994; Iedema 1997). Unlike traditional story genres, in a news story, "the need for a sensational lead to attract readers meant that a story might begin at any point in the sequence, and jump about in time as it presented different aspects of the events" (Martin & Rose 2008: 75). The multiplicity of sources for the story and the varying interests of readers lead to the shift of points of views. The purpose of a news story is to inform the reading public of the major happenings within a particular society (Caple 2009: 23).

According to White (1997: 101), news stories have developed a particular schematic structure: Nucleus ^ Satellite. The Nucleus reports the major happenings, while the satellites explain, contextualize and appraise a textually dominant nucleus. The satellites are more related to the Nucleus rather than to each other. However, since many other genres may also be organized in an orbital way, the terms "nucleus" and "satellite" are too general to indicate the schematic structure of the news story genre. In order to show the specific steps employed to report a news story, terms reflecting the specific contents of each step should be adopted. As the nucleus of a news story reports the major

Event, while the satellites provide additional information (including elaboration, specification, explanation, sourcing, etc.), the schematic structure of a news story will be suggested in this study as Major Event ^ Supplementary Information.

The news story genre is frequently employed on corporate websites to release corporate news, including product news and news about the corporations. Text 4 is a sample text extracted from the website of Microsoft. It will be analyzed in detail to show the realization of the news story genre.

Text 4 Microsoft's Bing Map

(1) Mar 12, 2010

(2) Microsoft's Bing Maps extends 'Bird's Eye' view of the world

(3) Microsoft has juiced up Bing Maps with fresh photos showing 2.6 million square miles of the planet. (4) The digital images were taken from satellites and camera-equipped airplanes.

(5) This latest expansion of Bing Maps includes 'Bird's Eye' aerial photos of much of Sweden; (6) you can view images of buildings and landscapes as if you're a modern day Phileas Fogg looking down at a 44-degree angle from the gondola of a balloon hovering at 10,000 feet.

(7) The more familiar satellite-view image maps show a direct overhead, or orthogonal, view. (8) Photos shot at an angle from low-flying aircraft are referred to as oblique-angle images. (9) Oblique-angle maps let you see a building's faade and (10) gives you better context of the surroundings. (11) 'We're trying to give you the sense of being there,' says Chris Pendleton, team evangelist for Bing Maps.

(12) Microsoft began sending airplanes aloft equipped with automatic-firing digital cameras and very large hard drives back in December 2007. (13) Those airplanes came back with photos of 12 U.S. cities. (14) The digital images were stitched together and correlated to road maps with some very sophisticated software from Pictometry and Blom, says Pendleton. (15) Microsoft has kept planes in the air taking photographs and amassing two petabytes of digital images. (One petabyte equals 1,000 terabytes.)

(16) Last December, Google launched its version of oblique-angle maps, adding the capacity to zoom in for tighter views, a feature Bing's Bird's Eye view lacks. (17) But so far Google's oblique-angle maps are only available for San

Diego and San Jose, says Pendelton.

(18) Meanwhile, Bing Maps supplies free Bird's Eye view maps that cover most of North America and Europe, with plans to move steadily east across Asia, wherever Microsoft can get approval from local authorities. (19) 'We're letting you explore a high-resolution view of the world,' says Pendleton.

(20) By Byron Acohido

(http://www.microsoft.com/presspass/presskits/bing/materials.aspx, accessed on March 12, 2010)

### 4.4.1 Teleological and Generic Structures

Based on the teleological model as developed in Chapter 3, the teleological structure of a news story can be analyzed as follows:

Purpose: to inform the reading public the major happenings in a particular society, which is concretized into:

Goal 1: to present the major happening to the public; semiotic organization

Goal 2: to provide supplementary information about the happening to the public; semiotic organization

Relation between Goal 1 and Goal 2: orbital

Realized by the generic structure: Major Event ^ Supplementary Information

Possible phasing in Stage 2: each aspect of supplementary information functioning as a phase

### 4.4.2 Realization at the Genre and Register Strata

As an instance of the news story genre, the teleological structure of Text 4 can be analyzed as follows:

Purpose: to inform the reading public of Microsoft's expansion of Bing Map

Goal 1: to report the major event-Microsoft's expansion of Bing Map

Goal 2: to (Messages 5-19) provide the supplementary information of the event

This teleological structure is realized by the following macro structure:

Major event (Microsoft's expansion of Bing Map) ^ Supplementary Information

Phasing in Stage 2:

Phase 1: details of the extension in the new Bing Maps

Phase 2: better quality of Microsoft's oblique-angle map compared with traditional orthogonal maps

Phase 3: the specific procedures for creating Bing Maps

Phase 4: Wider coverage of Bing Maps compared with Google's oblique-angle map

Phase 5: Other bird's eye view maps provided or to be provided by Microsoft

The field configuration of Text 4 is analyzed in Table 4.18:

**Table 4.18 Field Configuration of Text 4**

| | Activity Sequence/ Taxonomy | Degree of sharing | Degree of Specialization | Nature of Socialization |
|---|---|---|---|---|
| Stage 1 | Microsoft's extension of Bing Maps | low | low | Institutionalized |
| Stage 2 | Additional information concerning the event | low | low | Institutionalized |

As shown in Table 4.18, the major activity sequence in Stage 1 is concerned with Microsoft's extension of Bing Maps, while that of Stage 2 is concerned with additional information about the event (this will be shown more clearly in the analysis of ideational resources in Section 4.4.3). In news release, as the correspondent provides the news to the reading public, the news information in both stages is not shared by the interactants. The news information, though concerning technological activity, is represented mainly through common-sense words so that it can be understood by the reading public. In addition, news release is an institutionalized activity that requires appropriate education. It can be seen that the field configuration is largely conditioned by and realizes the representational aspect of the general purpose and the schematic structure of the news story genre.

The tenor configuration of Text 4 is analyzed in Table 4. 19.

**Table 4. 19 Tenor Configuration of Text 4**

| | Social Relation | Status | Contact | Affect |
|---|---|---|---|---|
| Stage 1 | Reporter-reading public | Equal | Uninvolved | Unmarked |
| Stage 2 | Reporter-reading public | Equal | Uninvolved | Unmarked |

As shown in Table 4. 19, in both stages, the news story is represented by the reporter to the reading public. They are of equal social status. The interaction is uninvolved as there is no too much contact between them. In addition, affect is unmarked, which is typical of hard news, especially news concerning technological events. Compared with the teleological structure of the text, it can be seen that this tenor configuration serves the realization of the interactional aspect of the general purpose of the genre.

The mode configuration of Text 4 is analyzed in Table 4. 20.

**Table 4. 20 Mode Configuration of Text 4**

| | Aural/Visual Contact | Modality | Monologue/Dialogue | Action/ Reflection |
|---|---|---|---|---|
| Stage 1 | Visual | Language | Monologue: publicly addressed, reply less likely; visually solidified, with high degree of consciousness | Reflection; Semiotically structured; serially organized |
| Stage 2 | Visual | Language | Monologue: publicly addressed, reply less likely, with high degree of consciousness | Reflection; Semiotically structured; serially developed |

As shown in Table 4. 20, in both stages, the text is presented visually in language in a form of monologue. It is addressed to the public in a well-prepared manner, with high degree of consciousness. In addition, as language plays the major role, the text is a reflection of the events. It is semiotically structured and developed in a serial way. This mode configuration appropriately realizes the organizational aspect of the news story genre and serves the pursuit of the general purpose (reporting happenings to the reading public) of the genre.

### 4.4.3 Realization at the Discourse Semantic Stratum

The ideational resources of Text 4 are analyzed in Table 4.21. It can be seen that there are three major activity sequences in this text. The first consists of the activities taken by the producers, including "Microsoft has juiced up Bing Maps...", "Microsoft began sending airplanes...", and "Microsoft has kept airplanes ...", as well as Google's activity ("launched its version of oblique angle maps"). The second is related to the maps (including the photos and images), mainly stating the quality, content, coverage, and effect of the maps. The third is the activity sequence of Pendleton (his comments on the new maps).

Table 4.21 Ideational Resources of Text 4

| Staging | Nuclear | Center | Nuclear | Peripheral |
|---|---|---|---|---|
| Stage 1 (1) | | | | Mar 12, 2010 |
| (2) | Microsoft's Bing Maps | extends | 'Bird's Eye' view of the world | |
| (3) | Microsoft | has juiced up | Bing Maps | with fresh photos showing 2.6 million square miles of the planet |

Table 4.21 continued

| Staging | Nuclear | Center | Nuclear | Peripheral |
|---|---|---|---|---|
| (4) | The digital images | were taken | | from satellites and camera-equipped airplanes |
| Stage 2 Phase 1 (5) | This latest expansion of Bing Maps | includes | "Bird's Eye" aerial photos of much of Sweden | |
| (6) | you | can view | images of buildings and landscapes | as if you're a modern day Phileas Fogg looking down at a 44-degree angle from the gondola of a balloon hovering at 10,000 feet |
| Phase 2 (7) | The more familiar satellite-view image maps | show | a direct overhead, or orthogonal, view | |
| (8) | Photos shot at an angle from low-flying aircraft | are referred to | as oblique-angle images | |
| (9) | Oblique-angle maps | let you see | a building's facade | |
| (10) | | gives | you better context of the surroundings | |

Table 4.21 continued

| Staging | Nuclear | Center | Nuclear | Peripheral |
|---|---|---|---|---|
| (11) | Chris Pendleton, team evangelist for Bing Maps | says | We're trying to give you the sense of being there | |
| Phase (3) (12) | Microsoft | began sending | airplanes aloft equipped with automatic-firing digital cameras and very large hard drives back in December 2007 | |
| (13) | Those airplanes | came back | | with photos of 12 U. S. cities |
| (14) | Pendleton | says | The digital images were stitched together and correlated to road maps with some very sophisticated software from Pictometry and Blom | |
| (15) | Microsoft | has kept | planes | in the air taking photographs and amassing two petabytes of digital images. (One petabyte equals 1,000 terabytes.) |
| Phase 4 (16) | Google | launched | its version of oblique-angle maps | Last December, adding the capacity to zoom in for tighter views, a feature Bing's Bird's Eye view lacks |

Table 4. 21 continued

| Staging | Nuclear | Center | Nuclear | Peripheral |
|---|---|---|---|---|
| (17) | Pendelton | says | but so far Google's oblique-angle maps are only available for San Diego and San Jose | |
| Phase 5 (18) | Bing Maps | supplies | free Bird's Eye view maps that cover most of North America and Europe | with plans to move steadily east across Asia, wherever Microsoft can get approval from local authorities |
| (19) | Pendleton | says | we're letting you explore a high-resolution view of the world | |
| (20) | | | | By Byron Acohido |

In addition, two major taxonomic relations can be identified in this text. The first taxonomy consists of entities concerning Bird's eye view maps. Specifically, bird's eye view maps fall into two types: orthogonal maps and oblique angle maps (typology). Oblique angle maps are made of oblique photos and digital images stitched together (meronymy) and include Google's maps and Microsoft's Bing Maps (hyponymy). Another major taxonomy consists of entities involved in the production of Bird's eye view maps, including the producers and tools. The producers include Google and Microsoft, while the tools include satellites, airplanes, cameras equipped on the airplanes, large hard drives, and sophisticated software from Pictometry and Blom. These entities are organized together mainly through hyponymy relation.

When the activity sequence and taxonomic relations are considered together, it can be seen that the ideational resources of the text

faithfully realizes the field configuration at the register configuration of the text.

The conjunction resources in Text 4 are analyzed in Table 4.22. According to the conjunction analysis, it can be seen that the overall text is mainly organized through internal conjunction resources. Specifically, each phase in Stage 2 provides some additional information concerning Microsoft's new Bing Maps. As satellites, they are related to the nucleus through internal additive conjunction, while the relations between the phases are very weak, either internally or externally. In addition, within each stage, the messages (ranking clauses) are also related to each other mainly through internal additive conjunction, though there are exceptions (including the external temporal successive conjunctions in Phase 3 and two external comparative conjunctions in Phase 1 and 2 respectively). The employment of internal additive conjunction relations between the stages and phases faithfully realizes the configuration of semiotical organization and serial development at the register stratum.

**Table 4.22 Conjunction Resources of Text 4**

| Staging | Internal Conjunction | | External Conjunction |
|---|---|---|---|
| Stage 1 | | (1) | |
| | | (2) | |
| | Rework, elaborating | (3) | |
| | Rework, elaborating | (4) | |
| Stage 2 Phase 1 (additive to Stage 1) | Rework, elaborating | (5) latest | Latest, compare |
| | Rework, elaborating (5) | (6) | |

Table 4. 22 continued

| Staging | Internal Conjunction | | External Conjunction |
|---|---|---|---|
| | | (7) more | More, compare (with 8) |
| Phase 2 (additive to Stage 1) | | (8) | |
| | additive | (9) | |
| | Additive | (10) | |
| | additive | (11) | |
| Phase 3 (additive to Stage 1) | | (12) | |
| | | (13) | Successive (to 12) |
| | | (14) | Successive (to 13) |
| | | (15) | Successive (to 15) |
| Phase 4 (additive to Stage 1) | | (16) | |
| | Additive to 17 | (17) | |
| Phase 5 (additive to Stage 1) | | (18) | |
| | Additive to 18 | (19) | |

The identification resources are analyzed in Table 4. 23 (on p. 155). As shown in the analysis, there are two entities that are tracked throughout the text. They are presented over and again in the text. In addition, two entities ("airplanes equipped with automatic-firing digital cameras and very large hard drives" and "photos of 12 U. S. cities") are first presented and then presumed (by "those airplanes" and "the digital images" respectively). But they are only distributed in two adjacent messages respectively rather than tracked throughout the text. Overall, the identification of the entities is mainly achieved through presenting rather than presuming.

Table 4.23 Identification Resources of Text 4

| Staging | Microsoft | Pendelton |
|---|---|---|
| Stage 1 (1) | | |
| (2) | Microsoft's | |
| (3) | Microsoft | |
| (4) | | |
| Stage 2 Phase 1 (5) | | |
| (6) | | |
| Phase 2 (7) | | |
| (8) | | |
| (9) | | |
| (10) | | |
| (11) | | Pendelton |
| Phase (3) (12) | Microsoft | |
| (13) | | |
| (14) | | Pendelton |
| (15) | | |
| Phase 4 (16) | | |
| (17) | | Pendelton |
| Phase 5(18) | | |
| (19) | | Pendelton |
| (20) | | |

As for the periodicity system, Stage 1 (the nucleus) functions as the macro-Theme of the whole text. Within Stage 1, the headline can be considered as the hyper-Theme of the lead, functioning as a kind of topic sentence. In addition, the nucleus also functions as a kind of marked macro-New of the text, summarizing the major content of the whole news report. Within the macro-New, the headline can be considered as a marked hyper-New of the lead, providing the major content to be elaborated in the lead. Within the lead, the messages are organized serially through additive relations. In addition, the phases in Stage 2 and the messages in each phase are also related with each other serially rather than hierarchically, without much logic relations between one another.

The appraisal resources of the text are analyzed in Table 4.24(on p.157). It can be seen that affect is unmarked in this news report as no affect is expressed explicitly. Judgment meanings are only invoked rather than explicitly inscribed. More specifically, the reporting of Microsoft's launch of high-resolution oblique-angle Bing Maps with wide coverage through the use of complicated technologies implies a positive judgment of Microsoft's technical strength and ability; while the description of the Microsoft's provision of free Bing Maps and its compliance with local laws helps invoke a benevolent and law-abiding image. As for appreciation, the high quality of the Bing maps is invoked by reporting the unique angle, high resolution, wide coverage, and better user experience. There are five pieces of inscribed appreciation resources, but they are embedded in messages for a judgment of Microsoft's technical strength.

The text is heteroglossic. There are two attributing resources, one (i.e. "by Byron Acohido") indicating the source of the whole news report, while the other ("says Chris Pendleton") indicating the source of specific comments in the text. The conjunction "but" also help opens the dialogic space though it is projected as Pendleton's verbiage. Heterogloss helps the author report the news from the angles of different persons. In addition, there are few resources for graduation, both in terms of force and focus. This can be attributed to the principle of objectiveness that is supposed to be followed by news reports.

As for resources for realizing social status, there are few resources for explicitly reflecting either domination or deference of the journalist, especially resources at the lexicogrammar or phonology stratum. Thus, they realize an equal social status between the journalist and the public. However, considering resources at the discourse semantic stratum, the journalist is the primary knower reporting the news to the public, initiating and controlling the reporting process according to his or the press's will. In this sense, the social status is not as equal as it seems.

The journalist and the press (in this case Microsoft) are in a more dominating position, while the reading public in a deferring position.

**Table 4.24 Appraisal Resources of Text 4**

| | | |
|---|---|---|
| Attitude | Affect | affect unmarked |
| | Judgment | Social esteem-invoked capacity: Microsoft has juiced up Bing Maps with fresh photos showing 2.6 million square miles of the planet... |
| | | Social sanction: invoked positive propriety: Bing Maps (i. e. Microsoft) supplies free Bird's Eye view Maps...; wherever Microsoft can get approval from local authorities ...; "we are letting you explore a high-resolution view of the world". |
| | Appreciation | Composition-inscribed complexity: very sophisticated software; very large hard drives |
| | | Valuation: Inscribed: fresh (photos); better (context); juiced up (Bing Maps) Invoked: this latest expansion of Bing Maps includes "Bird's Eye" aerial photos of much of Sweden; you can view images of buildings and landscapes as if you're a modern day Phileas Fogg looking down at a 44-degree angle from the gondola of a balloon hovering at 10,000 feet; oblique-angle maps let you see a building's facade and gives you better context of the surroundings; Bing Maps supplies free Bird's Eye view maps that cover most of North America and Europe, with plans to move steadily east across Asia, wherever Microsoft can get approval from local authorities |

Table 4.24 continued

| | | |
|---|---|---|
| Engagement | Heterogloss:<br>Attributing through projection: "by Byron Acohido"; "says Pendelton"<br>Entertaining through concession: "But so far Google's oblique-angle maps are only available for San Diego and San Jose" | |
| Graduation | Force | Very (large hard drives); very sophisticated software |
| | Focus | as if (you're a modern day Phileas Fogg looking down at a 44-degree angle from the gondola of a balloon hovering at 10,000 feet) |

As far as involvement resources are concerned, the text shows a low degree of involvement. In most parts of the text, the meanings are realized explicitly, as indicated by the use of major clauses with no ellipsis or contraction, use of full names (Microsoft, Google, Byron Acohido, Chris Pendleton, etc.) rather than nick names, the employment of standard and specific words, monologic forms, and experiential congruence. The low degree of involvement faithfully realizes the uninvolved contact relation as shown in the tenor analysis, and serves the official release of the news by Microsoft to the reading public.

When all the above analysis at the discourse semantic stratum is taken into consideration, it can be seen that the discourse semantic stratum well realizes the register configurations of the text, which in turn realizes the generic and teleological structure of the news story genre, and serves the achievement of the genre's general purpose to inform the reading public the major happenings (Microsoft's expansion of Bing Map in this case).

## 4.5 Summary

In Chapter 4, the telos-oriented genre realization is illustrated by the discussion of the realization of four genres frequently employed on corporate promotional websites: the operating procedure genre, the descriptive report genre, the compositional report genre and the news story genre. For an operating procedure, its general purpose (teaching the leaner the operating steps of a specialized activity) conditions its teleological structure, and in turn conditions the generic structure Objective ^ Steps. The teleological and generic structures in turn condition the configuration of register patterning and the configuration of discourse semantic resources, with the register patterning and discourse semantic resources all serving the pursuit of the general purpose. The purpose of a descriptive report (to classify and describe a phenomenon) and its concretization determines its generic structure (Classification ^ Description), while the corresponding register patterning and the configuration of discourse semantics resources are conditioned by the teleological configuration and serve the pursuit of this general purpose. Likewise, the respective purpose of a compositional report and a news story conditions the corresponding teleological and generic structures, which in turn condition the configuration at the register and discourse semantic strata.

This partial predictability (metaredundancy) relation among the semiotic resources configured at the different strata shows the realization process of each genre. In other words, the teleological structure of a genre partially conditions (predicts) the specific generic structure of the text, while the specific generic structure partially conditions the specific register patterning that realizes the genre, which in turn partially conditions the configuration of discourse semantic resources that realizes the register patterning. As the specific deployment of semiotic resources at each stratum is ultimately conditioned by the teleological configuration of a genre, such a realization process is telos-oriented, ultimately conditioned by the general purpose of the genre and serving the pursuit of the purpose.

# Chapter 5

# Instantiation of Corporate Website Genres

While the hierarchy of telos-oriented genre realization is responsible for interpreting the predicable configurations of meanings deployed for pursuing the purpose of a specific genre, the instantiation hierarchy is responsible for explaining how the same genre is instantiated into different text types, texts and readings to pursue the specific purposes of each genre instance (cf. Section 3.7). In this chapter, the instantiation of two genres will be discussed: the descriptive report genre and the corporate homepage genre, both of which are frequently employed on corporate websites. For each genre, two texts will be extracted from the corporate websites, analyzed comparatively at the discourse semantics, register and genre strata respectively. The analysis is intended to show how different texts instantiate the same genre through the different configurations of semiotic resources so as to achieve the specific purposes of each genre instance. The tools and methods of analysis as developed in Chapter 3 will be adopted again, though the focus will be on the differences in instantiation caused by the pursuit of different specific purposes.

## 5.1 Instantiation of the Descriptive Report Genre

As discussed in Section 4.2.1, descriptive reports are extensively employed on corporate websites for introducing company information. In this section, two texts are used to show the different instantiations of the same descriptive report genre through different ways of coupling and commitment. Text 5 is an overview of IBM citizenship, while Text 6 an overview of Dell social responsibility (which deals with basically the same topic as IBM citizenship). They are selected in this study because, on the one hand, both are typical instances of the descriptive report genre, on the other, they are representative of the different ways of telos-conditioned instantiations.

Text 5 IBM Corporate Citizenship: Helping to build a smarter planet

(1) The primary focus of our corporate citizenship activities is on developing initiatives to address specific societal issues, such as the environment, community economic development, education, health, literacy, language and culture. (2) We employ IBM's most valuable resources, our technology and talent, in order to create innovative programs in these areas to assist communities around the world.

(3) For example, our Corporate Service Corps program annually deploys teams of selected high potential employees to emerging regions to work with government, nonprofit and non-governmental organizations on critical local projects. (4) Teams have completed projects in Ghana, Romania, Tanzania, the Philippines and Vietnam around water quality, disaster preparedness and project management.

(5) Our World Community Grid initiative utilizes grid computing technology to harness the tremendous power of idle computers to perform specific computations related to critical research around complex biological, environmental and health-related issues. (6) The current projects include Help Fight Childhood Cancer, Clean Energy, and Nutritious Rice for the World, FightAIDS @ Home, Help Conquer Cancer, AfricanClimate @ Home, and a genomics initiative and research on Dengue Fever.

(7) Another example of our citizenship activities is our employee volunteer initiative, entitled On Demand Community. (8) Since its inception in 2003, over 145,000 employees and retirees have registered and (9) performed almost 10 million hours of volunteer service around the world. (10) This program equips our employee and retiree volunteers with a distinct set of on demand tools based on the successful technology solutions created exclusively by IBM for schools and community agencies. (11) These Web-based tools provide them with a myriad choice of meaningful volunteer opportunities, resources and specific activities designed to help make them more effective volunteers and to offer valuable assistance to schools and not-for-profit organizations.

(12) To learn more about our work in the context of IBM's broader corporate responsibility efforts, please visit Innovations in Corporate Responsibility.

(http://www.ibm.com/ibm/ibmgives/; accessed on April 4, 2010)

Text 6 Dell Responsibility

(1) Corporate responsibility at Dell is about being a responsible corporate citizen. (2) Dell focuses on the ideals of environmental responsibility, corporate accountability and social responsibility to further bolster the notion that addressing these issues support the attainment of financial goals and can be critical to long-term corporate success. (3) Our commitment means we must continue to build trust with customers and stakeholders by demonstrating our positive impact on our society and planet and developing meaningful measures for reporting our progress. (4) Corporate responsibility is a critical component of the company's overall business. (5) Learn more by reading our Corporate Responsibility summary report.

Dell Earth

(6) At Dell, environmental responsibility is being embraced throughout the company. (7) In fact, we aspire to be the greenest technology company on the planet. (8) That's why it's a central part of our commitment to continuously improve our business to help protect the environment while making it easier for customers to acquire, own and retire their computers responsibility.

(9) Join the Plant a Tree Program

Business Recycling — Invest in Peace of Mind

Driving Cost Savings for Customers

View More

Dell Difference

(10) For Dell, our commitment to social responsibility is about making a meaningful difference and seeking innovative ways to help others through our technology, resources and employees by partnering with non-governmental organizations to address key issues facing our world. (11) Through this collaboration, we hope to build a better, connected tomorrow

(12) Dell YouthConnect

Why Giving Back Makes Good Business Sense

Disaster Relief

View More

Diversity

(13) At Dell, and in any economic environment, we consider diversity and inclusion an integral part of our business strategy. (14) By continuing to drive

these initiatives throughout the company, we're able to harness each individual's full potential, drive innovation and become a better place to work — ultimately ensuring that we're providing the best customer experience.

(15) Customers with Disabilities

Dell Named As One of Working Mother 100 Best Companies

Gay, Lesbian, Bisexual and Transgendered (GLBT)

View More

Corporate Accountability

(16) Being a trustworthy company is the focus of our efforts in corporate accountability — and inspiring others to be principled as well. (17) Integrity and trust just don't happen; (18) you have to take measurable, transparent actions.

(19) Corporate Responsibility Policies

Public Policy

Political Disclosure and Accountability

View More

Report

(20) Inspire and innovate. These words embody our approach to achieving our corporate responsibility priorities. (21) We set out with a goal to inspire, to be inspired and to innovate-as a leader in our industry and as global citizens. (22) Dell's approach to being a responsible corporate citizen is a full-time commitment with the same goals, strategies and accountabilities that drive every element of our company.

(23) A Perspective on the U. S. Chamber of Commerce Climate Change Policy

A Message from Gil Casellas

Dell Supports Goals of the Conflict Minerals Act of 2009

View More

(http://content. dell. com/us/en/corp/cr. aspx? -ck = bt, accessed on April 6, 2010)

The messages (ranking clauses) of each text are numbered for the convenience of analysis. The resources employed by the two texts at the genre and register strata will be analyzed and compared first, which will be followed by a comparative analysis of the resources at the discourse semantic stratum. The similarities and differences in the instantiations of the two texts will be explained teleologically as conditioned by the pursuit of the specific purposes of each genre instance.

### 5.1.1 Instantiation at the Genre Stratum

The purpose of a descriptive report is to classify and describe a phenomenon to a reader (readers). This purpose is concretized into two goals: Goal 1 to classify the phenomenon to be described for the reader (readers), and Goal 2 to describe the specific features/aspects of the phenomenon for the reader (readers). The relation between Goals 1 and 2 is semiotic. Such a teleological structure is realized by a generic structure Classification ^ Description. The description of each feature or aspect of the phenomenon is likely to form a phase (cf. Section 4.2).

The teleological and generic structures are however instantiated differently in the two texts, as is shown by the generic analysis of the two texts in Table 5.1 (on p. 165). It can be seen from the analysis that at the genre stratum, the two texts have employed different couplings of interactional and representational aspects of the purpose. First, the representational aspects are different. In Text 5, the representational aspect is IBM's corporate citizenship, while in Text 6, it is Dell's responsibility that is represented. As for the interactional aspect, Text 5 is addressed to the potential customers/partners of IBM, while Text 6 to the potential customers/partners of Dell. The different couplings at the level of purpose will necessarily be reflected in the different couplings at the concretization process. Thus, in Text 5, the representational aspect of both Goal 1 and Goal 2 involves the IBM citizenship, while in Text 6 it is Dell responsibility that is involved. Moreover, the two goals in each text are related to the potential readers of IBM and Dell respectively.

The difference in teleological coupling leads to the difference in the specific macro structure of the two texts. In Text 5, IBM Citizenship is first introduced and then described, while in Text 6, Dell Responsibility is introduced and then described. As far as staging and phasing are concerned, both texts have only obligatory stages without

**Table 5.1 Teleological and Generic Structures of Texts 5 and 6**

| | Text 5 | Text 6 |
|---|---|---|
| Purpose | to describe IBM's corporate citizenship to IBM's customers/partners, concretized into | to describe Dell responsibility to Dell's customers/partners, concretized into |
| Goal 1 | to classify the phenomenon to be described as IBM corporate citizenship | to classify the phenomenon as Dell responsibility (roughly equivalent to citizenship) |
| Goal 2 | to describe IBM corporate citizenship | to describe Dell responsibility |
| Staging | Introducing IBM corporate citizenship as the Phenomenon to be Described ^ Describing IBM Corporate Citizenship | Introducing Dell responsibility as the Phenomenon to be described ^ Describing Dell responsibility |
| Phasing | Phasing in Stage 2: Corporate Service Corps program, World Community Grid initiative, On Demand Community (employee volunteer initiative) each described in a phase respectively | Phasing in Stage 2: Dell earth, Dell difference, diversity, corporate accountability and report, each described in a phase respectively |

any optional stage, as is shown in the staging analysis of the two texts in Table 5.1. A difference is exhibited in the degree of commitment in Stage 2 of the two texts. Specifically, in Text 5, Stage 2 has only three phases, while that of Text 6 is subpotentialized into 5 phases. Other things being equal, the more phases a stage has, the more committed it will be. In this sense, Stage 2 of Text 5 is less committed than that of Text 6. This difference seems to be conditioned by the specific purpose of the corresponding authors. Specifically, while the author of Text 5 intends to describe IBM citizenship by listing three programs/initiatives, the author of Text 6 intends to describe Dell responsibility by listing four different aspects.

### 5.1.2 Instantiation at the Register Stratum

The different instantiations at the genre stratum will necessarily be reflected in the instantiation process at the register stratum. At the register stratum, the two texts are similar in terms of tenor and mode. Specifically, in both texts, the social relation is between the respective promoter and the reading public (of IBM and Dell of course), with equal social status between the two sides, low degree of contact and marked affect. Both texts employ language as the only modality, instantiated in the form of monologue addressed to the public, with reply less likely and high degree of consciousness. Each text is a reflection of the authors' experience, semiotically structured and serially developed. The major difference lies in the field configuration. The field of each of the two texts is analyzed comparatively in Tables 5.2 and 5.3 (on p. 166 & 167).

**Table 5.2 Field Configuration of Text 5**

| | Activity Sequence/ Taxonomy | Degree of sharing | Degree of Specialization | Nature of Socialization |
|---|---|---|---|---|
| Stage 1 | General attribute of IBM citizenship | low | low | Institutionalized |
| Stage 2 | Specific initiative/programs taken by IBM to enact IBM corporate citizenship: including Corporate Service Corps program, World Community Grid initiative, and On Demand Community; Navigation for Additional Information | low | low | Institutionalized |

As far as field is concerned, in both texts, the field is institutionalized as its understanding requires institutionalized learning, is non-specialized and not shared by the interactants. The major difference lies in the activity sequence/taxonomy. In Text 5, the activity sequence/taxonomy focuses on IBM citizenship. Specifically, Stage 1 of Text 5 specifies the general attribute of IBM citizenship, while Stage 2 describes the specific initiatives and programs taken by IBM (including Corporate Service Corps program, World Community Grid initiative, and On Demand Community) to enact its role of a social citizen. In Text 6, the activity sequence/taxonomy focuses on Dell Responsibility, with Stage 1 specifying its general attribute, Stage 2 describing the specific aspects (including Dell earth/environmental responsibility, Dell difference/social responsibility, diversity, corporate accountability and report). Thus, at the register stratum, the similar tenor and mode values are coupled with different field values in the two texts. Such difference in register patterning is conditioned by the difference in the teleological configurations of the two texts at the genre stratum (i. e. with one classifying and describing the IBM citizenship and the other Dell responsibility).

**Table 5.3 Field Configuration of Text 6**

| | Activity Sequence/ Taxonomy | Degree of sharing | Degree of Specialization | Nature of Socialization |
|---|---|---|---|---|
| Stage 1 | General attribute of Dell Responsibility | low | low | Institutionalized |
| Stage 2 | Specific aspects of Dell Responsibility: including Dell earth, Dell difference, diversity, corporate accountability and report | low | low | Institutionalized |

When we compare the register patterning of Texts 5 and 6 with that of Text 2 (which is also an instance of the descriptive report genre), it can be seen that the field of Text 2 differs from the field of

Texts 5 and 6. In Text 2, the field is "general attribute of Linux Foundation followed by specific features/functions of the Foundation". This is more like a profile of the whole consortium. On the other hand, the field of both Texts 5 and 6 focuses on the social citizenship (responsibility), which is only one aspect of the overall information of the company concerned. In this sense, it can be said that the field of Text 2 is more general than that of Texts 5 and 6. In addition to the difference in field, Texts 5 and 6 also differ from the register patterning of Text 2 in terms of tenor: while the social relation, status and contact are basically the same, affect is unmarked in Text 2 but marked in Texts 5 and 6.

### 5.1.3 Instantiation at the Discourse Semantic Stratum

At the discourse semantic stratum, the two texts also instantiate the ideational, interpersonal and textual meaning potentials of the genre in different ways. In this section, the different ways of coupling and commitment at the discourse semantic stratum in the two texts will be analyzed.

The ideation resources of Text 5 are analyzed in Table 5.4 (on p. 169). As shown in the table, the nuclear elements to the left of the center include 2 Identified functions, 1 Carrier function, and 7 Actor functions; those to the right of the center include 2 Identifier functions, 1 Attribute function, 7 Goal functions, and 2 Recipient functions. The peripheral elements mainly include Purpose, Duration, Place, and Scope. In the center column, there are 3 relational processes (including two intensive identifying processes and one possessive attributive process), while the remaining 9 processes are all of the material type (the action type). Eight of the material processes describe the concerted efforts made by IBM through its citizenship programs (including the tools and employees) to address society issues. Specifically, the items "employ", "deploy", "complete", "utilize", "register", and "perform" can be considered as co-classes of the specific efforts made by IBM, while "equip" and "provide" are co-classes concerned with the resources and tools provided IBM to address specific issues. The other material process ("please visit") is used for webpage navigation.

**Table 5.4 Ideational Resources of Text 5**

| Staging | Nuclear | Center | Nuclear | Peripheral |
|---|---|---|---|---|
| Stage 1 (1) | The primary focus of our corporate citizenship activities | is | on developing initiatives | to address specific societal issues, such as the environment, community economic development, education, health, literacy, language and culture |
| (2) | we | employ | IBM's most valuable resources, our technology and talent | in order to create innovative programs in these areas to assist communities around the world |
| Stage 2 Phase 1 (1) | our Corporate Service Corps program | annually deploys | teams of selected high potential employees | to emerging regions to work with government, nonprofit and non-governmental organizations on critical local projects |
| (4) | Teams | have completed | Projects ... around water quality, disaster preparedness and project management | in Ghana, Romania, Tanzania, the Philippines and Vietnam |
| Phase 2 (5) | Our World Community Grid initiative | utilizes | grid computing technology | to harness the tremendous power of idle computers to perform specific computations related to critical research around complex biological, environmental and health-related issues |

Table 5.4 continued

| Staging | Nuclear | Center | Nuclear | Peripheral |
| --- | --- | --- | --- | --- |
| (6) | The current projects | include | Help Fight Childhood Cancer, Clean Energy, and Nutritious Rice for the World, FightAIDS @Home, Help Conquer Cancer, African Climate @Home, and a genomics initiative and research on Dengue Fever. | |
| Phase 3 (7) | Another example of our citizenship activities | is | our employee volunteer initiative, entitled On Demand Community | |
| (8) | over 145,000 employees and retirees | have registered | | Since its inception in 2003 |
| (9) | ø | performed | almost 10 million hours of volunteer service | around the world |
| (10) | This program | equips | our employee and retiree volunteers with a distinct set of on demand tools based on the successful technology solutions created exclusively by IBM for schools and community agencies | |

Table 5.4 continued

| Staging | Nuclear | Center | Nuclear | Peripheral |
|---|---|---|---|---|
| (11) | These Web-based tools | provide | them; a myriad choice of meaningful volunteer opportunities, resources and specific activities designed to help make them more effective volunteers and to offer valuable assistance to schools and not-for-profit organizations | |
| Phase 4 (12) | | Please visit | Innovations in Corporate Responsibility | to learn more about our work in the context of IBM's broader corporate responsibility efforts |

As for taxonomic relations of Text 5, the participants in the text can be grouped into several taxonomies. The most important is the hyponymic taxonomy of IBM corporate citizenship activities (initiatives), including such items as Corporate Service Corps program, World Community Grid initiative, and On Demand Community (employee volunteer initiative). Projects and services undertaken by these programs can also be regarded as subordinates in this taxonomy, which include projects undertaken in the first program (projects ... around water quality, disaster preparedness and project management), projects undertaken in the second (Help Fight Childhood Cancer, Clean Energy, and Nutritious Rice for the World, FightAIDS@Home, Help Conquer Cancer, AfricanClimate@Home, and a genomics initiative and research on Dengue Fever), and the service undertaken by the third (almost 10 million hours of volunteer service). Another hyponymic taxonomy is about the societal issues addressed by IBM, including such items as environment, community economic development, education, health, literacy, language and culture. Among them, community economic development is addressed in the program by Corporate Service Corps program, environment and health issues are addressed by World Community Grid Initiative, while education, literacy, language and culture are addressed by On Demand Community (employee volunteer initiative). Still another taxonomy is the resources employed by IBM, including human resources (its employees), technology (e. g. grid computing technology), and on demand tools (web-based tools). The staging of the whole text is indicated by the taxonomy of IBM corporate citizenship activities as the superordinate indicates Stage 1 while the three subordinates constitute Stage 2.

Taken as a whole, Text 5 is more committed to the description of the citizenship activities taken by IBM to address the special societal issues, rather than its tenets or policies for dealing with the issues.

The ideational resources of Text 6 are analyzed in Table 5.5.

**Table 5.5 Ideation Resources of Text 6**

| Staging | Nuclear | Center | Nuclear | Peripheral |
|---|---|---|---|---|
| Stage 1 (1) | Corporate responsibility at Dell | is | about being a responsible corporate citizen | |
| (2) | Dell | focuses on | the ideals of environmental responsibility, corporate accountability and social responsibility | to further bolster the notion that addressing these issues support the attainment of financial goals and can be critical to long-term corporate success |

Table 5.5 continued

| Staging | Nuclear | Center | Nuclear | Peripheral |
|---|---|---|---|---|
| (3) | Our commitment | means | we must continue to build trust with customers and stakeholders by demonstrating our positive impact on our society and planet and developing meaningful measures for reporting our progress | |
| (4) | Corporate responsibility | is | a critical component of the company's overall business | |
| (5) | | learn | more | by reading our Corporate Responsibility summary report |
| Stage 2 Phase 1 | Dell Earth | | | |
| (6) | environmental responsibility | is being embraced | | at Dell, throughout the company |
| (7) | we | aspire to be | the greenest technology company on the plane | |
| (8) | That | is | Why… | |
| | to continuously improve our business to help protect the environmentwhile making it easier for customers to acquire, own and retire their computers responsibility | is | a central part of our commitment | |

Table 5.5 continued

| Staging | Nuclear | Center | Nuclear | Peripheral |
|---|---|---|---|---|
| (9) | Join the Plant a Tree Program<br>Business Recycling — Invest in Peace of Mind;<br>Driving Cost Savings for Customers<br>View more | | | |
| Phase 2 | Dell Difference | | | |
| (10) | our commitment to social responsibility | is | about making a meaningful difference and seeking innovative ways to help others through our technology, resources and employees by partnering with non-governmental organizations to address key issues facing our world | For Dell |
| (11) | we | hope to build | a better, connected tomorrow. | Through this collaboration |
| (12) | Dell YouthConnect<br>Why Giving Back Makes Good Business Sense<br>Disaster Relief<br>View More | | | |
| Phase 3 | Diversity | | | |
| (13) | we | consider | diversity and inclusion; an integral part of our business strategy | At Dell, and in any economic environment |
| (14) | we | are able to harness<br>drive<br>become | each individual's full potential<br>innovation<br>a better place to work | By continuing to drive these initiatives throughout the company; ultimately ensuring that we're providing the best customer experience |

Table 5.5 continued

| Staging | Nuclear | Center | Nuclear | Peripheral |
|---|---|---|---|---|
| (15) | Customers with Disabilities<br>Dell Named As One of Working Mother 100 Best Companies<br>Gay, Lesbian, Bisexual and Transgendered (GLBT)<br>View More | | | |
| Phase 4 | Corporate accountability | | | |
| (16) | Being a trustworthy company; and inspiring others to be principled as well | is | the focus of our efforts in corporate accountability | |
| (17) | Integrity and trust | just don't happen | | |
| (18) | you | have to take | measurable, transparent actions | |
| (19) | Corporate Responsibility Policies<br>Public Policy<br>Political Disclosure and Accountability<br>View More | | | |
| Phase 5 | Report | | | |
| (20) | Inspire and innovate;<br>These words | embody | our approach to achieving our corporate responsibility priorities | |
| (21) | we | set out | | with a goal to inspire, to be inspired and to innovate; as a leader in our industry and as global citizens |

Table 5.5 continued

| Staging | Nuclear | Center | Nuclear | Peripheral |
|---|---|---|---|---|
| (22) | Dell's approach to being a responsible corporate citizen | is | a full-time commitment with the same goals, strategies and accountabilities that drive every element of our company | |
| (23) | A Perspective on the U. S. Chamber of Commerce Climate Change Policy<br>A Message from Gil Casellas<br>Dell Supports Goals of the Conflict Minerals Act of 2009<br>View More | | | |

In the above analysis, the nuclear elements to the left of the center column include 2 Identified functions, 4 Identifier functions, 2 Carrier functions, 4 Senser functions, and 4 Actor functions, while those to the right include 4 Identifier functions, 2 Identified functions, 2 Attribute functions, 4 Phenomenon functions, and 2 Goal functions. Most (actually twenty) of these nuclear elements are concerned with the different responsibilities of Dell (e. g. the specific contents, the significance as seen by Dell, its attribute, etc.). The peripheral column includes 2 Purpose functions, 3 Manner functions, 4 Place functions, and 1 Role function (the processes used for navigating webpages are not included in the analysis). In the center column, there are 8 relational processes (6 intensive identifying ones and 2 intensive attribute ones), 5 mental ones (being embraced is treated as mental here), and 3 material ones. Among the 3 material processes, only 1 ("set out") describes Dell's action, 1 ("happen") is of the happening type, while the other ("you have to take ... actions") actually describes IBM's belief.

As for the taxonomic relations, a major taxonomy is Dell's

corporate responsibilities based on hyponymy, including such co-hyponyms as environmental responsibility (Dell Earth), corporate accountability, and social responsibility (Diversity and Difference). This taxonomic relations help scaffold the macro structure of the text, with the superordinate indicating the first stage, while the co-hyponyms indicating each phase of the second stage (together with a phase describing the approach to achieve the responsibilities). In addition, among the items listed at the end of each phase, 6 ("why giving back makes good business sense", "disaster relief", "gay, lesbian, bisexual and transgendered", "public policy", "political disclosure and accountability", "a perspective on the U. S. Chamber of Commerce Climate Change Policy") describe Dell's ideas or policies concerning the corresponding aspect, while the other 10 items are concerned with specific activities or decisions.

When the ideational meanings of the two texts are compared, it can be seen that though both texts describe corporate responsibility (which is called corporate citizenship by IBM), they are committed to different aspects. Specifically, Text 5 focuses on the development of specific activities and initiatives to address the issues, which are indicated by the large proportion of material processes, and by the taxonomies concerning the activities, resources, and specific projects for addressing the societal issues. Text 6 also has mentioned 6 special projects and activities, but they are only briefly listed without any elaboration. Thus, Text 5 is more committed than Text 6 to the description of the specific activities for realizing its responsibility. From a teleological perspective, the representation of the specific activities that it has taken enables the author to provide the reader with a more concrete and vivid image of IBM's citizenship policies and achievements.

On the other hand, Text 6 focuses on the description of Dell's ideas and policies concerning its corporate responsibility (called citizenship in this case), as indicated by the frequent employment of relational and mental processes (as shown in the center column in Table 5.5) as well as the taxonomy concerning the different aspects of corporate responsibility. Text 5 also describes the different aspects of its corporate citizenship and its policies and ideas, but only very briefly and generally at the first stage. Thus, Text 6 is more committed than Text 5 to the abstract description of the general ideas and policies concerning different responsibilities. This enables the author to provide the readers with a more general and comprehensive description of its social responsibility tenets.

In terms of cross-stratum coupling, in Text 5, greater commitment to specific activities is coupled with more frequent employment of material processes, while in Text 6, greater commitment to general ideas and policies is coupled with more frequent use of relational and mental processes (as shown in Table 5.5). The different ways of cross-stratum coupling help the authors to pursue their respective purposes of describing IBM's citizenship and Dell's social responsibility.

In the examination of the instantiation of interpersonal meanings, the focus will be on the appraisal resources of the two texts though attention will also be paid to involvement resources.

The inscribed appraisal resources of Text 5 are analyzed in Table 5.6 (on p. 179). It can be seen that there are some (but not too many) inscribed appraisal resources in Text 5. Most of the attitude resources are of the appreciation type, coupled with the factors involved in the citizenship activities. There are two pieces of inscribed judgment resources (judgment of capacity), also coupled with factors (objective and employees) of citizenship activities. Affect is not inscribed in this Text. In addition, all the targets are not directly related to IBM corporate citizenship. Moreover, except for IBM employees, the other targets are even not directly related to IBM Corporation, but are only factors involved in IBM's citizenship activities.

**Table 5.6 Inscribed Appraisal Resources of Text 5**

| Inscribed Appraisal Resources | Target | Type Analysis |
|---|---|---|
| primary | focus… | appreciation-valuation |
| smarter | planet | force-raise; judgment-capacity |
| most valuable | resources | force-raise; appreciation-valuation |
| innovative | programs | appreciation-valuation |
| high potential | employees | force-raise; judgment-capacity |
| critical | local projects | appreciation-valuation |
| tremendous | power | force-raise |
| complex | …issues | appreciation-composition |
| successful | technology | appreciation-valuation |
| meaningful | volunteer opportunities | appreciation-valuation |
| effective | volunteers | judgment-capacity |
| valuable | assistance | appreciation-valuation |

As indicated by the analysis of the inscribed appraisal meanings, neither IBM corporate citizenship nor IBM itself is directly appraised in the texts. However, the text is not as neutral as it seems. There are many resources that can evoke appraisal meanings, as shown in Table 5.7.

**Table 5.7 Evoked Appraisal Resources of Text 5**

| Type | Trigger/ Target | Evoked Appraisal Resources |
|---|---|---|
| Judgment-social esteem-capacity; positive | IBM | Teams of high potential employees; teams have completed projects …; utilizes grid computing technology to harness the tremendous power of idle computers to perform specific computations related to critical research around complex biological, environmental and health-related issues; the successful technology solutions created exclusively by IBM; |

Table 5.7 continued

| Type | Trigger/ Target | Evoked Appraisal Resources |
|---|---|---|
| Judgment-social sanction-propriety; positive | IBM | IBM Corporate Citizenship: Helping to build a smarter planet; developing initiatives to address specific societal issues; in order to create innovative programs in these areas to assist communities around the world; Help Fight Childhood Cancer, Clean Energy, and Nutritious Rice for the World, FightAIDS @ Home, Help Conquer Cancer, AfricanClimate@ Home, and a genomics initiative and research on Dengue Fever; employee volunteer initiative |

According to the analysis in Table 5.7, Text 5 employs many resources to positively appraise IBM indirectly. These evoking appraisal resources fall into two types: they either help highlight the capacity of IBM by describing the potential of its employees, its technical strength, and the great number of completed projects, or invoke a responsible image by describing IBM's efforts to address societal issues. In addition, the resources themselves are concerned with the specific factors of corporate citizenship activities. The employment of invoked appraisal resources thus helps the author to positively appraise IBM in a seemingly neutral way.

The inscribed appraisal resources of Text 6 are analyzed in Table 5.8 (on p. 181). It can be seen that in Text 6, the inscribed appraisal resources also fall into two major types: judgment and appreciation, with affect unmarked. This is similar to Text 5. Unlike Text 5, however, in addition to appreciation resources, judgment resources in Text 6 account for a large proportion. The judgment resources include veracity and propriety in addition to capacity (which is the only type in Text 5). The targets of the judgment resources are the company (Dell) rather than the specific factors in citizenship activities.

**Table 5.8 Inscribed Appraisal Resources of Text 6**

| Inscribed Appraisal | Trigger/Target | Type Analysis |
|---|---|---|
| responsible | corporate citizen (Dell) | judgment-social sanction-propriety |
| critical | addressing these issues | appreciation-valuation |
| positive | impact | appreciation-valuation |
| critical | component | appreciation-valuation |
| meaningful | measures | appreciation-valuation |
| greenest | technology company (Dell) | judgment-social sanction-propriety |
| meaningful | difference | appreciation-valuation |
| innovative | ways | appreciation-valuation |
| key | issues | appreciation-valuation |
| better | connected tomorrow | force-raise; appreciation-valuation |
| better | place to work | force-raise; appreciation-valuation |
| integral | part | appreciation-composition-balance |
| best | customer experience | force-raise; appreciation-valuation |
| best | companies (including Dell) | force-raise; appreciation-valuation |
| trustworthy | company (Dell) | judgment-social sanction-veracity |
| principled | others | judgment-social sanction-veracity |
| transparent | actions | judgment-social sanction-propriety |
| inspire and innovate | our approach | Appreciation-valuation |
| As a leader in our industry and as global citizens | we (Dell) | judgment-social esteem-capacity judgment-social sanction-propriety |
| responsible | corporate citizen (Dell) | judgment-social sanction-propriety |

The appreciation resources are of the valuation type, coupled with either the company (Dell), or abstract ideas/approaches held by the company, or general measures (actions). Taken as a whole, the targets of the appraisal resources in Text 6 are quite different from those in Text 5. The company itself (Dell) accounts for a large proportion of the targets, which is simply absent in Text 5. Some targets are abstract approaches, ideas and policies embraced by Dell concerning its corporate responsibility, which forms a sharp contrast with the specific factors of corporate citizenship activities functioning as targets in Text 5. The coupling of the ideational targets with the inscribed interpersonal resources in Text 6 enables the author to positively evaluate Dell and its social responsibility policies explicitly, while that in Text 5 can only help its author evoke positive evaluation of IBM and its citizenship.

With the inscribed appraisal resources as a signpost of the reading position, there are many other resources in Text 6 which can invoke positive appraisal meanings, as shown in Table 5.9 on p. 183 (negative appraisal meanings are rarely employed in the text).

As shown in Table 5.9, there is only one clause employed to invoke the positive judgment of Dell's capacity, while other resources in Text 6 focus on the positive judgment of Dell's propriety. Compared with those resources in Text 5, the evoked resources in Text 6 are more committed to the judgment of corporate propriety and less committed to the judgment of capacity. Most of the resources themselves are concerned with the abstract aspects of corporate responsibility. In terms of coupling, in Text 6, the invoked judgment of Dell's propriety is coupled with the abstract representation of its corporate responsibility, while the invoked judgment of IBM's propriety in Text 5 is coupled with the representation of specific factors involved in corporate citizenship activities.

When the instantiations of appraisal meanings of the two texts are compared, it can be seen that Text 6 is more committed to the instantiation of attitudinal meanings. Both texts employ many ideational resources to invoke specific attitudinal meanings. But Text 5 has few inscribed attitudes, while Text 6 has many. The difference makes Text 5 more objective and less emotional, whereas Text 6 is more subjective and more emotional.

**Table 5.9 Evoked Appraisal Resources of Text 6**

| Type | Trigger /Target | Evoking Appraisal Resources |
|---|---|---|
| Judgment -social esteem-capacity | Dell | we're able to harness each individual's full potential, drive innovation and become a better place to work — ultimately ensuring that we're providing the best customer experience |
| Judgment -social sanction-propriety | Dell | Dell Responsibility; Dell focuses on the ideals of environmental responsibility, corporate accountability and social responsibility; our commitment; Corporate responsibility is a critical component of the company's overall business; environmental responsibility is being embraced throughout the company; help protect the environment; making it easier for customers to acquire, own and retire their computers responsibility; our commitment to social responsibility; Corporate Responsibility Policies; Political Disclosure and Accountability; Disaster Relief; Dell Supports Goals of the Conflict; Minerals Act of 2009; we consider diversity and inclusion an integral part of our business strategy; Customers with Disabilities; Gay, Lesbian, Bisexual and Transgendered(GLBT), etc. |

In addition, Text 6 is more committed to the direct judgment of the propriety of the company concerned, achieved through the coupling of judgment resources with the company itself as well as the abstract principles and policies held by the company. This enables the author of Text 6 to explicitly express his/her attitude to IBM and invite the readers to share the same attitude. In Text 5, the judgment of the propriety is more often indirect, achieved by the coupling of judgment resources with the representation of specific factors of corporate citizenship activities. The roundabout manner enables the author of

Text 5 to implicitly express his/her attitude and influence the reader's attitude in a more subtle way.

In addition to the instantiation of ideational and interpersonal meanings, the textual meanings need also be instantiated in the two texts. The conjunction resources of the two texts are analyzed in Tables 5.10 and 5.11 (on p. 184 & 185) respectively. According to the above analysis, it can be seen that both texts are mainly organized through internal additive conjunctions. That is, one message is added to another, and one phase is also added to another. There are no external conjunction resources.

**Table 5.10 Conjunction Resources of Text 5**

| Internal Conjunction | Message | External Conjunction |
|---|---|---|
| | Stage 1 | |
| | (1) | |
| Developing-additive to (1) | (2) | |
| | Stage 2 (Phase 1) | |
| | (3) | |
| Additive to (3) | (4) | |
| Additive to Phase 1 | Phase 2 | |
| | (5) | |
| Additive to (5) | (6) | |
| Additive to Phase 2 | Phase 3 | |
| | (7) | |
| Additive to (7) | (8) | |
| Additive to (8) | (9) | |
| Additive to (9) | (10) | |
| Additive to (10) | (11) | |
| Additive to Phase 3 | Phase 4 | |
| | (12) | |

**Table 5.11 Conjunction Resources of Text 6**

| Internal Conjunction | Message | External Conjunction |
|---|---|---|
| | Stage 1 | |
| | (1) | |
| Additive to (1) | (2) | |
| Additive to (2) | (3) | |
| Additive to (3) | (4) | |
| Additive to (4) | (5) | |
| | Stage 2 Phase 1 | |
| | (6) | |
| | (7) | |
| Cause to (7), expectant | (8) | |
| Additive to (6) | (9) | |
| Additive to Phase 1 | Phase 2 | |
| | (10) | |
| Purpose to (10) | (11) | |
| Additive to (10) | (12) | |
| Additive to Phase 2 | Phase 3 | |
| | (13) | |
| Means to (13) | (14) | |
| Additive to (13) | (15) | |
| Additive to Phase 3 | Phase 4 | |
| | (16) | |
| Additive to (16) | (17) | |
| Additive to (17) | (18) | |
| Additive to (16) | (19) | |
| Additive to Phase (4) | Phase 5 | |
| | (20) | |
| Additive to (20) | (21) | |
| Additive to (21) | (22) | |
| Additive to (22) | (23) | |

In both texts, Stage 1 can be considered as a hyper-Theme of Stage 2. However, there is no hyper-New in Stage 2. Both texts are organized in a serial way rather than through periodical hierarchies. This serial organization, coupled with the loosely additive internal conjunction resources, is typical of corporate promotional texts. The serial organization enables the author to string the messages of the text loosely, and can add or delete information in a real-time way according to the specific demand. This facilitates the description of IBM citizenship and Dell responsibilities in a flexible way.

When all the analysis above is considered together, it can be seen that conditioned by the different specific purposes (instances) of the general purpose of the descriptive report genre (to describe IBM citizenship and to describe Dell responsibility respectively), the same genre is respectively instantiated into the IBM citizenship text and Dell responsibility text through their unique ways of coupling and commitment during the configuration of the semiotic resources at each stratum. Each instantiation process is governed by the pursuit of the corresponding purpose, and is therefore teleological.

## 5.2 Instantiation of the Corporate Homepage Genre

While the genres discussed in the previous sections are uni-modal ones realized by language, the corporate homepage genre to be discussed in this section is multimodal. The discussion is intended to show the specific ways of instantiation of the corporate homepage genre in particular, and to illustrate the applicability of the telos-oriented model of genre analysis as established in Chapter 3 for multimodal genres in general.

### 5.2.1 Corporate Homepage as a Genre

Website homepages have been explored in different ways by many authors from a functional perspective (cf. Knox 2009: 176). Thurstun (2004) considers homepages as a text type and defines it as "the external pages of a site, the pages that provide a map of the website and which are the user's introduction to the site". Kok (2004: 140) maintains that a website homepage serves the function of welcoming and introducing the (hypertext) reader to a series of linked webpages, is held to be the locus of point to all the other linked webpages, and may also serve as an index of varying degrees. Nielsen & Tahir (2002: 2) holds that "The most critical role of the homepage is to communicate what the company is, the value the site offers over the competition and the physical world, and the products or services offered".

Based on the work of the previous authors, Knox (2009) argues that the major function of homepages is orientation. Knox focuses on the study of homepages of online newspapers. According to him, the homepages can be distinguished from other webpages according to their structure. For example, the basic elements of online newspaper homepages include a brand realized by a header, which identifies the identity of the newspaper, the navigation realized by the navigation zone, which functions to allow the reader to navigate beyond the current page to other pages and sections of the newspaper, the signature realized by the footer, which signifies ownership of the content of the newspaper, the marketing, which sells products or publicizes other parts of the newspaper, and the news coverage, which functions to give an overview of the events and/or issues in one or more news domains and is realized by a visual or visual-verbal taxonomy (Knox 2009: 177-178).

Knox holds that online newspaper homepages (and homepages in general) are macro-genres rather than elementary genres. His view is based on Baldry's findings concerning the text-types (or mini-genres) identified on the homepages (Knox 2009: 187). However, from the point of view of SFL's genre theory, some of the so-called mini-genres as identified by Baldry cannot be considered as elementary genres. For example, captions, headings/titles, and tree structures are not genres, but rather some realization forms (cf. Balrdy 2000: 59). In this study, homepages will be considered as elementary genres, rather than macro-genres, though there may be other genres embedded in each elementary genre. These elementary genres constitute a genre family, comparable to the family of story genres as studied by Martin & Rose (2008). Within the family, online newspaper homepage (as studied by Knox), corporate homepage, blog homepage and others each constitute a separate genre. This section will focus on the study of corporate homepage as a genre.

On the corporate websites in the corpus adopted in this study, all homepages have a similar general purpose, with several steps employed to achieve this purpose. Based on the above discussions of the functions of general website homepages, the general purpose of a corporate homepage genre can be considered as providing the readers with an orientation to the overall contents of the corporate website (while the homepage of online newspapers can be considered as providing an orientation to the overall contents of online newspapers). The basic structure of a corporate homepage genre is similar to that of online newspaper homepage, though there is no Marketing stage, and the News Coverage stage is changed into Corporate Highlights.

According to the telos-oriented model of genre analysis as developed in Chapter 3, the corporate homepage genre can be analyzed as follows:

Purpose: to provide the readers with an orientation to the overall contents of the corporate websites, which is concretized into:

Goal 1: to establish the identity of the corporation

Goal 2: to navigate the reader beyond the current page to other pages and sections of the website

Goal 3: to describe the highlight contents of the website

Goal 4: to signify the ownership of the content of the website

Realized by the schematic structure: Identity ^ Navigation ^ Highlights ^ Signature

In the following sections, the different instantiations of the corporate homepage genre by China-based Lenovo and US-based Cisco will be explored, with a view to illustrate the multimodal instantiation of a specific genre.

In order to show the instantiation of the corporate homepage genre, two multimodal texts are extracted, the homepage of Lenovo's website (Text 7) and the homepage of Cisco's website (Text 8). The two homepages are accessed and snapped at the same day (April 27, 2010). The discussion will proceed from the genre stratum, to the register stratum, and finally to the discourse semantic stratum. The basic assumption is that the telos-oriented genre theory as developed in Chapter 3 is also applicable to multimodal texts. The analysis at the genre and register strata will be basically the same as the analysis of mono-modal texts realized by language. The discourse semantic resources of multimodal texts will necessarily be different. As in websites, the major modality other than language is image, the analysis will be based on the work of Kress & Leeuwen (1996, 2006, 2000, 2001) and Leeuwen (2005).

Text 7 Lenovo's Homepage

(http://www. lenovo. com/us/en/index. html, accessed on April 10, 2010)

Text 8 Cisco's Homepage

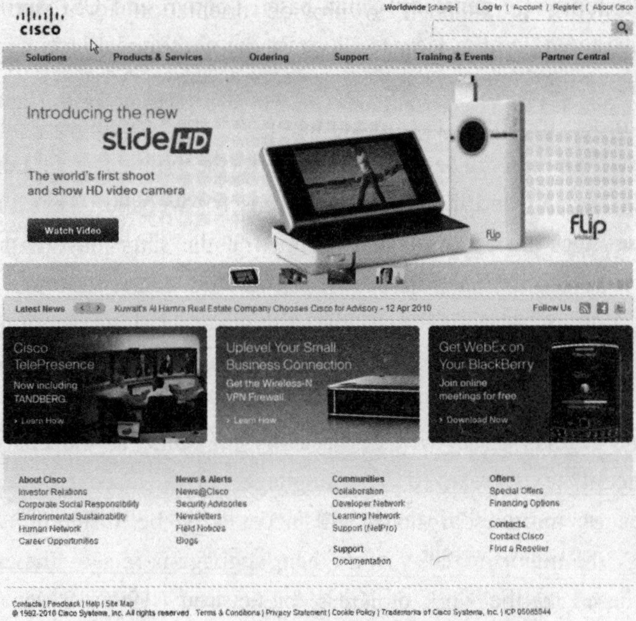


(http://www.cisco.com/, accessed on April 10, 2010)

## 5.2.2 Instantiation at the Genre Stratum

At the genre stratum, the two texts instantiate the same genre in different ways. This is mainly reflected in the different instantiations of the general purpose, and the different concretizations of the purpose into specific goals, which are then realized by different specific schematic structures. See the analysis in Table 5.12 (on p. 191).

Based on the above analysis, it can be seen that as far as the instantiation of purpose and its concretization into specific goals are concerned, the two texts are quite similar in many aspects. The major difference is that they serve the interest of different companies. Specifically, Text 7 is intended to provide orientation information for Lenovo website readers, and therefore help promote Lenovo corporation (including both the corporation itself and its products and services), while Text 8 is intended to provide orientation for Cisco website readers, and therefore help promote Cisco Systems.

**Table 5.12 Teleological and Generic Structures of Texts 7 and 8**

| | Text 7 | Text 8 |
|---|---|---|
| Purpose | to provide the readers with an orientation to the overall contents of the Lenovo website | to provide the readers with an orientation to the overall contents of Cisco website |
| Goal 1 | to establish the identity of Lenovo | to establish the identity of Cisco |
| Goal 2 | to navigate the reader to other information of Lenovo website rather than the current one | to navigate the reader to other information of Cisco website other than the current one |
| Goal 3 | to describe the highlight contents of Lenovo website | to describe the highlights of Cisco website |
| Goal 4 | to describe the ownership of Lenovo website | to signify the ownership of Cisco website |
| Staging | Lenovo Identity ^ Navigation of Lenovo Website ^ Lenovo Highlights ^ Signature | Cisco Identity ^ Navigation for Cisco Website ^ Cisco Highlights ^ Cisco Signature |
| Phasing | Identity: logo ^ slogan<br>Navigation: short navigation bar for shopping ^ navigation bar for whole websites ^ detailed navigation section (with five sub-phases)<br>Highlights: product offer/news ^ four products promoted in four phases through Flash<br>Signature: no | Identity: no<br>Navigation: shortcut navigation bar ^ navigation bar for whole websites ^ detailed navigation section (four sub-phases)<br>Highlights: four products in Flash (each in a sub-phase) ^ latest news ^ products in static images<br>Signature: no |

This difference, though seemingly insignificant, has lead to the different couplings of the representational, interactional and organizational aspects of the goals. Specifically, in Text 7, the representational aspect of the purpose and specific goals is concerned with Lenovo, coupled with the interactional aspect that is concerned with Levono website readers; in Text 8, the representational aspect is concerned with Cisco Systems, coupled with the interactional aspect that is concerned with Cisco website readers.

The two texts have a similar schematic structure. However, the stages of Text 7 center on Lenovo, while those of Text 8 center on Cisco Systems. This difference in coupling is caused by the different teleological couplings.

In addition, the stages of the two texts also differ in the degree of commitment. Specifically, the Identity stage of Text 7 is realized by two phases, with one phase indicating the logo of Lenovo, and the other indicating its tenet. In Text 8, the same stage has only one phase, which only shows the logo of Cisco. Thus, as far as phasing is concerned, the Identity stage of Text 7 is more committed than that of Text 8.

The Navigation stage of both texts has three phases. Phases 1 and 2 in both texts are very similar in terms of commitment. However, Phase 3 of Text 8 is much more committed than that in Text 7, because the former has 5 subphases, while the latter only 4, and each subphase in Text 7 has more items than that in Text 8. As a whole, the Navigation stage of Text 7 is more committed than that of Text 8.

The Highlights stage in Text 7 has two phases: Phase 1 is a sign-up box for promoting product offers and news, and Phase 2 promotes Lenovo's products/services, with each product/service promoted in a subphase. In contrast, the Highlights stage in Text 8 has three phases: Phase 1 has 4 subphases, each promoting a specific product; Phase 2 shows the latest news of Cisco; Phase 3 has three subphases, each of which also promotes a product. Thus, the Highlights stage of Text 7 is less committed than that of Text 8.

The Signature stage of Lenovo homepage is less committed than that of Cisco's. The former has only five items, while the latter has two phases, with the first phase including 4 items and the second phase including 6 items.

The varying degrees of commitment in the different stages of the two texts are conditioned by the different considerations of the author, specifically, conditioned by what the author considers as important for achieving the general purpose of the text.

### 5.2.3 Instantiation at the Register Stratum

In order to show the difference and similarity of register instantiation in the two texts, the register configurations of the two texts are analyzed in Tables 5.13 and 5.14 respectively:

**Table 5.13 Register Patterning of Text 7**

| | Field (activity sequence/taxonomy; degree of sharing/specialization, nature of socialization) | Tenor (social relation, status, contact, affect) | Mode (aural visual contact); modality; monologue/dialogue; action/reflection |
|---|---|---|---|
| Stage 1 | Establishing the identity of Lenovo through the Lenovo logo and its tenet; low degree of sharing; non-specialized; | Promoter-public reader; equal status; uninvolved contact; affect unmarked | Visual contact; language; monologue; +reflection |
| Stage 2 | Providing navigation information; low degree of sharing; non-specialized; | Promoter-public reader; equal status; uninvolved contact; affect unmarked | Visual contact; language, image; monologue; +reflection |
| Stage 3 | Promoting Lenovo products; low degree of sharing; specialized | Promoter-public reader; equal status; uninvolved contact; affect marked | Visual contact; language, image; +reflection |

Table 5.13 continued

| | | | |
|---|---|---|---|
| Stage 4 | Ownership information; legal information; sitemap; interaction; lowest degree of sharing; non-specialized | Promoter-public reader; equal status; uninvolved contact; affect unmarked | Visual contact; language; monologue; + reflection |

**Table 5.14 Register Patterning of Text 8**

| | Field (activity sequence/taxonomy; degree of sharing/specialization, nature of socialization) | Tenor (social relation, status, contact, affect) | Mode (aural visual contact); modality; monologue/dialogue; action/reflection |
|---|---|---|---|
| Stage 1 | Establishing Cisco identity though a logo; low degree of sharing; non-specialized | Promoter-public reader; equal status; uninvolved contact; unmarked affect | Visual contact; image and language; monologue; + reflection |
| Stage 2 | Navigation information; low degree of sharing; non-specialized | Promoter-public reader; equal status; uninvolved contact; affect unmarked | Visual contact; language; monologue; + reflection |
| Stage 3 | Promoting Cisco products and three services, low degree of sharing, specialized; releasing company news of Cisco; low degree of sharing; non-specialized | Promoter-public reader; equal status; uninvolved contact; affect marked | Visual contact; image and language; monologue; + reflection |
| Stage 4 | Ownership and legal information; sitemap; interaction; low degree of sharing; non-specialized | Promoter-public reader; equal status; uninvolved contact; affect unmarked | Visual contact; language; monologue; + reflection |

The analysis above shows that the instantiations of the genre by the two texts at the register stratum are similar in many aspects. For example, the tenor configurations of the two texts at each of the four stages are similar in all aspects. The social relation is of promoter-public reader, with equal status between the two sides; the social distance is relative large, with low degree of involvement; affect in Stages 1 and 2, and 4 is unmarked but is marked in Stage 3 for promoting the products/services. However, the same tenor configuration in each stage is coupled with different field or mode configurations. Specifically, the Identity stage in Text 7 is more committed than Text 8 in terms of activity sequence/taxonomy, as it includes both a logo and a slogan distributed in different zones of the homepage, while that in Text 8 only has a logo. In addition, in Text 7, Stage 1 is configured with only one modality (language), while that in Text 8 is configured with two modalities (language and image). It should be noted that the action/reflection analysis here is based on the role of language in the text, because as a whole, the meanings realized by language play a more important than those realized by image, even in Stage 3. At the Navigation stage, both the tenor and mode configurations of the two texts are similar. However, the taxonomies are different, as will be shown in more detail in the taxonomy analysis at the discourse semantic stratum. Thus, the same tenor and mode configurations are coupled with different field configurations.

At the Highlights stage, the tenor and mode configurations of the text are similar, as shown by the analysis above. However, the field configurations in the two texts are quite different. Specifically, the field in Text 7 only includes the promotion of five kinds of Lenovo PC products; in Text 8, the field covers not only the promotion of Cisco products, but also the promotion of services and the release of news. Thus, the field in Text 8 in this stage is much more committed than that in Text 7. At the Signature stage, the two texts are also similar in terms of tenor and mode configurations. The field of Text 8 is slightly more committed than that in Text 7 as the former includes more information than the latter.

In short, at the register stratum, the two texts instantiate the same homepage genre through different ways of register patterning. The different instantiations are realized by varying degrees of commitment in one or more register variables, coupled with the same configurations of other variables. Each register patterning is a unique way for instantiating the same genre, hence a unique way for achieving the same general purpose and its unique aspect of the individualized purpose.

### 5.2.4 Instantiation at the Discourse Semantic Stratum

The instantiation of a genre at the discourse semantic stratum is conditioned by the instantiation at the genre/register stratum, and ultimately governed by the realization of the purpose of the genre. In order to show the different instantiations of the same genre at the discourse semantic stratum, in this section, the instantiations will be discussed stage by stage.

The Identity stage of Text 7 is replayed in Figure 5.1 for convenience of analysis. It consists of two phases: a logo at the upper left corner, and a slogan at the lower left corner of the homepage (note that the two phases are placed together in the figure though they are actually distributed at different places in the text). The logo is represented by a word "Lenovo" in the modern "sans serit" font. The word "Lenovo" is a coinage consisting of "le + novo". The former half "le" is inherited from the former logo "legend", which indicates the origin and the tradition of the company. The latter half "novo" is a Latin word that means "new", which symbolizes the company's belief of creation and innovation. The deep blue color of the logo is a typical symbol of the IT industry. As a whole, ideationally the logo represents the identity of the company, while interpersonally, it evaluates the company as modern and innovative but also with its own tradition. The slogan "NEW WORLD NEW THINKING" represents the tenet held by Lenovo, but also helps invoke an image of an innovative company that is always ready to change its way of thinking according to the change of the world. The slogan is also in deep blue, which is symbolic of IT companies.

lenovo

NEW WORLD. NEW THINKING.

**Figure 5.1 The Identity Stage of Lenovo Homepage**

The Identity stage of Text 8 (as is replayed in Figure 5.2) is realized by the Cisco logo in a zone established by covert framing (through white spaces) at the upper left corner of the homepage, which consists of an icon and a word. The icon is a symbol of a suspension bridge. On the one hand, this is synonymous with San Francisco's Golden Gate Bridge, which reminds the readers of the location of Cisco Systems. On the other, it symbolizes Cisco's role as a bridge for interconnection and communications in the society. The deep blue color gives the readers an impression of serenity and profoundness, which is often employed to symbolize high technologies. The word CISCO, which holds an extension relation with the icon, clearly indicates the identity of the corporation, while the bold font, the upper case and the red color makes it eye-catching. The sharp contrast between the deep blue and red colors and the slight cartooning help make the whole logo more lively and lovely. The use of the shortened name (Cisco rather than the full name Cisco Systems as used before), which sounds like the name of an ordinary people, also makes the logo more intelligible to ordinary customers. As a whole, the logo ideationally establishes the identity of Cisco Systems and interpersonally defines the role of Cisco as bridging communications that serves both enterprise and ordinary customers.

When the different instantiations of the Identity stage by the two

CISCO

**Figure 5. 2 The Identity Stage of Cisco Homepage**

texts are compared, it can be seen that the two texts are equally committed to the ideational meaning of their respective identities, as in both texts the identity of the company is appropriately established. Interpersonally, Text 7 is more committed to the appreciation of the company concerned. On the one hand, it invokes an image of both creative and traditional company through the coinage of a new word. On the other, it intensifies appreciation by provoking the appreciation of the innovative spirit of the company through a highly interpersonally-loaded slogan. The evaluative meaning of Text 8 is much more implicit as it is mainly achieved by the bridge icon (which functions as a kind of metaphor) and the use of color and its understanding requires much more imagination. Moreover, Cisco as a bridge for communications only indirectly invokes some sort of judgment or appreciation meanings.

At the Navigation stage, the field of each of the text is mainly realized by taxonomies. The Navigation stage of Texts 7 and 8 are replayed in Figures 5. 3 (on p. 199) and 5. 4 (on p. 201) respectively. The different phases of each stage, though distributed in different places on the corresponding homepage, are again placed together for the convenience of analysis. In Text 7, Phase 1 of the Navigation stage includes location selection and a loose taxonomy related to shopping, which includes account, cart, order, shopping help, and contact phone number. Phase 2 of the Navigation stage in Text 7 is a loose taxonomy without superordinate, including five items, i. e. "products", "services & warranty", "solutions for", "support", and "about Lenovo". Except for the last item, the other four items are all concerned with the products and services provided by Lenovo to the customers. In addition, there is a search engine for intra-site retrieval.

Phase 3 includes five taxonomies: products, solutions, support, resources, and what is new. Under each superordinate, a range of items are listed. It is very interesting that these five taxonomies are actually a more detailed elaboration of the first four items in Phase 2. Taken as a whole, the ideational resources of the Navigation stage in Text 7 is more intended to navigate the reading public to different kinds of products and services promoted by Lenovo.

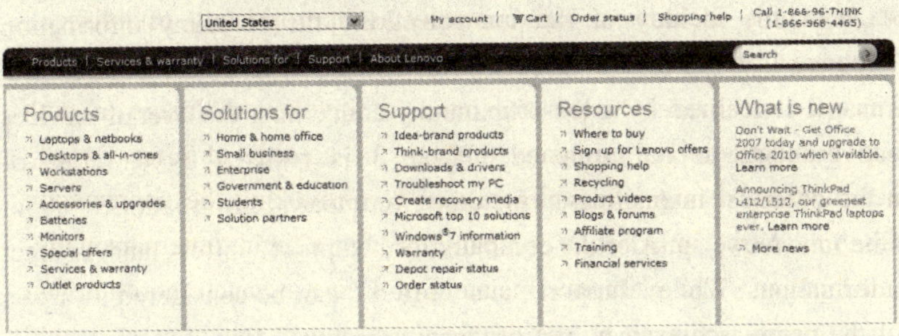


**Figure 5.3　The Navigation Stage of Lenovo Homepage**

Interpersonally, the Navigation stage of Text 7 is more concerned with establishing a potential seller-buyer relation with the readers. The affect in this stage is unmarked as there is only one piece of inscribed evaluation resources ("our greenest enterprise ThinkPad laptops ever" in the last taxonomy of Phase 3). As for involvement resources, there are a few resources which are typically employed to show a relatively high degree of involvement, for example, the homophoric form ("my account", "our greenest..."), and the use of mood contraction and minor clauses ("where to buy" and "Don't wait"). Though the actual contact between the Lenovo promoter and the reading public is more likely to be distant, these resources are intended to shorten the social distance and thus help promote the products, services and the corporation itself.

Textually, the three phases of the stage are clearly indicated by framing resources, Phase 1 by covert framing (through white space), while Phases 2 and 3 by overt framing (through boxes). The use of explicit framing raises the intelligibility and readability of the text. Moreover, in a way, Phases 1 and 2 can be considered as a kind of hyper-Theme for Phase 3, as Phase 3 is actually an elaboration of the former two phases. The last sub-phase of Phase 3 can also be regarded as a kind of hyper-New for the whole stage, which helps the author to better promote the latest products and services.

In Text 8, the ideational resources of Phase 1 of the Navigation stage mainly includes a location selection, the company information ("about Cisco") and a loose taxonomy related to customer account. Phase 2 is realized by a loose taxonomy concerning the overall services and products to be promoted. Phase 3 is realized by a series of heterogeneous taxonomies, including company information (about Cisco), News & Alerts, communities, support, offers and contact information. While "support" and "offers" can be considered as a part of the promoted services and products, the other taxonomies are more concerned with the information of a large Cisco community. Compared with the ideational resources of the same stage in Text 7, it can be said that Text 8 is more committed to the navigation of the public readers to different aspects of Cisco community, while that of Text 7 more committed to the navigation of the readers to different products and services (as discussed above).

Interpersonally, in addition to the definition of a seller-buyer relation, the Navigation stage of Text 8 employs many resources to establish a community-membership relation with the public readers. Thus, Text 8 is more committed to the establishment of a community-membership relation, while Text 7 more committed to the establishment of a seller-buyer relation. In addition, in Text 8, there is no resources inscribing evaluative meaning, and the degree of involvement is also lower than that in Text 7.

Textually, the boundaries between the phases in the stage are also realized by overt framing (through boxes). Within Phase 3, the different subphases are indicated both by subheading and covert framing. This

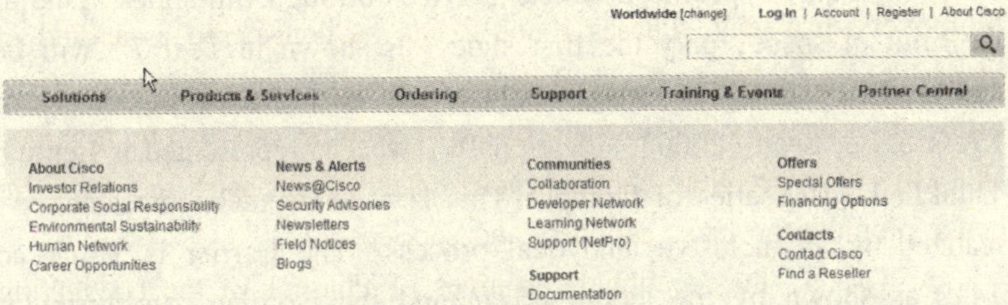


**Figure 5.4 The Navigation Stage of Cisco Homepage**

also helps increase the intelligibility and readability of the text. The phases are related to each other serially rather than periodically, as there is no hyper-Theme or hyper-New in the Stage, which enables the author to loosely organize the text and delete or add relevant contents when appropriate. The different instantiations of Stage 2 by the two texts at the discourse semantic stratum are summarized in Table 5.15.

**Table 5.15 Discourse Semantic Resources of Texts 7 and 8 (Navigation Stage)**

| | Ideational | Interpersonal | Textual |
|---|---|---|---|
| Stage 2 of Text 7 | Both products/services and community information represented, but More committed to the navigation of readers to different products and services; | More committed to the establishment of Seller-buyer relation with the readers; affect slightly marked; higher degree of involvement | Phase boundaries realized by both overt and covert framing; hierarchical development with hyper-Theme and hyper-New |
| Stage 2 of Text 8 | Both products/service and community information represented, but more committed to the navigation of readers to Cisco-related community | More committed to the establishment of a community-member relation with the readers; affect totally unmarked; lower degree of involvement | Phase boundaries realized by overt and covert framing; serial rather than hierarchical development |

The Highlights stage of Text 7 (which is replayed in Figure 5.5 on p. 202) consists of two phases (cf. Section 6.2.2.1). Phase 1 is a sign-up box intended to promote product offers and news. Phase 2 is the promotion of specific products/services through flip slides. Due to the limit of space, only the first slide (as shown in Text 7) will be analyzed in detail. The image analysis will be based on the theory of Kress & Leeuwen (2006). Ideationally, what is represented is Lenovo ThinkPad T410 series of laptops. This is a conceptual representation, realized by an inclusive analytical process. The Carrier is ThinkPad T410 as shown by the laptop image and the wording. Its attributes include its popularity (represented both by the phrase "ThinkPad best sellers" and the medal image), the target customers ("ideal for businesses that seek outstanding performance"), its price (represented by "free shipping", "save up to $546 on our best-selling laptops. Savings end Wednesday, May 5"), a critical component the Intel core (represented by the words and the image), and its quality (represented metaphorically by "There is more thinking in a ThinkPad"). The configuration of the ideational resources enables the Lenovo Homepage designer to promote the latest Lenovo products and services.

**Figure 5. 5 The Highlights Stage of Lenovo Homepage**

Interpersonally, the absence of gaze at the viewer from the image indicates that it is an offer rather than demand of information. The laptop image is taken by a medium shot, which indicates a social (medium level) distance between the viewer and the laptop. In addition, the laptop image is taken from a frontal and eye-level angle, which indicates that the viewer is involved and the relation between the viewer and the participant (the laptop) is equal. Moreover, the modality of the slide is at the lower-medium level. This is indicated by the medium color saturation and differentiation, a slightly articulated background, and the medium-level representation. In addition, there are some appraisal resources realized by language, for example, "best sellers", "best-selling", "ideal" (inscribed high force + positive appreciation of reaction), and "there's more thinking in a ThinkPad" (evoked positive appreciation of valuation). In short, the specific configuration of the interpersonal resources enables the author to promote the product in a highly involved and sensory manner.

Textually, the laptop image and the phrases "ThinkPad best sellers" are most salient due to their largest size and highest tonal values. This enables the author to highlight the most important information and makes it most eye-catching.

While the Highlights stage of Text 7 has only two phases, the same stage of Text 8, which is replayed in Figure 5.6, has three phases. Phase 1 is a promotion of Cisco products, services and events through flip slides, which is comparable to Phase 2 of the same stage in Text 8. Phase 2 is the news release, while Phase 3 is the promotion of products and services by static images. Due to the limit of space, only the first slide of Phase 1 (as shown in Text 8) will be analyzed in detail.

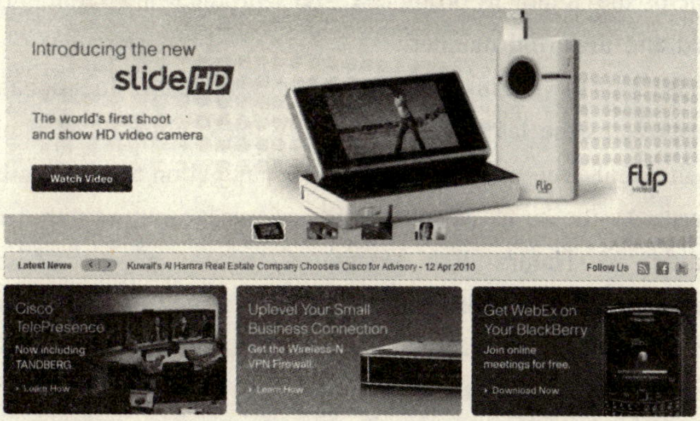


**Figure 5.6 The Highlights Stage of Cisco Homepage**

Like the first slide of Text 7 analyzed above, ideationally the slide in Text 8 as a whole is also an analytical process, representing an HD. The carrier is the HD, represented by the two images, and by the words "slide HD". The attributes of the carrier represented here include its horizontal image, its vertical image, and its working principle ("slide HD", "flip video", "the world's first shoot and show HD video camera"). Interpersonally, the pictures are taken from an oblique, eye-level angle with medium shots, which indicates a detached attitude towards the image, an equal relation and a social (medium-level) distance between the viewer and the images. The modality of the picture is also at the lower-medium level, basically the same as that in Text 7, as is indicated by the low-level color saturation, differentiation, contextualization and representation. In addition, there are no inscribed appraisal resources, though the words "new slide HD" and "word's first shoot and show HD video camera" can evoke a positive appreciation of the valuation of the camera. Textually, the words on the left are given information, while the images on the right are new information. In addition, the words "Slide HD" and the two images are also the most salient. As a whole, the coupling of the ideational, interpersonal and textual resources at this phase helps the author to promote Cisco's product in a seemingly more detached and impartial manner.

Phase 2 of the Highlights stage is a news release. Ideationally, the phase represents the latest news (actually the caption of each piece of news) in a real-time manner and also the navigation to the details of all the news. At the time when the picture was captured, the news is "Kuwait's Al Hamra Real Estate Company chooses Cisco for Advisory". Interpersonally, it establishes a news releaser-audience relation. Textually, the news phase is realized by overt framing with maximum disconnection from other phases. The instantiation in this phase enables the author to release the latest news in a highly real-time manner while keeping the accessibility and readability of the news.

Phase 3 consists of three static images. Ideationally they respectively represent Cisco TelePresence Wireless-N VPN Firewall and Cisco WebEx products/services through three analytical processes. Interpersonally, the modality of the pictures is at a relatively high level, as indicated by the high-level color saturation and modulation. The images are also taken from oblique, eye-level angles with medium shots, indicating detachment, equality and social distance. In addition, there is evoked appreciation of the specific products concerned. Textually, the boundaries between the images are realized by covert framing with maximum disconnection, and they are serially developed. This way of instantiation is also instrumental to the author's promotion of the relevant products in a seemingly detached and impartial manner.

The different instantiations of the Highlights stage by the two texts are summarized in the following table:

**Table 5.16 Discourse Semantic Resources of Texts 7 and 8 (Highlights Stage)**

| | Ideational | Interpersonal | Textual |
|---|---|---|---|
| Phase 1, Stage 3 of Text 7 | Sign up for Exclusive product offers/news | Low modality; positive appreciation of valuation (exclusive) | Covert framing |
| Phase 2, Stage 3 of Text 7 | Lenovo ThinkPad T410 series laptops and its attributes (popularity, target customers, price, core component, quality) | Offering information, involved attitude, equal relation, and social distance; low modality; high force, inscribed positive appreciation of reaction; raising force, evoked positive appreciation of valuation | Covert framing; important information highlighted through salience (through large size and high tonal value) |
| Phase 1, Stage 3 of Text 8 | HD video camera and its attributes | Offering information, Detached attitude, equal relation, and social distance between the viewer and image; low modality; evoked appreciation of valuation | Covert framing; important information highlighted through salience |

Table 5.16 continued

| | Ideational | Interpersonal | Textual |
|---|---|---|---|
| Phase 2, Stage 3 of Text 8 | Release of latest news | News releaser-reader relation | Covert framing |
| Phase 3, Stage 3 of Text 8 | Cisco TelePresence; wireless-N VPN firewall, WebEx | Offering information; detached attitude, equal relation and social distance; relative high modality; evoked appreciation | Covert framing, serial development |

The Signature stage of Text 7 (replayed in Figure 5.7) consists of "site map", "terms of use", "privacy", "contact", "jobs at Lenovo" and "email signup". However, only "terms of use" and "privacy" are obligatory elements of this stage. They help clarify the ownership and legal affairs concerning the contents of the website. The other items are all optional ones, providing supplementary information considered as useful for public readers. Thus, ideationally, the stage consists of two loose taxonomies, i. e. the signature information and supplementary information. Interpersonally, the stage defines an owner-user relation between Cisco Systems and the reading public. In addition, the affect is unmarked, and there are no inscribed evaluation resources in the Text. However, the signature information concerning the ownership and legal affairs can invoke a positive judgment of the propriety of Cisco Systems. The degree of involvement is relatively low, which is indicated by the use of formal and standard words.

Site map | Terms of use | Privacy | Contact | Jobs at Lenovo | E-mail signup

**Figure 5.7 The Signature Stage of Lenovo Homepage**

The Signature stage of Text 8 (replayed in Figure 5.8) also

consists of two taxonomies: signature information and supplementary information. In addition to terms & conditions (comparable to terms of use in Text 7) and privacy statement (comparable to privacy in Text 7), the signature taxonomy also includes information about copyright, cookie policy, trademark and registration. Thus, the stage in Text 8 is more committed in terms of signature information than that in Text 7. The taxonomy of supplementary information includes contact, site map, help, and feedback. The first two items are similar to those in Text 7, while the latter two are simply absent and replaced by job and email information. In other words, where parts of the supplementary information are similar, different choices are made concerning other supplementary information. The difference in commitment is conditioned by the different specific purposes of the two texts.

Contacts | Feedback | Help | Site Map
© 1992-2010 Cisco Systems, Inc. All rights reserved. Terms & Conditions | Privacy Statement | Cookie Policy | Trademarks of Cisco Systems, Inc. | ICP 05085544

**Figure 5.8 The Signature Stage of Cisco Homepage**

Interpersonally, the Signature stage of Text 8 also defines a content owner-user relation between Cisco Systems and the reading public. Similar to the same stage in Text 7, there are no inscribed evaluation meanings. The representation of the ownership and legal affairs information may also evoke a positive judgment of the propriety of the behavior of Cisco Systems. Moreover, the greater degree of commitment to this information may lead to an intensification of such evoked evaluative meanings, and thus make the stage more committed to the propriety judgment compared with that in Text 7. Textually, the boundary between the two taxonomies is clearly indicated by framing (through white space and typesetting), while that in Text 7 is vague. In both texts, the stage is developed serially rather than hierarchically. The different instantiations of the Signature stage by the two texts are summarized in Table 5.17.

**Table 5.17 Discourse Semantic Resources of Texts 7 and 8 (Signature Stage)**

| | Ideational | Interpersonal | Textual |
|---|---|---|---|
| Stage 4 of Text 7 | Signature and supplementary information provided; less committed to signature information; different choices of parts of supplementary information | Establishing content ownership-user relation; less degree of evoked judgment of propriety | Boundary between taxonomies realized by covert framing; serial development |
| Stage 4 of Text 8 | Signature and supplementary information provided; high degree of commitment to signature information; different choices of parts of the supplementary information | Establishing content owner-user relation; higher degree of commitment of evoked judgment of propriety | Heterogeneous taxonomies without clear boundary; serial development |

As a whole, the instantiation process as shown in Texts 7 and 8 can be briefly summarized as follows. The general and abstract purpose of the homepage genre is first instantiated into different specific purposes (to provide the readers with an orientation to the overall contents of the websites of Lenovo and Cisco respectively). The different instantiations of the abstract purpose condition the different ways of coupling and commitment during the semiotic configurations of the two texts at each stratum. The unique ways of coupling and commitment of each instantiation process are strategies to achieve their respective specific purposes.

## 5.3 Summary

In Chapter 5, the instantiation processes of two genres are discussed: the descriptive report genre and the corporate homepage genre. The instantiation of the descriptive report genre is illustrated by a comparative analysis of the IBM citizenship text and Dell responsibility text, while the instantiation of the corporate homepage genre is illustrated by the comparative analysis of the homepages of Lenovo and Cisco respectively. For each genre, the different instantiations by the two texts are first analyzed at the genre stratum to show the instantiations of the teleological structure and generic structure, then at the register stratum to explore the different ways of register patterning, and at last at the discourse semantic stratum to show the different configurations of ideational, interpersonal and textual resources. The different ways of coupling and commitment at each stratum are explained in relation to the specific effect that they have for achieving the user's purpose.

The analysis in the chapter shows that for each genre, the general abstract purpose will be instantiated into a unique purpose and concretized into a unique teleological structure. Unique ways of coupling and commitment at every stratum will be adopted as strategies to achieve this purpose (which is an instance of the general abstract purpose of the genre). The instantiation at a lower stratum are conditioned by the instantiation at a higher stratum, and finally conditioned by the general purpose of the specific user. Specifically, the unique configurations of ideational, interpersonal, and textual resources at the discourse semantic stratum are conditioned by and serve the instantiation at the register stratum, while the unique configurations of register variables are in turn conditioned by and serve the instantiation at the genre stratum.

# Chapter 6

# Individuation and Complexing of Corporate Website Genres

While genre instantiation deals with the ways for achieving the specific purpose of a genre by employing specific instances of semiotic resources, genre individuation is concerned with the achievement of the specific purpose of a genre by employing user-specific semiotic resources. When actualized in social life, every genre will be imbued with the unique purpose of the user, and every user will employ the semiotic potential of the genre to achieve their own purpose and serve their own interests. In Chapter 5, the instantiation of the descriptive report genre and corporate homepage genre has been explored. In this chapter, the individuation of the descriptive report genre will be discussed, with a view to show how the same genre is individualized by different companies to serve their own purposes, how their different identities are established through the individualized employment of genre resources, and how they negotiate with each other into the collective identity of the IT industry.

## 6.1 Individuation of the Descriptive Report Genre

In order to illustrate genre individuation, three texts of the descriptive report genre are extracted from the websites of Acer, Motorola and Cisco respectively, each of which is a profile of the corresponding company. All the texts belong to the descriptive report genre (cf. 4.2.1). They are intended to give an overview of the company and are concerned with the establishment of the identities of the corresponding company. The texts will be analyzed comparatively, first at the discourse semantic stratum, and then at the register and genre strata respectively. Then the individuation/affiliation processes as shown by them will be discussed.

### 6.1.1 Individuation at the Discourse Semantic Stratum

At the discourse semantic stratum, the analysis will focus on the ideation system, appraisal system, periodicity system and conjunction system, as long as it is adequate to illustrate the different ways of individuation conditioned by the specific purposes of the authors of the three texts.

#### 6.1.1.1 Individuation in Motorola Profile Text

To start, the Motorola Profile text will be first analyzed. The original text is numbered as Text 9 below.

Text 9 Motorola Profile

(1) We are a global communications leader powered by a passion to invent and an unceasing commitment to advancing the way the world connects. (2) Our communication solutions allow people, businesses and governments to be more connected and more mobile.

(3) Motorola (NYSE: MOT) has been at the forefront of communication inventions and innovations for more than 80 years. (4) We have achieved extraordinary accomplishments along the way — such as making the equipment that carried the first words from the moon and leading the cellular communication revolution with the development of the world's first handheld cellular phone. (5) More recently, Motorola has taken leadership positions in solutions for public safety, enterprises, mobile computing, 4G broadband, and high definition video.

(6) Today, Motorola's portfolio of technologies, solutions and services includes wireless handsets, wireless accessories, digital entertainment devices, wireless access systems, voice and data communications systems, and enterprise mobility products. (7) We operate in numerous countries around the globe, tapping the creativity of diverse cultures and individuals.

(8) With the rapid convergence of fixed and mobile broadband Internet and the growing demand for next-generation mobile communication solutions, our

mission is to lead the next wave of innovative products that meet the expanding needs of our customers around the world. (9) The trends toward media mobility, ubiquitous connectivity and wireless flexibility, coupled with mobile lifestyles and business, continue to expand.

(10) Our history is rich. (11) Our future is dynamic. (12) We are Motorola and (13) the spirit of invention is what drives us. (14) See this Motorola 2010 Corporate Profile in a printable format (2 page PDF; 113 KB).

( http://www. motorola. com/web/Business/Corporate/US-EN/about-motorola/corporate-overview. html; accessed on April 15, 2010)

For the convenience of analysis, the messages (ranking clauses) of the text are numbered. The ideational resources are analyzed first, as shown in Table 6. 1.

**Table 6. 1 Ideational Resources of Text 9**

| Message | Nuclear | Center | Nuclear | Peripheral |
|---|---|---|---|---|
| (1) | We | are | a global communications leader powered by a passion to invent and an unceasing commitment to advancing the way the world connects | |
| (2) | Our communication solutions | allow | people, businesses and governments to be more connected and more mobile | |
| (3) | Motorola (NYSE: MOT) | has been | at the forefront of communication inventions and innovations | for more than 80 years |
| (4) | We | have achieved | extraordinary accomplishments; such as making the equipment that carried the first words from the moon and leading the cellular communication revolution with the development of the world's first handheld cellular phone | along the way |

Table 6.1　continued

| Message | Nuclear | Center | Nuclear | Peripheral |
|---|---|---|---|---|
| (5) | Motorola | has taken | leadership positions | more recently, in solutions for public safety, enterprises, mobile computing, 4G broadband, and high definition video |
| (6) | Motorola's portfolio of technologies, solutions and services | includes | wireless handsets, wireless accessories, digital entertainment devices, wireless access systems, voice and data communications systems, and enterprise mobility products | today |
| (7) | We | operate | | in numerous countries around the glob; tapping the creativity of diverse cultures and individuals |
| (8) | our mission | is | to lead the next wave of innovative products that meet the expanding needs of our customers around the world | With the rapid convergence of fixed and mobile broadband Internet and the growing demand for next-generation mobile communication solutions |

Table 6.1 continued

| Message | Nuclear | Center | Nuclear | Peripheral |
|---|---|---|---|---|
| (9) | The trends toward media mobility, ubiquitous connectivity and wireless flexibility, coupled with mobile lifestyles and business | continue to expand | | |
| (10) | Our history | is | rich | |
| (11) | Our future | is | dynamic | |
| (12) | We | are | Motorola | |
| (13) | the spirit of invention | is | what drives us | |
| (14) | | See | this Motorola 2010 Corporate Profile in a printable format | At… |

According to the analysis of Table 6.1 (Message 14 is not included in the discussion as it is not a direct description of Motorola), it can be seen that the processes of the messages (ranking clauses) fall into two types: 8 relational processes and 5 material processes. Specifically, there are 4 identifying relational processes (all are of the intensive type), 4 attributive ones (including 1 circumstantial process, 1 possessive and 2 intensive ones). The material processes are not concrete actions directed to specific goals, but are rather abstract, specifying either the current state of Motorola or a trend (including its leading position and accomplishment). The nuclear elements to the left of the center column include Identifier, Identified, Carrier, and Actor.

Among them, 5 elements are Motorola, and 5 are about Motorola's products/services or other aspects (such as mission, history and future); 1 element ("the spirit of invention") is the Identifier of the corresponding Identified ("what drives us") related to Motorola; only that of Message 9 has no direct relation to the company. The nuclear elements to the right of the center column include Identified, Identifier, Attribute, and Goal. The peripheral elements include circumstances of Duration, Time, Place and Accompaniment.

The major taxonomy in the text is Motorola's characteristics, including such items as its leading position ("mentioned for"), its mission, its accomplishment/achievement, its production range, its customers, its history/future and its momentum. The items of this taxonomy are distributed throughout the whole text. The item "Motorola" (as the superordinate) has been most frequently mentioned (for 11 times in various forms including "Motorola", "we", "our" and "us"), its leading position has been mentioned for 4 times ("a global communications leader", "at the forefront", "leadership positions" and "to lead the next wave"), its momentum (the spirit of invention) has been mentioned for 3 times, while Motorola customers have only been mentioned for 2 times. Other minor taxonomies are Motorola's accomplishment (with two subordinates), its product range (including 6 subordinates) and the range of its leadership position (with 5 subordinates). These taxonomies are much local, each distributed only in one message. They are also directly related to Motorola. The customers are only mentioned for two times, in Message 2 ("allow people, businesses and governments to be more connected and more mobile") as Goal and in Message 8 ("that meet the expanding needs of our customers around the world") as a part of the Goal in an embedded qualifying clause.

The taxonomic relations, combined with the activity sequences and nuclear relations as analyzed above, show that the author of the text is most committed to the description of Motorola's characteristics, specifically, to its leading position in the industry, its achievements and the wide variety of products. The momentum (the spirit of invention) receives less commitment, while the commitment to the description of the customers is the least. As the author is most possibly a member of Motorola's staff, this is a self-centered description, focusing on the high status and the technical strength of the company. The author as shown in this text is also self-centered, with little consideration of the customers or partners.

Interpersonally, the inscribed appraisal resources of the text are analyzed in Table 6.2. In addition, the whole text is full of resources that invoke positive appraisal meanings. They are analyzed in Table 6.3.

**Table 6.2 Inscribed Appraisal Resources of Text 9**

| Source | Force/Focus | Inscribed Appraisal Resources | Trigger/Target | Type Analysis |
|---|---|---|---|---|
| Author | | leader in Message 1 | We (Motorola) | Judgment-social esteem-capacity |
| Author | | a passion to invent | We | Judgment-social esteem-capacity |
| Author | | unceasing in Message 1 | commitment (Motorola indirectly) | Judgment-social esteem-tenacity |
| Author | Inscribed quantification: for more than 80 years | at the forefront of communication inventions and innovations | Motorola | Judgment-social esteem-normality |
| Author | Inscribed intensification: extraordinary | accomplishments | we (Motorola) | Judgment-social esteem-capacity |
| Author | | leadership position | Motorola | Judgment-social esteem-capacity |
| Author | | diverse | cultures and individuals | Appreciation-composition-complexity |

Table 6.2 continued

| Source | Force/Focus | Inscribed Appraisal Resources | Trigger/Target | Type Analysis |
|---|---|---|---|---|
| Author | | lead the next wave | Our mission (Indirectly Motorola) | Judgment-social esteem-capacity |
| Author | | rich | Our history | Appreciation - composition-complexity |
| Author | | dynamic | Our future | Appreciation-reaction-impact |

**Table 6.3 Evoked Appraisal Resources of Text 9**

| Source | Force/Focus | Invoked Appraisal Resources | Trigger/Target | Type Analysis |
|---|---|---|---|---|
| Author | | Message 2 | Our communication solutions | Appreciation-valuation |
| Author | Evoked quantification in Message 4 through enumeration | Messages 3, 4, and 5 | Motorola | Judgment-social esteem-capacity |
| Author | Evoked quantification through enumeration | Message 6 | Motorola's portfolio of technologies, solutions, and services | Appreciation-composition-complexity |
| Author | Inscribed quantification: in numerous (countries) around the globe | Message 7 | We (Motorola) | Judgment-social esteem-capacity |
| Author | Inscribed quantification: around the world in Message 8 | Messages 8 and 9 | Motorola | Judgment-social esteem-capacity; social sanction-propriety |

Table 6.3 continued

| Source | Force/Focus | Invoked Appraisal Resources | Trigger/Target | Type Analysis |
|---|---|---|---|---|
| Author | | Messages 12 and 13 | We | Judgment-social esteem/ normality |

Based on the analysis of both inscribed and evoked appraisal resources, it can be seen that the appraisal meanings of Text 9 have several features. First, as shown in the "Source" column, all appraisal and other meanings come from the author of the text. In terms of engagement, it is a kind of monologue, and the appraisal meanings are the voices of the author. The choice of monogloss helps the author control the semantic configurations of the company. Specifically, the author can select meanings that help establish a positive image of the company, and prevent any negative meanings.

However, the source of the meanings is not inscribed, which make the messages become barely asserted propositions. Bare assertions often appear intersubjectively neutral, objective or even "factual" (cf. Martin & White 2005: 98-102). Through the use of bare assertions, the author makes both the ideational and appraisal meanings of the company look factual and hides the promotional intention.

Second, there are a few graduation resources (cf. Martin & White 2005: 150-153). Specifically, there is only one word used as isolated intensification: "extraordinary" in Message 4. Intensification through semantic infusion is rare as most of the processes and qualities are relatively mild and neutral. There are three pieces of inscribed quantification (extent) resources, and two pieces of evoked quantification (number) resources. There are no resources for graduation in focus. As a whole, the author seems to promote Motorola in a relatively mild and objective tone. Compared with an exaggerative tone through abundant use of graduation resources, a mild and objective tone is more acceptable to the reading public, and more consistent with Motorola's identity as a world-renowned high-tech company.

Third, the text employs many inscribed appraisal resources. Most of them are positive judgment of the social esteem of the company (Motorola in this case), with judgment of Motorola's capacity accounting for the major proportion, while the tenacity and normality each only appraised once. The triggers/targets of all the inscribed judgment resources are Motorola. In addition, there are some appreciation resources (appreciation of complexity and impact). Their triggers/targets include "cultures and individuals" (of Motorola's target markets), "our history", and "our future", all related to Motorola. Affect is not inscribed in the text. The text also has many resources that can evoke specific appraisal meanings. Most of them evoke positive judgment of Motorola, including the judgment of capacity and normality. Judgment of social sanction (specifically, propriety) of the company is only evoked once in the text. In addition, appreciation meanings are also invoked, including the positive appreciation of the valuation of Motorola's communication solutions and the complexity of its product portfolio.

The employment of abundant inscribed appraisal resources indicates that an important way for the author to promote the company is to directly and explicitly evaluate it. In addition, he/she also evaluates the company indirectly. As far as the type of appraisal resources is concerned, the author promotes the company mainly by treating the company as a person and positively judging its behavior. The judgment focuses on the social esteem, especially the capacity of the company; social sanction is rarely mentioned. This indicates that the author mainly judges the company as powerful and capable, with a high status in the industry. The insignificance of social sanction seems to indicate that the author pays little attention to the morality of the company. In a few cases the author treats the company as a phenomenon as is indicated by the appreciation resources, focusing on the history, future and technology of the company. The absence of inscribed affect indicates that the author does not resort to subjective personal affect for promotion. This adds to the impartial tone of the text.

Interpersonally, the author is thus construed as a mild promoter in a seemingly impartial tone, promoting the company by both explicitly and implicitly highlighting its capacity and high status but with little attention to its morality.

Textually, Text 9 is serially structured rather than structured through hierarchies of periodicity. Messages 1 and 2 can be considered as the macro-Theme of the whole text as they present the general meanings that are elaborated in the following parts of the text. However, there is no corresponding macro-New at the end of the text. After the macro-Theme is presented, the following text just elaborates the different aspects of the macro-Theme one by one in serial way, and comes to an end after the last aspect is elaborated. Thus, there is no hierarchy of periodicity.

As for conjunction resources, except for the two circumstances of time ("more recently" in Message 5 and "today" in Message 6) that function as external conjunction resources, the messages are interconnected with one another mainly through internal additive conjunction relations, with one message simply added to another. In some cases, they are organized through reworking (comparative) conjunctions (Messages 4 and 5 elaborating Message 3). This is another indication of the serial development of the text.

The employment of serial organization is conditioned by the purpose of the promoter. Specifically, as serial organization is much looser and much more flexible than hierarchical organization, it enables the author to add, delete, and replace promotional contents whenever appropriate. As a result, the author can update the contents of a text in a real time way according to the changing market demand. The employment of serial organization establishes the identity of the author more like an offhand promoter that has improvised the promotional contents rather than a well-prepared promoter that has carefully designed the contents and the organization of the text.

#### 6.1.1.2 Individuation in Acer Profile Text

In this section, the Acer profile text titled "About Us" will be analyzed in comparison with Text 9. It is numbered as Text 10 below.

Text 10 Acer Profile

About Us

(1) Since its founding in 1976, Acer has achieved the goal of breaking the barriers between people and technology. (2) Globally, Acer ranks No. 2 for total PCs and notebooks. (3) A profitable and sustainable Channel Business Model is instrumental to the company's continuing growth, (4) while its multi-brand approach effectively integrates Acer, Gateway, Packard Bell, and eMachines brands in worldwide markets. (5) Acer strives to design environmentally friendly products and establish a green supply chain through collaboration with suppliers. (6) Acer is proud to be a Worldwide Partner of the Olympic Movement in staging the Vancouver 2010 Olympic Winter and London 2012 Olympic Games. (7) The Acer Group employs 7,000 people worldwide. (8) Estimated revenue for 2009 is US $17.9 billion.

(9) Overcoming the barriers between people and technology: This is Acer's long-term mission, to allow anyone to use and benefit from technology. (10) Acer is renowned for the development and manufacture of sophisticatedly and intuitively designed, easy to use products.

(11) Acer's product range includes PC notebooks and Desktops, servers and storage systems, monitors, peripheral devices, digital devices, LCD TVs and e-business solutions for business, Government, Education and home users. (12) Acer employs 5,400 people throughout the world and (13) has created a consolidated sales and service network in more than 100 countries. (14) Revenues reached US $11.32 billion in 2006.

(http://us.acer.com/acer/about_us.do?LanguageISOCtxParam=en&ctx2.c2att1=25&CountryISOCtxParam=US&ctx1g.c2att92=453&ctx1.att21k=1&CRC=3529792491, accessed on April 15, 2010)

The ideational resources of Text 10 are analyzed in Table 6.4.

**Table 6.4 Ideational Resources of Text 10**

| Message | Nuclear | Center | Nuclear | Peripheral |
|---|---|---|---|---|
| (1) | Acer | has achieved | the goal of breaking the barriers between people and technology | since its founding in 1976 |
| (2) | Acer | ranks | No. 2 | globally, for total PCs and notebooks |
| (3) | A profitable and sustainable Channel Business Model | is | instrumental to the company's continuing growth | in worldwide markets |
| (4) | its multi-brand approach | effectively integrates | Acer, Gateway, Packard Bell, and eMachines brands | in worldwide markets |
| (5) | Acer | strives to design, establish | environmentally friendly products, a green supply chain | through collaboration with suppliers |
| (6) | Acer | is proud to be | a Worldwide Partner of the Olympic Movement | in staging the Vancouver 2010 Olympic Winter and London 2012 Olympic Games |
| (7) | The Acer Group | employs | 7,000 people | worldwide |
| (8) | Estimated revenue for 2009 | is | US $ 17.9 billion | |

Table 6.4 continued

| Message | Nuclear | Center | Nuclear | Peripheral |
|---|---|---|---|---|
| (9) | Overcoming the barriers between people and technology: this | is | Acer's long-term mission | to allow anyone to use and benefit from technology. |
| (10) | Acer | is | renowned | for the development and manufacture of sophisticatedly and intuitively designed, easy to use products |
| (11) | Acer's product range | includes | PC notebooks and Desktops, servers and storage systems, monitors, peripheral devices, digital devices, LCD TVs and e-business solutions for business, Government, Education and home users | |
| (12) | Acer | employs | 5,400 people | throughout the world |
| (13) | (Acer) | has created | a consolidated sales and service network | in more than 100 countries |
| (14) | Revenues | reached | US $11.32 billion | in 2006 |

In Text 10, there are altogether 14 messages (ranking clauses). As indicated in the center column, there are 7 relational processes, of which 6 are of the attributive type and the other one is of the identifying type. In addition, 6 of them are of the intensive type, and 1 (realized by "includes") is of the possessive type. The other 7 processes are material ones; 4 of them are concrete actions with clear Actors and Goals, while the other 3 ("achieved", "integrate" and "reached") describe status rather than concrete actions. The great proportion of relational processes and abstract material ones is typical for the description of a phenomenon, which is quite similar to the model in Text 9. The nuclear elements to the left of the center column include Carrier, Actor and Identifier. Of them 8 indicate the company to be described (Acer), five indicate different aspects of Acer, while the remaining one is the Identifier whose Identified is also directly related to Acer. The nuclear elements to the right of the center column include Attribute, Goal, and Identified. The peripheral elements include Duration, Place, Time, Manner, Reason, and Purpose.

The major taxonomy in the text is the features of Acer Group, including its goal (mission), its ranking position, its business model, its multi-brand approach, its service/sales model, its product range, its staff, and its cooperation with partners/suppliers. The items of this taxonomy are distributed throughout the whole text, and account for a major part of the experiential meanings. The item "Acer" has been most frequently mentioned (for 12 times in different forms) and functions as the nuclear elements (Carrier or Actor) for 6 times. In addition, there are some minor taxonomies related to Acer: its brands (including Acer, Gateway, Packard Bell, and eMachines), its range of products (including PC notebooks and Desktops, servers and storage systems, monitors, peripheral devices, digital devices, LCD TVs and e-business solutions), and the target users of its products (including business, Government, Education and home users). The items of the minor taxonomies are much more local, as all the items of each taxonomy are only distributed in one message. Moreover, the customers of Acer have not been directly mentioned, though the target users and "the people" can be considered as potential customers.

When the activity sequence, nuclear relations and taxonomic relations are all taken into consideration, it can be seen that like Text 9, Text 10 is also mainly committed to the description of the various features and aspects of the company concerned (Acer in this case). However, the major focus is on the goal/long-term mission as it functions as a macro-Theme of the two stages of the text (which will be discussed in more detail in the analysis at the genre stratum). Moreover, though the potential customers have been mentioned only for 3 times, since the item "people" is included as a part for its goal and long-term mission, the author of Text 10 is not as self-centered as that of Text 9. Rather, he/she is more oriented to the needs of the people (its potential customers). In addition, while the author of Text 9 focuses on the description of Motorola's leading position in the industry, the author in this text pays more attention to the description of Acer's business models.

Thus, ideationally, compared with the author of Text 9, the author of Text 10 is more customer/partner-oriented and less self-centered, and prefers a more indirect way of promotion by describing Acer's goal and business models rather than by directly emphasizing its leading status in the industry and its technical capacity.

Interpersonally, the inscribed appraisal resources of Text 10 are analyzed in Table 6.5. In addition, there are many resources in the text that can evoke appraisal meanings indirectly, as shown in Table 6.6.

**Table 6.5 Inscribed Appraisal Resources of Text 10**

| Source | Force | Inscribed Appraisal Resources | Trigger/Target | Type Analysis |
|---|---|---|---|---|
| Author | - | effectively integrates | its multi-brand approach | Appreciation-valuation |

Table 6.5 continued

| Source | Force | Inscribed Appraisal Resources | Trigger/Target | Type Analysis |
|---|---|---|---|---|
| | - | Profitable and sustainable | channel business model | Appreciation-valuation |
| Author | - | environmentally friendly | products | Appreciation-valuation |
| Author | - | green | supply chain | Appreciation-valuation |
| Author | - | proud | Acer | Affect-satisfaction-disposition |
| Author | - | renowned | Acer | Judgment-social esteem-normality |
| Author | - | sophisticatedly and intuitively designed, | products | Appreciation-composition-complexity |
| Author | - | easy to use | products | Appreciation-reaction-impact |
| Author | - | consolidated | sales and service network | Appreciation-composition-balance |

**Table 6.6 Evoked Appraisal Resources of Text 10**

| Source | Force | Evoked Appraisal Meanings | Trigger/Target | Type Analysis |
|---|---|---|---|---|
| Author | | Message 1 | Acer | Judgment-social esteem-capacity |
| Author | Inscribed quantification: globally | Message 2 | Acer | Judgment-social esteem-capacity |

Table 6.6 continued

| Source | Force | Evoked Appraisal Meanings | Trigger/Target | Type Analysis |
| --- | --- | --- | --- | --- |
| Author | Inscribed quantification worldwide (markets) | Messages 3 and 4 | Acer's business model and multi-brand approach | Appreciation-valuation |
| Author | | Message 5 | Acer | Judgment-social sanction-propriety |
| Author | worldwide | Message 6 | Acer | Judgment-social esteem-capacity |
| Author | Inscribed quantification: worldwide | Messages 7 and 8 | The Acer group | Judgment-social esteem-capacity |
| Author | | Message 9 | Acer | Judgment-social esteem-tenacity; Judgment-social sanction-propriety |
| Author | | Message 10 | Acer | Judgment-social esteem-capacity |
| Author | | Message 11 | Acer's product range | Appreciation-composition-complexity |
| Author | Inscribed quantification: enumeration of products, throughout the world, in more than 100 countries | Messages 11, 12, 13 and 14 | Acer | Judgment-social esteem-capacity |

It can be seen from the analysis that the deployment of the appraisal meanings in Text 10 shows the following features. First, like Text 9, the whole text is a monogloss. This means that all the ideational and interpersonal meanings are voices of the author. Moreover, the description of the company is presented in the form of bare assertions, which makes it look impartial and factual. In this way, the author manipulates the description and covers the promotional intention.

Second, there are a few graduation resources in Text 10. Most of them are of the quantification type, specifying the extent ("worldwide") of the processes concerned. There are no intensification resources. As a whole, the description of Acer is expressed in a relatively mild tone rather than in an exaggerative way. Such a tone is harmonious with the author's effort to establish Acer's identity as a world-renowned IT company in a relatively impartial way. This is also similar to Text 9.

Third, the author employs many inscribed appraisal resources to promote the company. Unlike Text 9 where the company (Motorola) functions as the trigger/target in most cases, in Text 10, most of the triggers/targets of the inscribed appraisal resources are factors involved in the commercial operation of Acer. As a result, while judgment accounts for the major part of the appraisal meanings in Text 9, in Text 10, the major type of appraisal meanings is appreciation. The affect to the company (Acer) is inscribed only once in the text. Thus, the author of Text 10 focuses on the positive appreciation of the products, multi-brand approach, business model, supply chain and service/sales network of Acer rather than the direct judgment of Acer's behavior. In other words, while the author of Text 9 promotes Motorola by directly judging Motorola's performance, the author of Text 10, promotes Acer in a more indirect way, mainly by positively evaluating the products, services and business models of the company.

Fourth, like Text 9, Text 10 also has many resources that can evoke appraisal meanings. In fact, almost all the messages in the text can evoke specific appraisal meanings that are different from the inscribed ones. Interestingly, while the inscribed resources of the text mainly express appreciation meanings as described above, the evoked appraisal meanings are mainly positive judgment of the company, particularly the judgment of the social esteem (capacity) of Acer. The targets of the invoked appreciation meanings are its products and business modes, which is consistent with the inscribed appreciation resources. In addition, unlike Text 9 which lacks appraisal meanings about social sanction, the propriety of Acer's performance is also evoked, mainly by the description of its green products and supply chain and the description of its people-oriented long-term mission.

In summary, interpersonally, the author of Text 10 promotes the company mainly in two ways, by explicitly appreciating Acer's business modes (including its products, multi-brand approach, business model, supply chain and service/sails network), and by implicitly evaluating the propriety of the performance of Acer. In Text 9, on the other hand, the author promotes Motorola mainly by evaluating the performance (especially the capacity) of Motorola both explicitly and implicitly. While Text 9 construes Motorola more as a promising person of high status, with powerful capacity and full of creative spirit, Acer in this text is described as a capable and responsible company with well-designed business modes.

As far as the author's identity is concerned, the author of Text 9 is construed as a monogloss but mild promoter in a seemingly impartial tone, promoting the company by both explicitly and implicitly highlighting its capacity and high status but with little attention to its morality. Compared with the author of Text 9, the author of Text 10 is a much more roundabout promoter, promoting the company mainly by positively evaluating Acer's business modes and other related aspects, and by indirectly evaluating the company through evoking resources.

Like Text 9, Text 10 is also serially organized. There is neither macro-Theme or macro-New in the whole text, and the different stages of the text are simply added one after another without any periodical hierarchy. Within Stage 1, Message (1) can be considered as the hyper-Theme of the whole stage, but there is no hyper-New at the end of the stage. Moreover, the messages in the text are mainly organized through implicit internal additive conjunction relations, with one message added to another. Like Text 9, this serial organization is conducive to the real-time variation of the contents of the text according to the change of market situations. It helps establish the identity of the author as an offhand promoter that has improvised the promotional contents, rather than as a well-prepared promoter that has carefully designed the contents and the organization of the text.

#### 6.1.1.3 Individuation in Cisco Profile Text

The individuation at the discourse semantic stratum in Cisco profile text will be analyzed in this section, in comparison with Texts 9 and 10 when appropriate. It is shown in Text 11 below, titled "Cisco Overview". The messages are also numbered for convenience of analysis.

Text 11 Cisco Overview

(1) At Cisco (NASDAQ: CSCO) customers come first and (2) an integral part of our DNA is creating long-lasting customer partnerships and working with them to identify their needs and provide solutions that support their success. (3) The concept of solutions being driven to address specific customer challenges has been with Cisco since its inception. (4) Husband and wife Len Bosack and Sandy Lerner, both working for Stanford University, wanted to email each other from their respective offices located in different buildings but (5) were unable to due to technological shortcomings. (6) A technology had to be invented to deal with disparate local area protocols; (7) and as a result of solving their challenge-the multi-protocol router was born. (8) Since then Cisco has shaped the future of the Internet by creating unprecedented value and opportunity for our customers, employees, investors and ecosystem partners (9) and has become the worldwide leader in networking-transforming how people connect, communicate and collaborate.

Please view Cisco's Corporate Overview Presentation for more information.

( http://newsroom. cisco. com/dlls/corpinfo/corporate _ overview. html, accessed on April 15, 2010)

The ideational resources of Text 11 are analyzed in Table 6.7.

**Table 6.7 Ideational Resources of Text 11**

| Message | Nuclear | Center | Nuclear | Peripheral |
| --- | --- | --- | --- | --- |
| (1) | customers | come | first | At Cisco (NASDAQ: CSCO) |
| (2) | an integral part of our DNA | is | creating long-lasting customer partnerships and working with them | to identify their needs and provide solutions that support their success |
| (3) | The concept of solutions being driven to address specific customer challenges | has been | with Cisco | since its inception |
| (4) | Husband and wife Len Bosack and Sandy Lerner, both working for Stanford University | wanted | to email each other from their respective offices located in different buildings | |
| (5) | | were | unable to | due to technological shortcomings |
| (6) | A technology | had to be invented | | to deal with disparate local area protocols |
| (7) | the multi-protocol router | was | born | as a result of solving their challenge |
| (8) | Cisco | has shaped | the future of the Internet | since then; by creating unprecedented value and opportunity for our customers, employees, investors and ecosystem partners |

Table 6.7 continued

| Message | Nuclear | Center | Nuclear | Peripheral |
|---|---|---|---|---|
| (9) | (Cisco) | has become | the worldwide leader | in networking; transforming how people connect, communicate and collaborate |

It can be seen that there are 9 messages (ranking clauses) in Text 11, of which 5 are relational processes, 3 material ones, and 1 mental process. Among the relational processes, 4 are of the attributive type, and 1 of the identifying type. In addition, 1 relational process is circumstantial, while the other four are intensive ones; there is no possessive relation process. The three material processes are concrete ones with specific goals. In addition, based on the tense of the process verbs, the processes can be group into two activity sequences, with those in past tense describing the founding of Cisco Systems, while those in present tense describing the current features and status of Cisco.

The nuclear elements to the left of the center column include Carrier, Senser, Goal, and Actor, while those to the right include Attribute, Phenomenon, and Goal. The peripheral elements include Location (Place), Purpose, Duration, Reason, Manner, and Accompaniment.

There is one major taxonomy, i. e. the loose taxonomy of customer-related matters, including such items as customer partnership, customer needs, customers' success, and customer challenges. The items are distributed throughout the whole text and are critical to its organization. Another minor taxonomy is Cisco community, including its customers, employees, investors and ecosystem partners. This taxonomy is local, distributed only in one message.

The analysis of activity sequence, nuclear relations and taxonomic relations shows that Text 11 is much less self-centered compared with the previous two texts. Though it is also a description of the company concerned (Cisco Systems in this case), the whole text is much more committed to the description of the customers and other members of the Cisco community than Texts 9 and 10. In fact, experientially, it seems that Text 11 is intended to describe Cisco as a customer servant. Considering that the author is most probably a representative of Cisco Systems, he/she is the least self-centered but most customer/partner-oriented compared with the authors of Texts 9 and 10.

In addition, as a large part of the processes is committed to the account of the founding and development of Cisco rather than a simple description of its current state, Text 11 has many features of historical account infused into the descriptive report genre (cf. Martin & Rose 2008: 114-117). Thus, the author is established as a promoter in the guise of a story teller, while those of the previous two texts are simply promoters.

The inscribed appraisal resources of Text 11 are analyzed in Table 6.8. In addition, there are some resources that can evoke appraisal meanings, as shown in Table 6.9.

**Table 6.8 Inscribed Appraisal Resources of Text 11**

| Source | Force | Inscribed Appraisal Resources | Trigger/Target | Type Analysis |
|---|---|---|---|---|
| Author | | comes first | customers | Appreciation-valuation |
| Author | | long-lasting | customer partnerships | Appreciation-valuation |
| Author | Infused intensification: high force | unprecedented | value and opportunity | Appreciation-valuation |
| Author | | worldwide leader | Cisco | Judgment-social esteem-capacity |

**Table 6.9 Evoked Appraisal Resources of Text 11**

| Source | Force | Evoked Appraisal Meanings | Trigger/Target | Type Analysis |
|---|---|---|---|---|
| Author | Inscribed quantification in Message 2: since its inception | Messages 1 – 7 | Customers | Appreciation-valuation |
| Author | | Messages 2 (provide solutions that support their success) | Cisco | Judgment-social esteem-capacity |
| Author | | Message 7 | Cisco | Judgment-social esteem-capacity |
| Author | | Message 8 (shaped the future of the Internet by creating unprecedented value and opportunity) | Cisco | Judgment-social esteem-capacity |
| Author | | Message 8 (for customers, employees, investors and ecosystem partners) | Customers, employees, investors and ecosystem partners Cisco | Appreciation-valuation Judgment-social sanction-propriety |
| Author | | Message 9 (transforming how people connect, communicate and collaborate) | Cisco | Judgment-social sanction-propriety; Judgment-social esteem-capacity |

According to the analysis of the appraisal resources, it can be seen that interpersonally Text 11 show the following characteristics. First, like Texts 9 and 10, all the meanings are derived from the author in a monogloss way, and the descriptions are presented in the form of bare assertions. The monogloss and bare assertions enable the author to promote the Cisco in a seemingly detached way and to hide the promotional intention.

Second, except a case of infused intensification and a phrase of quantification of extent, there are little graduation resources, which means that the appraisal meanings are expressed in a moderate rather than an exaggerative way. Like Texts 9 and 10, the author of Text 11 is also a relatively moderate rather than sensational promoter.

Third, compared with the previous Texts 9 and 10, Text 11 has much less inscribed appraisal resources. Among the four pieces of inscribed appraisal resources, only one is a judgment of the company concerned (Cisco in this case), two are appreciations of the valuation of customers, and the remaining one is an appreciation whose target is also related to Cisco's customers. The greater proportion of customers as triggers/targets indicates that the author focuses on the evaluation of Cisco's customers rather than the company itself. Naturally, as the customers appraised are Cisco's, the appraisal of customers also serves indirectly the evaluation of Cisco itself (which will be discussed in more detail below). But this is a much roundabout way.

Fourth, while Text 11 employs few inscribed appraisal resources, it has resources that can evoke specific evaluation meanings. The invoked evaluation meanings fall into two types: the evoked judgment of Cisco, including its capacity and propriety, and the invoked appreciation of the valuation of Cisco's customers and other members of Cisco-related community. It should be noted that the judgment of Cisco in Text 11 is mainly achieved indirectly through evoked appraisal resources. Moreover, the great importance attached to Cisco's customers also helps evoke the positive judgment of the propriety of

Cisco's behavior, and thus describing Cisco as a moral, customer-centered company.

In summary, the author of Text 11 is also a moderate promoter in a seemingly impartial tone. But he/she promotes Cisco mainly by evaluating the valuation of its customers through both inscribed and evoked resources. Judgment of Cisco is only made indirectly through evoked appraisal resources, and with focus on its propriety (morality) and capacity. Thus, the author of Text 11 is the most roundabout compared with the authors of Texts 9 and 10.

Textually, Messages 1 and 2 of Text 11 can be considered as a hyper-Theme, presenting the overall information that is to be developed in the following messages. However, as there is no hyper-New at the end of the text, the text as a whole is serially rather than hierarchically organized.

The individual messages of Text 11 are not as loosely strung as those of Texts 9 and 10. This is indicated by the conjunction resources (as shown in Table 6. 10 on p. 237), which are different from the previous two texts. While Texts 9 and 10 are mainly organized through internal conjunction relations, in Text 11, external conjunctions play a more important role in the organization of the text than internal ones. Specifically, Messages 3-9 are organized through external successive conjunctions as indicated by the use of circumstances of time ("since its inception", "since then", etc.) and other implicit resources. Internal conjunctions only exist between Messages 1 and 2, and between Messages 8 and 9. Moreover, while addition and rework are the major types of conjunctions in the previous two texts, the author of Text 11 employs a variety of conjunction types such as concessive means, consequence, cause, purpose, and succession in addition to rework and addition for the organization of the messages. The use of a variety of external successive conjunctions as the major organization resources of Text 11 is conditioned by the author's purpose, i. e. to promote Cisco's customer-centered principle of operation through a brief account of its development. As a result, while the authors of Texts 9 and 10 seem to be off-hand and prefer loosely strung serial organization, the author of Text 11 is much better prepared.

**Table 6.10 Conjunction Resources of Text 11**

| Internal Conjunction | Message | External Conjunction |
|---|---|---|
| | Stage 1 | |
| | (1) | |
| Additive to 1 | (2) | |
| | Stage 2 (Phase 1) | |
| Reworked (elaborated by) 4-9 | (3) Hyper-theme | |
| | (4) | |
| | (5) | Means (concessive) to (4) |
| | (6) | Causal: expect to (4) and (5) |
| | (7) | Consequence to (6) |
| | Phase 2 | Successive to Phase 1 |
| | (8) | |
| Additive to (8) | (9) | |

### 6.1.2 Individuation at the Register and Genre Strata

In Section 6.1.1, the different individuations of the authors in the three texts are analyzed at the discourse semantic stratum. However, according to Martin (2010a), every stratum of the realization hierarchy individuates. This means that individuation will also appear at the register and genre strata. As the discourse semantics is the realization of register and genre, individuation at the discourse semantic stratum is also conditioned by the individuation at the register and genre strata and ultimately conditioned by the individuation of the specific goals and general purpose of each author. In this section, the individuation at the register and genre stratum as shown in Texts 9, 10 and 11 will be analyzed.

### 6.1.2.1 Individuation at the Register Stratum

In order to better show the different individuations at the register stratum, the register patterning of the three texts are analyzed in Table 6.11 in a comparative way, focusing on the minute difference in the configurations of register variables.

**Table 6.11 Field Configurations of the Profile Texts**

| | Activity Sequence/Taxonomy | Degree of sharing | Degree of Specialization | Nature of Socialization |
|---|---|---|---|---|
| Text 9 | Most promoter-centered and least customer-oriented: focusing on the description of Motorola's leadership position, accomplishment, and technical strength | low | Medium | Institutionalized |
| Text 10 | Middle degree of promoter-centeredness, focusing on the description of Acer's barrier-breaking goal, and its business model and technical strength | low | Medium | Institutionalized |
| Text 11 | Least promoter-centered, and most customer-oriented: focusing on the critical importance of customers in Cisco's operation since its inception to present | low | Medium | Institutionalized |

As far as the authors' configuration of field is concerned, their choices of field as shown in the three texts are similar in three aspects:

low degree of sharing between the author (the promoter) and readers (potential customers/partners/investors), middle degree of specialization, and institutionalized field. However, the specific activity sequences are different. Specifically, in Text 9, the author/promoter focuses on the description of the company concerned (Motorola in this case), particularly its leadership position, accomplishments and technical strength, but with little attention to the customers. In Text 10, the author's focus is on the company's (Acer's) goal/mission for breaking the barrier between the technology and people, and the business models and technical strength for achieving such a goal. Thus, the author is not so self-centered, but more oriented to the needs of the customers. The author of Text 11 is more concerned with the critical role of the customers' needs in Cisco's development and operation, and is therefore least self-centered but most customer-oriented.

The choices of tenor by the three authors are shown in Table 6.12 (on p. 240). All three authors have chosen the same type of social relation: promoter-(potential) customer/partner. This is conditioned by the general purpose of all three texts, that is, to promote the respective company concerned to the potential customers/partners. As for the social status, in three texts, the relation between the promoter and the customer is basically equal. However, the author of Text 9 attaches more importance to the promoter (which is a representative of the Company promoted) as the text is promoter-centered, while the customers receive much less attention. Customers of Text 10 have obtained a higher status as they are treated as an integral part of Acer's goal. In Text 11, customers are given the highest status as customer demand is described as the basic momentum for the development of the company, while the company is described as playing a role for serving the customers. The affect (attitude, realized by appraisal resources) is inscribed most explicitly by the author of Text 9, less inscribed by the author of Text 10, and least inscribed by the author of Text 11.

Contact in the three texts is basically the same, with low degree of involvement.

**Table 6.12 Tenor Configurations of the Profile Texts**

| | Social Relation | Status | Contact | Affect/Attitude |
|---|---|---|---|---|
| Text 9 | Motorola's promoter-Motorola's customer/partner | Basically equal, more importance attached to promoter, and least importance to customer | Uninvolved | Explicitly inscribed, and also evoked |
| Text 10 | Acer's promoter-Acer's potential customer/partner | Basically equal, less promoter-centered but more customer-oriented | Uninvolved | Less inscribed, more evoked |
| Text 11 | Cisco's promoter-Cisco's customer/partner | Basically equal, most importance attached to customers | Uninvolved | Least inscribed affect |

The authors' configuration of mode are analyzed in Table 6.13 (on p. 241). As shown in Table 6.13, the mode configurations by the three authors are similar in many aspects, that is, all the promotions are carried out through visual contact, with language as the only modality, in a form of publicly addressed monologue, and with high degree of consciousness. However, though language is assigned a constitutive role by all three authors, minute difference is shown in the specific ways of the organization. While the authors of Texts 9 and 10 have structured the two texts semiotically and serially throughout, the author of Text 11 has organized the text in a more well-designed way. Particularly, though Text 11 as a whole is still semiotically structured, Stage 2 is organized temporally and the degree of serial organization is lower than the previous two texts. This difference in mode is conditioned by the goal configuration at the genre stratum.

**Table 6.13 Mode Configurations of the Profile Texts**

| | Aural/ Visual Contact | Modality | Monologue/Dialogue | Action/Reflection |
|---|---|---|---|---|
| Text 9 | Visual | Language | Monologue: publicly addressed, reply less likely; visually solidified, with high degree of consciousness | Reflection; semiotically structured, serially organized throughout the text |
| Text 10 | Visual | Language | Monologue: publicly addressed, reply less likely, with high degree of consciousness | Reflection; semiotically structured and serially developed throughout the text |
| Text 11 | Visual | Language | Monologue: publicly addressed, reply less likely, with high degree of consciousness | Reflection; semiotically structured as a whole, but temporally structured in the account part; lower degree of serial organization |

### 6.1.2.2 Individuation at the Genre Stratum

The individuation at the genre stratum is conditioned by the unique purpose and configuration of goals by the individual genre user, and will be reflected in the unique staging and phasing in the realization of the generic structure. In order to study the respective individuation of the authors of the three texts, the teleological structure of each text is analyzed first, followed by the analysis of the unique staging and phasing, as shown in Table 6.14.

**Table 6.14 Individuation of the Profile Texts at the Genre Stratum**

| | Text 5 | Text 6 | Text 7 |
|---|---|---|---|
| Purpose | to promote Motorola by describing its profile | to promote Acer by describing its profile | to promote Cisco by describing its profile |
| Goal 1 | Classifying the phenomenon to be described as Motorola | Classifying the phenomenon to be described as Acer | Classifying the phenomenon to be described as Cisco |
| Goal 2 | Describing Motorola | Describing Acer | Describing Cisco |
| Stage 1 | Introducing Motorola | Introducing Acer | Introducing Cisco |
| Stage 2 | Describing Motorola: Phase 1: Motorola's leadership position and accomplishments Phase 2: Motorola's mission Phase 3: Motorola's history/future/momentum | Describing Acer: Phase 1: Acer's achievement of the barrier-breaking goal Phase; Phase 2: Acer's long-term mission; Phase 3: Acer's product range | Describing Cisco: Phase 1: Customer's importance in Cisco's operation Phase 2: Customer's role in Cisco's development (realized in an account) |

It can be seen that the individuations of the three authors at the genre stratum are similar in many aspects. As all the authors have employed the descriptive report genre, the basic teleological structure and generic structure are similar: they all intend to promote a company by describing its profile, and concretize this general purpose into two specific goals, which are realized by a two-stage generic structure (introduction/classification ^ description). A major difference lies in the specific companies that the authors select to describe, which are Motorola, Acer and Cisco respectively. The different choices of the target companies in the teleological and generic structures by the author indicate their respective identity: the author of Text 9 is a promoter of Motorola, that of Text 10 Acer's promoter, and that of Text 11 Cisco's promoter.

In addition, the three authors have adopted different ways of phasing at the description stage. Specifically, the author of Text 9 promotes Motorola by describing its leading position/accomplishments, its mission and its history/future/momentum, the author of Text 11 promotes Acer by describing its achievement of its goal, its long-term mission and product range, while the author of Text 11 promotes Cisco by describing the customers' importance in its operation and their role in its development. The different choices of phasing are conditioned by the specific considerations of the authors. In other words, the author of each text has selected the aspects that they think are most important for and conducive to the general purpose of company promotion.

## 6.2 Affiliation—Another Side of Individuation

Affiliation is the reverse process of individuation. They are two sides of the same phenomenon. In a sense it can be said that while the dimension of individuation focuses on the difference between the identities of different genre users, affiliation focuses on their commonalities and the ways through which the individual persona are affiliated into persona types, master identities and finally into a cultural community (cf. Section 3.8). In order to better show the affiliation process as shown by the three authors in Texts 9, 10 and 11, the differences and commonalities of the individual identities of the three authors are summarized in Tables 6.15 and 6.16 respectively (on p. 244 & 245).

As shown in Tables 6.15 and 6.16, during the individuation process, each author has shown their individual identities at the discourse semantics, register and genre strata. When they are compared with one another, it can be seen that each author has shown his/her unique identity that is different from the other two.

**Table 6.15 Different Identities of the Authors of the Profile Texts**

| | Author of Text 9 | Author of Text 10 | Author of Text 11 |
|---|---|---|---|
| Discourse Semantic Stratum | (1) Ideationally, a self-centered and straightfoward promoter (centering on Motorola), focusing the high status and the technical strength of Motorola, with little consideration to the customers (2) Interpersonally, promoting the company by both explicitly and implicitly highlighting its capacity and high status of the company but with little attention to its morality; (3) Textually, more like an offhand promoter that has improvised and loosely organized the promotional contents | (1) ideationally more customer/partner-oriented and less self-centered, more roundabout, promoting Acer indirectly by describing Acer's goal and business models (2) Interpersonally, more roundabout, promoting Acer mainly by positively evaluating Acer's business modes and other related aspects, and indirectly judging the company through evoking resources (3) Textually, more like an offhand promoter that has improvised and loosely organized the promotional contents | (1) Ideationally, least self-centered but most customer/partner-oriented, promoting Acer by describing the significant role of its customers in its operation and development (2) Interpersonally most roundabout, promoting Cisco mainly by appreciating the valuation of its customers both explicitly and implicitly, with only implicit judgment of Cisco (3) Better prepared, organizing the text in a better designed manner |
| Register Stratum | Company-oriented/elevating promoter, | Customer-company balanced promoter | Customer-oriented/elevating promoter |
| Genre Stratum | Motorola's promoter through the use of descriptive report genre | Acer's promoter through the use of descriptive report genre | Cisco's promoter through the use of descriptive genre, with an embedded historical account genre. |

**Table 6.16 Commonalities of the Three Authors**

| | | | |
|---|---|---|---|
| Discourse Semantic Stratum | Ideationally, as a promoter representing the different aspects of the target company | Interpersonally, as a monogloss promoter in a relatively mild and seemingly objective/factual tone, without resort to personal affect | Textually, a promoter preferring a serial rather than hierarchical organization |
| Register Stratum | A promoter representing an unshared and non-specialized field | A promoter of basically equal status and low degree of involvement with the customer | A monologuizing promoter addressing to the public in language, with high degree of consciousness |
| Genre Stratum | Promoter of a company through the use of a descriptive report genre | | |

However, there are also many commonalities among the three authors. Specifically, at the discourse semantics genre, all authors are promoters representing the different aspects of the respective target company, controlling the communication through the use of monogloss, promoting the target company in a mild and seemingly impartial tone without resort to personal affect, and preferring loosely strung serial structure. At the register stratum, all have selected an unshared and non-specialized field, are basically equal with the customer and uninvolved, and are monologuizing to the public with high degree of consciousness. At the genre stratum, each of the authors is a promoter of a specific company through the use of a descriptive report genre.

In addition, the authors of Texts 9 and 10 share some characteristics that are different from the author of Text 11. Textually, authors of Texts 9 and 10 are more like an offhand promoter that has improvised and loosely organized the promotional contents, while the author of Text 11 seems better prepared. At the genre stratum, the authors of Texts 9 and 10 only employ the descriptive report genre, while the author of Text 11 employs an embedded historical account genre in addition to the descriptive report genre. The commonalities between the authors of Texts 9 and 10 help group them into a smaller personality type, while the commonalities among all three authors further group all three into a larger personality type. In fact, the authors of all profile texts and other promotional texts in the corpus of this study also share the commonalities at the strata of discourse semantics and register as shown in Table 6.16. For example, though their general purpose is to promote the company and its products/service, they all adopt a relatively mild and seemingly impartial/factual tone, which is closer to a technological rather than sensory coding orientation (cf. Kress & van Leeuwen 2006: 163-166). They all prefer serial rather than hierarchical organization and are more like off-hand rather than well-prepared promoters. In addition, the ubiquitous use of homepage and content-page genres (cf. Section 6.2) shows that they are website-based promoters. The common characteristics shared by all the promoters of the companies in the corpus thus constitute the master identity of the sub-culture of the high-tech IT industry, which, together with other master identities, constitute the general culture of a society.

The affiliation/individuation process as shown in this study is illustrated in Figure 6.1 (on p. 247). In the figure, the top-down dimension illustrates the individuation process as shown by the three texts, whereas the bottom-up dimension illustrates the affiliation process. Each of the authors' identities is realized by the unique ways of meaning making, whereas the commonalities shared by one or more authors establish a personality type. The Personas A, B, and C represent the identities (personalities) of the authors of Texts 9, 10 and 11 respectively. As Personas A and B share some characteristics, these commonalities establish a sub-personality type, while the commonalities among the three authors establish a more general personality type. The commonalities (e.g. the technological coding orientation) among the personas of authors of other websites in the corpus will establish other personality types, while the commonalities among all the personas of the high-tech industry companies will constitute a master identity. Finally, all the coding orientations of a society/community will constitute the culture of the society. Along the individuation dimension, the different ways of meaning making help classify the system/culture of the western society step by step and recognize the individual master identities, personality types and personas.

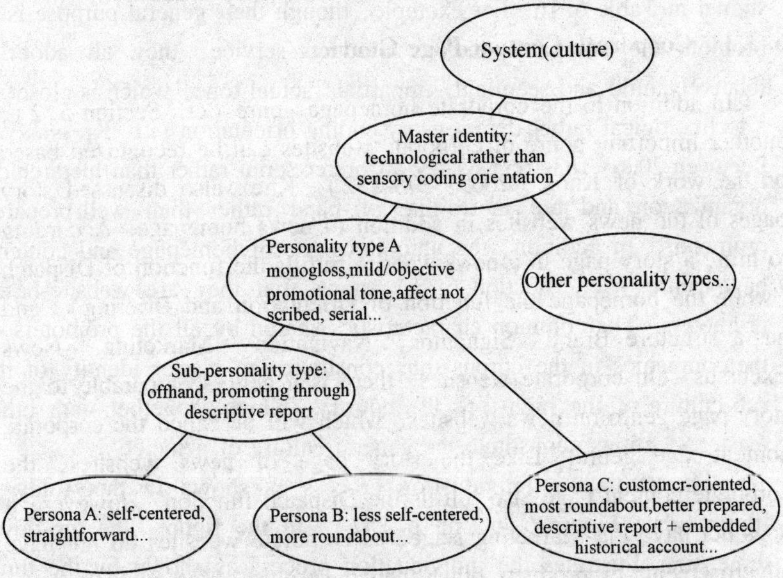


**Figure 6.1 Individuation/Affiliation of the Company Profile Texts**

## 6.3 A Note on Macro-Genres

In previous chapters, five genres on corporate websites have been identified and discussed: the operating procedure genre, the descriptive report genre, the compositional report genre, the news story genre, and the corporate homepage genre. There are naturally many other genres employed on corporate websites. The five genres are selected for detailed study in this book only because they are among the most common ones and are sufficient to the purpose of this study. The genres, however, are not randomly distributed on the websites, but have to be combined organically into macro-genres and work together to help promote the corresponding companies, their products and services. In this section, the complexing of the individual genres into macro-genres will be explored by studying the "about" or "company information" section of the corporate websites. Before proceeding to the study, however, another genre need be briefly introduced.

### 6.3.1 Corporate Content-Page Genre

In addition to the corporate homepage genre (cf. Section 5.2), another important genre of corporate websites can be recognized based on the work of Knox (2009: 179-182). Knox also discussed story pages of the news websites in addition to news homepage. According to him, a story page in a news website fulfills the function of Dispatch (while the homepage the function of Orientation and Briefing), and has a structure Brand ^ Signature ^ Navigation ^ Marketing ^ News Excursus. On corporate websites, there is a genre comparable to the story page genre on news websites, which will be called the corporate content-page genre. Like the story page of news websites, the corporate content page also fulfills the Dispatch function. However, it does not have the Marketing stage, as corporate websites do not have advertisements of products other than their own. Moreover, it has a Content Dispatch stage rather than News Excursus. The teleological structure of the content-page genre can be analyzed as follows:

Purpose: to dispatch the specific promotional contents to the website readers, which is concretized into:

Goal 1: to establish the identity of the corporation

Goal 2: to navigate the readers beyond the current page to other pages or sections of the website

Goal 3: to dispatch the specific promotional contents of the current page

Goal 4: to signify the ownership of the contents of the website

Realized by the schematic structure: Identity ^ Navigation ^ Content Dispatch ^ Signature.

Like the corporate homepage genre, neither the numbering of the goals nor the use of the carets "^" indicates the sequencing of the stages. Rather, the goals and the corresponding stages are connected through their internal logical ordering. This means that the same stage may be realized by resources distributed all over the content page wherever appropriate. Moreover, the Content Dispatch stage is always realized by another genre such as a descriptive report, a compositional report, a news story or any other applicable genre, or by a macro-genre consisting of these genres.

Text 12 is an instance of the corporate content-page genre. In this text, while the Identity, Navigation, Content Dispatch, and Signature are clearly shown, the Content Dispatch stage is realized by an embedded descriptive report genre. With the content-page genre established, genre complexing on corporate promotional websites will be explored in the following section.

Text 12　Philanthropy of Sony Corporation of America

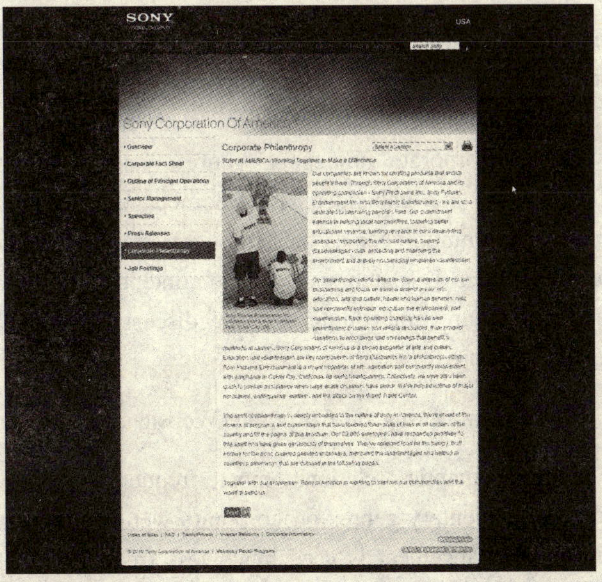


(http://www.sony.com/SCA/philanthropy.shtml, accessed on April 20, 2010)

### 6.3.2 Macro-genres on Corporate Websites

Macro-genres are texts or hypertexts that combine several elementary genres through genre complexing or genre embedding. Genre complexing can be achieved through the employment of either expansion or project relations. Expansion includes three subtypes: elaboration, extension, and enhancement, while projection includes locution and idea (cf. Section 3.5.1). Corporate websites (in fact websites of any kind) are hypertexts with underlying macro-genres. The elementary genres integrated in the macro-genre include, first and foremost, the corporate homepage (including sub-homepage) genre and the content-page genre, and also a variety of other genres as long as they are applicable. As far as the corpus in this study is concerned, the most common genres other than the homepage and content-page ones include the descriptive report genre, the compositional report genre, the news story genre, and the operating procedure genre among others.

Generally speaking, the skeleton of a corporate website is established by the employment of the corporate homepage genre (note that homepages and sub-homepages are the same in nature as both are instances of the corporate homepage genre) and the content-page genre. Other genres are embedded in the homepage genre and content-page genre, functioning either as the Highlights stage of the homepage genre, or the Content Dispatch stage of the content-page genre. Genre complexing and genre embedding will be discussed in detail in the following two sections.

#### 6.3.2.1 Genre Complexing on Corporate Websites

The logico-semantic relations most frequently employed for connecting the elementary genres on corporate websites are elaboration and extension. Enhancement is used much less frequently, while idea and locution are rarely employed. Specifically, a homepage genre is connected with a sub-homepage genre through elaboration, because a sub-homepage always elaborates a part of the contents that is presented as a section on the homepage. For example, Text 13 is Siemens's homepage, while Text 14 (on p. 252) is its "About us" sub-homepage. The sub-homepage elaborates the "about us" item in the homepage, providing more detailed information. In addition, as the situation requires, a sub-homepage may be further elaborated by one or more sub-subhomepages. For example, the "about us" sub-homepage in Text 14 is further elaborated by the "business" sub-homepage as shown in Text 16 (on p. 253), because Text 16 provides more details on the "business" item in the Navigation stage of Text 14. Theoretically, the number of recursive use of homepage/sub-homepage genres through elaboration is unlimited. Practically, however, it is quite limited, and generally will be no more than 5 or 6 times. Such restriction may be partly attributed to the consideration of the availability of information.

Text 13 Siemens' Homepage

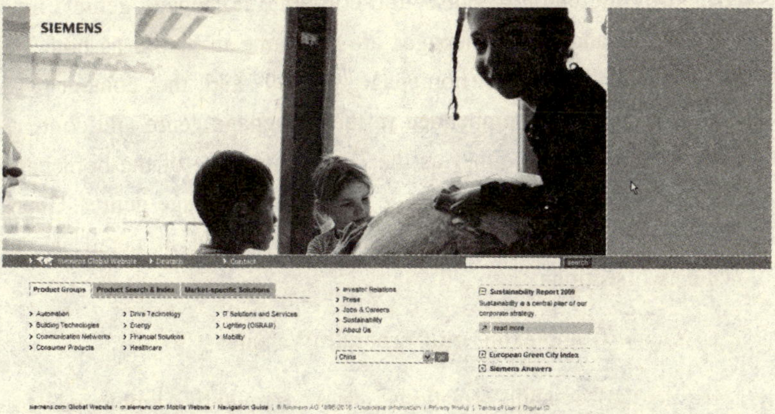


(http://www. siemens. com/entry/cc/en/, accessed on April 20, 2010)

Text 14 Siemens Home_ About us

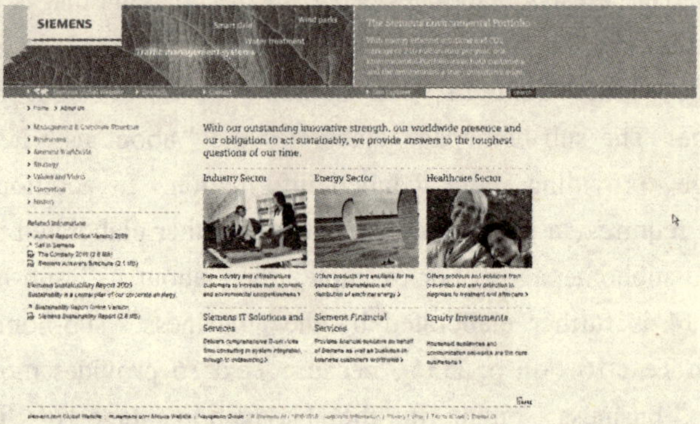


(http://www. siemens. com/about/en/, accessed on April 20, 2010)

Any homepage/sub-homepage genre needs to be elaborated by at least one content page genre. For example, Text 15 elaborates Text 14, because it provides detailed information concerning the "our values and vision" item on the sub-homepage. Likewise, Text 17 (on p. 253) and other content-pages concerning the "energy sector" and "healthcare sector" elaborate the corresponding parts of Text 16.

Text 15 Siemens Home_ About us_ Values and Vision

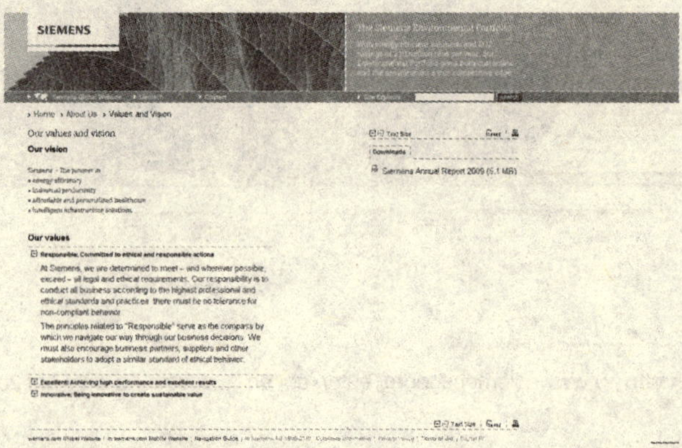


(http://www. siemens. com/about/en/index/values. htm, accessed on April 20, 2010)

Text 16 Siemens Home_ About us_ Business

( http://www. siemens. com/about/en/businesses/index. htm, accessed on April 20, 2010)

Text 17 Siemens Home_ About Us_ Business_ Industry Sector

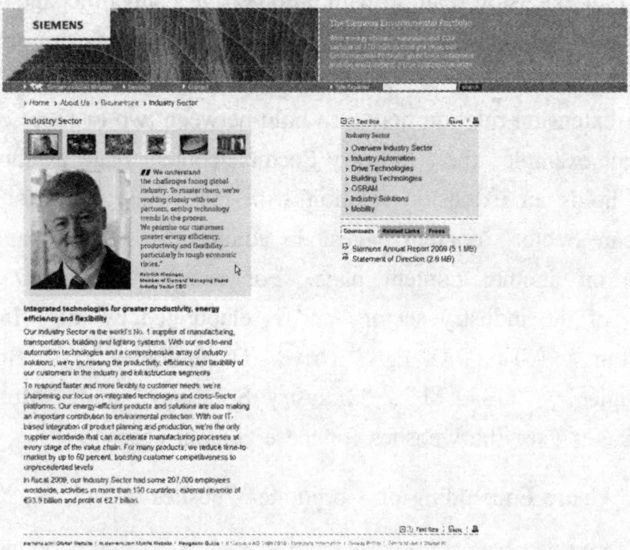


( http://www. siemens. com/about/en/businesses/industry. php, accessed on April 20, 2010)

In addition to elaboration, extension also plays an important role for genre complexing on corporate websites. Extension is widely used to complex any two or more genres that have parallel status on the website. For example, the "About Us" sub-homepage holds an extension relation with any of the "investor relations", "press", "jobs & careers", and "sustainability" sub-homepages, as it has a similar status on the whole website (which is clearly indicated by the equal status of the corresponding navigation items on the homepage as shown in Text 13).

Likewise, the "Values and Vision" content page in Text 15 (there is no sub-homepage for this part on Siemens's website) also holds an extension relation with the "Business" sub-homepage as shown in Text 16, and with any of the "Management & Corporate Structure", "Siemens Worldwide", "Strategy", "Innovation" and "History" sub-homepages. It should be noted that a content page genre may hold an extension relation with a homepage (subhomepage) genre in addition to the more common elaboration relation, as this example indicates.

The extension relation may also hold between two or more content pages. For example, the "Industry Sector" content page as shown in Text 17 holds an extension relation with the "Energy Sector" and "Healthcare Sector" content pages. In addition, a content page may elaborate on another content page. For example, Text 17 is an overview of the industry sector, and is elaborated by the "Industry Automation" (Text 18), "Drive Technologies", "Building Technologies", "OSRAM", "Industry Solutions" and "Mobility" content pages (see the websites for these content pages).

#### 6.3.2.2 Genre Embedding on Corporate Websites

In addition to genre complexing through expansion relation, another important way for creating macro-genres on corporate websites (in fact on any kind of websites) is genre embedding. Genre embedding is an essential way for the realization of a content page. As discussed at the beginning of Section 6. 3. 1, the homepage genre and the content-page genre work together to establish the basic framework of a website. However, a skeleton is obviously not enough. In order to present the specific contents of each webpage, a basic way is to embed a genre in the homepage and make it function either as the Highlights stage (or a part of the Highlights stage), or embed a specific genre in the content-page genre and make it function as the Content Dispatch stage (or a part of the Content Dispatch stage). Theoretically, any genre can be embedded, though practically the embedding is conditioned by the purpose of the super-ordinate genre and the general purpose of the website. Moreover, theoretically the number of recursive use of embedding is unlimited; but practically, on corporate websites, it generally will be no more than 2 or 3 times.

In a content-page genre, a wide variety of genres can be embedded. In the corpus of this study, the most frequently embedded is the descriptive report genre. For example, in Text 15, the Content Dispatch stage is realized by a descriptive report that describes the values and vision of Siemens. In Text 17, it is a descriptive report that presents an overview of Siemens' industry sector. The same stage in Text 18 (on p. 256) is a descriptive report describing the industry automation of Siemens. The frequent embedding of this genre is conditioned by the general purpose of the "About Us" part of a corporate website, i. e. to describe different aspects of the company concerned the customers and partners.

Text 18 Siemens Home_ About Us_ Business_ Industry Sector_ Industry Automation

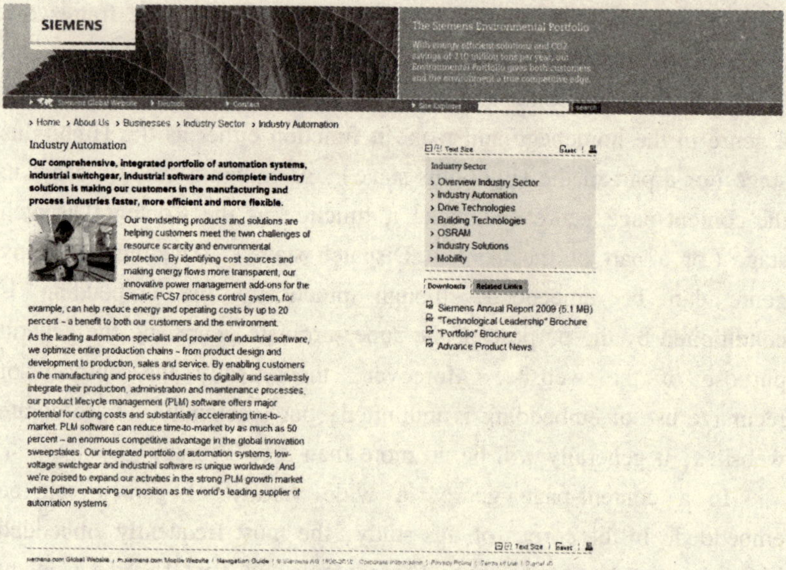


(http://www.siemens.com/about/en/businesses/industry/industry_automation.htm, accessed on April 20, 2010)

Another genre that is frequently embedded in a content-page genre is the compositional report genre (cf. Section 5.4). It is often employed in webpages that describe the governance/management of the company concerned. For example, in Text 19 (on p. 257), the Content Dispatch stage is realized by a compositional report describing the composition of Siemens' managing board (the members are indicated by pictures and described in more detail through words). Interestingly, at each phase of the composition stage of the genre, a resume genre is embedded. This recursive use of genre embedding makes the text rather complicated.

Text 19 Siemens Home_ About Us_ Management & Corporate Structure_ Managing Board

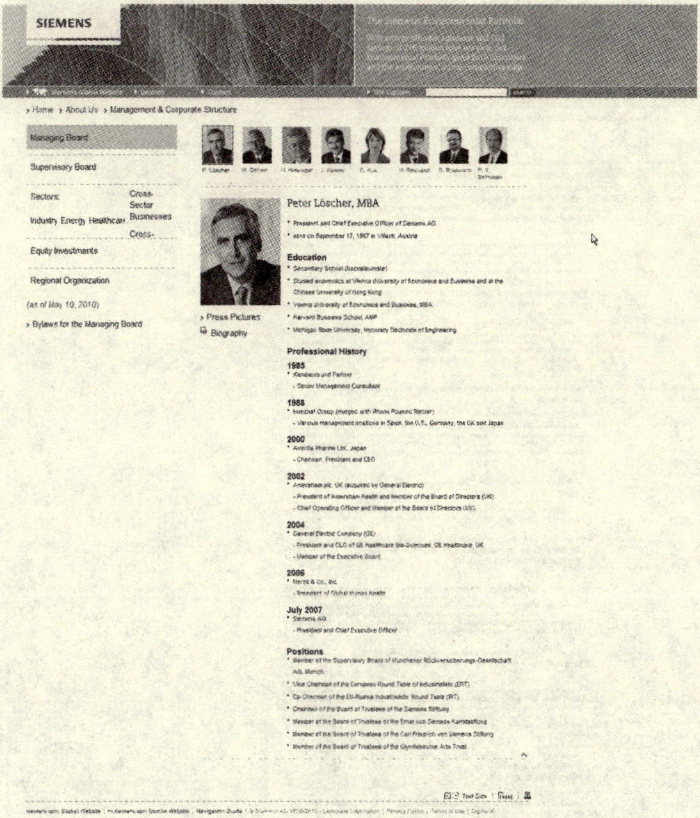


( http://www. siemens. com/about/en/management-structure. htm, accessed on April 20, 2010)

News story genre is also often embedded in the content-page genre in the press/company news section of a corporate website. For example, in Text 20 (on p. 258), the Content Dispatch stage is realized by a macro-genre that consists of a series of news story genres. The relation among the news story genres is extension.

Text 20 Siemens Home_ Press_ Press Release

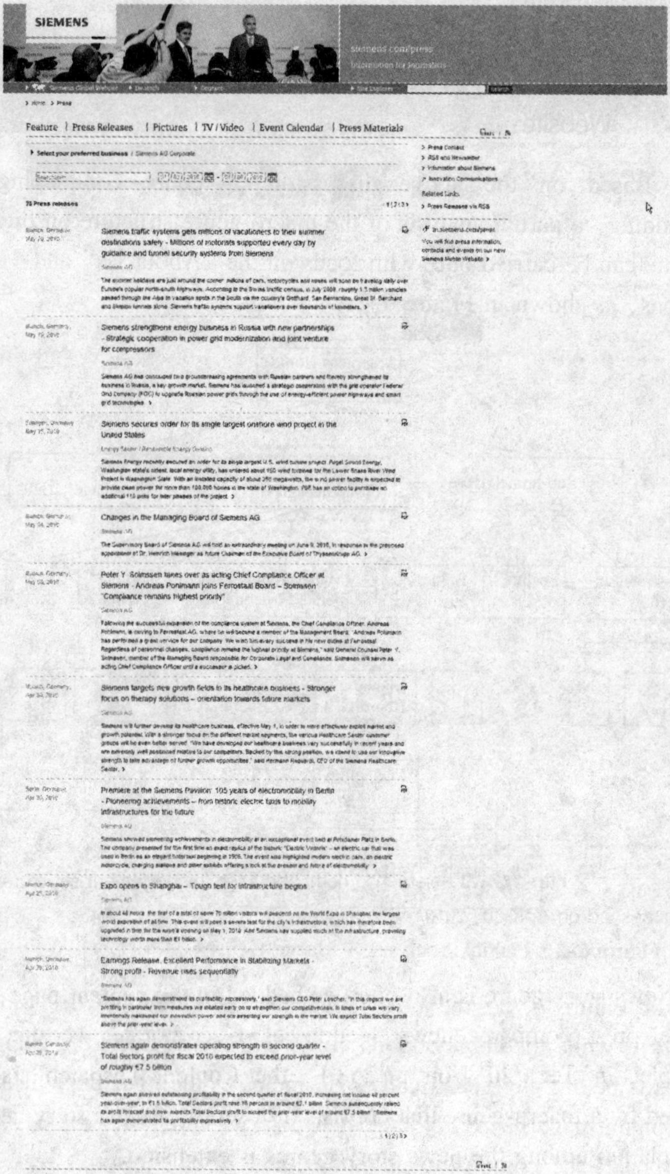

(http://www. siemens. com/press/en/pressrelease/index. php, accessed on April 20, 2010)

#### 6.3.2.3 Partial Analysis of the Macro-Genre Structure on Siemens' Website

Based on the above discussion of genre complexing and embedding, a partial analysis of the macro-genre structure on Siemens' website can be carried out, with focus on the "About Us" and "Press" sections, as shown in Figure 6.2.

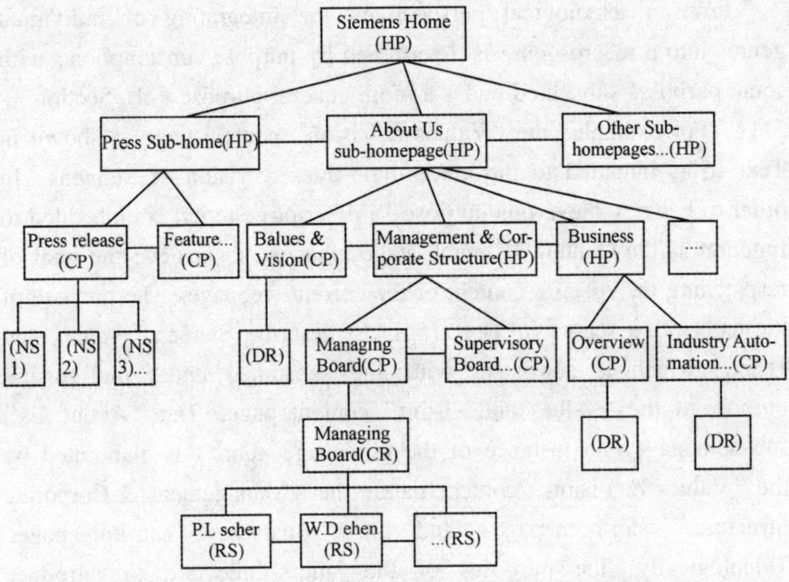


**Figure 6.2 Partial Analysis of Macro-Genres on Siemens Website**

In Figure 6.2, the boxes indicate the names of the webpages (texts), while the abbreviations in the brackets indicate the genres that the texts belong to. Specifically, HP indicates the homepage genre, CP the content-page genre, NS the news story genre, DR the descriptive report, CR the compositional report, and RS the resume genre. The oblique lines connecting the boxes indicate the relation of elaboration, with the upper-level box elaborated by the lower-level one. The horizontal lines indicate the relation of extension, while the vertical lines the relation of embedding, with the genre in the lower-level box embedded in the genre of the upper-level box. The square brackets indicate a macro-genre consisting of several other genres. Based on the analysis in Figure 6. 2, it can be seen that the whole website of Siemens is a macro-genre consisting of a series of lower-level macro-genres created by integrating individual genres (instances of individual genres) through elaboration, extension, and embedding.

From a teleological perspective, the integrating of individual genres into a macro-genre is determined by purpose subsumption, with some purposes subsumed under a more general purpose (cf. Section 3. 5.1). For example, the "Values & Vision" content-page as shown in Text 15 is intended to introduce the values & vision of Siemens. In order to better achieve this purpose, a descriptive report is embedded to function as the Content Dispatch stage, that is, to achieve the goal of dispatching the specific content of the current webpage. The purpose of the descriptive report in Text 15 is to describe Siemens' values and vision, which is consistent with and subsumed under the general purpose of the "values and vision" content page. The "About Us" sub-homepage (an instance of the homepage genre) is elaborated by the "Values & Vision" content page, the "Management & Corporate Structure" sub-homepage, and the "Business" sub-homepage. Teleologically, the purposes of the latter three are to introduce Siemens' values and vision, its management and corporate structure, its business, and so on. These are all subsumed under the more general purpose of the "About Us" sub-homepage, i. e. to introduce Siemens' company information. Likewise, the purposes of "Press", "About Us" and other sub-homepages are to present Siemens' press-related information, company-related information, and other relevant information, which are in turn subsumed under the general purpose of promoting Siemens.

## 6.4 Summary

This chapter explores the individuation and complexing of corporate website genres. The individuation process is illustrated by the analysis of three corporate profile texts: Motorola profile text, Acer "about us" text and Cisco overview text. For each text, the meaning making resources at the strata of discourse semantics, register, and genre are analyzed in a comparative way, and are explained as strategies for each author to achieve his underlying purpose. The commonalities and differences among the authors' purposive choices of meaning-making resources are recognized, and treated as showing the commonalities and differences in the authors' personalities. As a result, the personality/persona of each author (and each individual in general) is pinned on his unique way of purposive choice of semiotic resources. From the perspective of affiliation, the shared ways of meaning making among the individual authors help them affiliate into different personality types. The shared characteristics of the personalities together establish a master identity of the high-tech IT industry as defined by the technological rather than sensory coding orientation. This master identity and other master identities together constitute the culture of the whole society.

Genre complexing on corporate websites is based on two backbone genres (the homepage genre and the content-page genre) and other "application" genres such as descriptive reports, compositional reports, news stories, operative procedures, resumes, etc. The basic logico-semantic relations among the genres include elaboration, extension and embedding. Specifically, a homepage (an instance of the homepage genre) may be elaborated by sub-homepages, which may be further elaborated by content pages (instances of the content page genre). A sub-homepage may be extended by other sub-homepages or content pages at the same level of the website, while a content page may also be extended by other homepages at the same level. The application genres are embedded into the homepage genre or content page genre, functioning either as the Highlights stage or Content Dispatch stage (or a part of the corresponding stage). In addition to elementary application genres, macro-genres may also be embedded. The creation of macro-genres from elementary genres on corporate websites through genre complexing and embedding is conditioned by the purpose of the website designer to promote the companies and their products. From a teleological perspective, the designer subsumes the individual purpose of the elementary genres into the most general purpose of promotion, and achieves this supreme purpose by dividing it into specific individual purposes of the elementary genres.

# Chapter 7

# Conclusion

In this study, a telos-oriented model of genre analysis is developed and applied to a case study of corporate website genres. In this chapter, the major findings of the study will be summarized, the significance of the research will be examined, and the limitations of the study and suggestions for future work will be presented.

## 7.1 Summary of the Findings

Through the teleological study of genre in the previous chapters, an integrated model of genre analysis is established based on an integration of the theories of teleology, sociology and SFL. Such a model is telos-oriented and the genre analysis based on this model is teleologically conditioned. The interpretation of the model leads to the following findings, which are respectively concerned with the necessity of a teleological perspective, the telos-oriented genre system, telos-oriented genre structure, inter-genre relation, genre operationalization, analytic tools and the application procedures.

1. The necessity of a teleological perspective: A teleological perspective to genre is entailed by the teleological nature of genre. Genre is first and foremost a social process, or social action. As a human action, genre is teleological, because a human action as the realization of activities is driven by a motive/object and directed toward a conscious purpose, which is in turn realized by specific operations subordinate to specific conditions. It is social because the activity of

each individual depends on his place in society and the appearance of goal-directed actions in activity is a result of the transition of man to social life. In other words, a genre is a typification of telos-oriented human social actions, and is both medium and outcome of the recursive social practices. As a type of routinized social actions, a genre can be identified on the basis of its unique purpose. Genre as a typification of social actions presupposes a semiotic perspective as typification is based on semiotic interpretation.

2. The telos-oriented genre system: The critical role of telos in genre identification leads to the establishment of a telos-oriented genre system. Three basic teleological units can be identified: purpose, goal and end. An abstract purpose can only be pursued through its concretization into specific goals. Goals are in turn pursued through more specific ends that hold both a "means-to" and a "parts-of" relation with the goals. Several purposes can be subsumed under a more general purpose until the supreme purpose is reached. Purpose is the unconditioned meanings of our actions, while ends and goals constitute the unique individuality of our actions. Each of the three units can form complexes based on appropriate logico-semantic relations.

Three structural units of genre are established in relation to the teleological orders. Specifically, purpose is the aim of a genre, goals are the aims of the different stages of a genre, and ends are the aims of the messages. Messages are realized in language by ranking clauses (each of which can function as an independent rank unit), which are in turn realized by one or more clauses at the lexicogrammatical stratum. Since the macro-structure of a text (a genre instance) is generated at the genre stratum, the structural units of genre analysis are also the basic units for text analysis.

With a slight adaptation of Smith's classification of ends into physical, mental and interpersonal types, two basic aspects in the configuration of ends, goals and purposes can be recognized:

representational aspect ( including both physical and mental aspects) and the interactional aspect. In addition, an organizational aspect can be added, which organizes the representational and interactional aspects during their realization process. The three aspects form a trinity in a purpose, a goal, or an end, and are realized respectively by field, tenor, and mode at the register stratum and by the ideational, interpersonal and textual metafunctions at the discourse semantic stratum.

Based on the teleological structure of social actions, a teleological genre system is established, which includes two subsystems: simplex and complex. The simplex subsystem includes two conjunctive features, goal configuration and goal complex. Goal configuration is a process through which the representational, interpersonal and organizational aspects are configured into a specific goal; its recursion leads to the configuration of two or more goals. Goal complexing is a process whereby the multiple goals are organized into a specific genre based on the conjunctive selection of two types of relations: temporal/spatial/semiotic and serial/orbital. It may also be recursive. The complex subsystem describes the resources employed to organize two or more genres into a genre complex (a macro-genre) based on the teleological ordering of purpose subsumption. The complexing may be carried out either through logico-semantic expansion or projection, and may also recur.

This tentative genre system is capable of capturing the underlying principle for the derivation of generic structure, the principle for macro-genre generation, and the principle of genre agnation. Its feasibility is approved by its application to the study of corporate website genres.

3. Genre structure: Genre staging (structure) is the result of the realization of the telos-oriented simplex subsystem, and may be explained teleologically by the concretization of a general and abstract purpose into several specific goals. The specific content of a stage is

the result of the specific goal configuration, including an organic integration of the representational, interactional and organizational aspects of the goal, while the relation among the different stages is determined by the choice of the relation between the different goals during the goal complexing process. The generic structure (schematic structure) of a specific genre is then the result of the realization of the goal configuration and goal complexing subsystems. The generic structure reflects the order of the stages, which is realized by specific sequences during the instantiation process. The derivation of the generic structure and its ordering and sequencing are shown in the analysis of the teleological and generic structures of the elementary genres on corporate websites, while the difference between ordering and sequencing is most clearly shown in the analysis of the distribution of the Navigation and other stages of the homepage genre.

In addition, as each stage is the result of a specific goal configuration process, the specific goal configuration of one stage will be necessarily different from that of another. The register configuration as a realization of the goal configuration process will correspondingly vary from stage to stage. This text dynamics is illustrated by the stage-based register analysis of the sample texts in the three application chapters.

4. Inter-genre relation: Two types of inter-genre relations are teleologically discussed: genre complexing and genre agnation. A macro-genre (genre complex) is generated through the process of genre complexing. Teleologically, it is realized by a process where two or more purposes are subsumed under a more general purpose. Several elementary genres may be complexed either through expansion (including elaboration, extension, and enhancement) or through projection (including idea and locution). In addition, one elementary genre may also be embedded into another, functioning as a stage of the superordinate genre. Genre complexing and embedding are the basic ways for generating hyper-texts. On corporate websites, promotional

macro-genres are organized mainly through extension and elaboration. Enhancement, locution and idea may also be employed, but much less frequently. In addition, embedding is also fundamental to the organization of website hyper-texts. Specifically, the homepage (including sub-homepages) and content page genres constitute the framework of the whole website, within each of which another genre or macro-genre is embedded to display the unique content of that page. The macro-genres created through complexing and embedding on the websites all serve the purpose of promotion. In other words, the general purposes of the elementary genres are subsumed under the websites' supreme purpose of promotion.

Genre agnation can be explored along two dimensions: typology and topology. Teleologically, the criteria for genre typology should be based on the differences and similarities between the general purposes of different genres. Each feature of the goal configuration and goal complexing subsystems can function as a criterion for sub-classifying a genre family. As a result, genre typology focuses on the different values of the same system feature realized in different genres. On the other hand, genre topology is the result of the sharing of feature values in the genre system among several genres. The degree of feature sharing determines the degree of similarity and difference among the genres. This is conditioned by the number of shared features of two genres, and by the adjacency of the values of the shared features realized in different genres.

5. Genre operationalization: The abstract purpose of a genre need be pursued through a specific operationalization process, which can be explored along three dimensions: realization, instantiation and individuation.

Genre realization deals with the way that resources at lower strata are employed to achieve the telos of a genre. Teleologically, the general purpose of genre is concretized into specific goals. The specific configurations of the representational, interactional and organizational aspects of the goals condition (probablistically predict) the configurations of the field, tenor, and mode values of the corresponding stages, which in turn condition the ideational, interpersonal, and textual meanings of the stages at the discourse semantic stratum. The goal complexing process conditions the patterning of the register configurations at the different stages, which in turn conditions the patterning of the resources at the discourse semantic stratum. This probablistic predictability is bidirectional. In addition, as a redundancy relation exists between the configurations of the three teleological aspects at the same genre stratum, the configuration of any one of the teleological aspect also conditions the configurations of the other two, and thus exerts influence on the configuration of the corresponding register variables. Genre realization is applied to the study of four genres: the operating procedure genre, the descriptive report genre, the compositional report genre and the news story genre. The detailed analysis of resources at the genre, register, and discourse semantics strata shows the metaredundancy relation between the three strata and the teleological nature of the realization process (i. e. the configurations of semiotic resources at all strata ultimately serve the pursuit of the general purpose of each genre).

Genre instantiation deals with the pursuit of a specific purpose of a genre by deploying specific instances of semiotic resources. Every stratum along the realization hierarchy instantiates. Genre instantiation can be explored along two basic dimensions: coupling and commitment, both of which are conditioned by the general purpose of a specific genre. Commitment is concerned with the amount of meaning potential activated in a particular process of instantiation, i. e. the relative semantic weight of a text. Conditioned by the purpose of the genre, choices must be made for optional systems at each stratum, and after the choice is made, a specific delicacy of the meaning resources within the selected system should be determined. Coupling deals with the way in which meanings combine, and constrains the possible combinations in order for the meaning potential of the culture to be manifested in a specific act of communication. Couplings can be inter-stratum, cross-metafunction, inter-modality or inter-system. The different ways of coupling as allowed by the culture are conditioned in a specific text instance by the general purpose of the genre and the individualized purpose of the user. Genre instantiation is applied to the study of the descriptive report genre and the corporate homepage genre. The comparative study of IBM citizenship text and Dell responsibility text shows that the unique ways of coupling and commitment at all the three strata help instantiate the same descriptive report genre into the respective texts. In each case, the instantiation at all the strata are conditioned by the specific purposes for describing IBM citizenship and Dell responsibility respectively. Likewise, the unique ways of coupling and commitment, conditioned by the purposes to provide orientations to Cisco and Lenovo customers respectively, also instantiate the homepage genre into Cisco and Lenovo homepage texts correspondingly.

Genre individuation is concerned with the achievement of the specific purpose of a genre by a user through the employment of user-specific semiotic resources. It can be explored along two trajectories: individuation and affiliation, which are two aspects of the same phenomenon. Individuation in the narrow sense is concerned with the pursuit of the unique purpose of the user by employing user-specific resources that show his unique identity among a genre community, while affiliation is concerned with the negotiation of the specific purposes of different users into a general purpose of a genre community. Every stratum of the realization hierarchy individuates. At the genre stratum, the user will have his unique purpose and unique way of goal configurations in addition to the collective aspect of the purpose and goal configurations, which will result in variation in the generic structure. At the register stratum, the user will make register configurations appropriate for the realization of his individualized teleological and generic structures of the genre. In order to realize the unique register configuration, the user will in turn configure the ideational, interpersonal and textual resources at the discourse semantic stratum in a unique way. Considered in relation to instantiation, the unique ways of coupling and commitment of a specific user at all levels of a semiotic establishes the user's unique identity and serves his purpose, while the shared ways of coupling and commitment at each strata of a semiotic generalizes persona into personality types, further into different master identities and finally into a culture system. The individuation dimension is applied to the comparative analysis of three corporate overview texts of Motorola, Acer and Cisco, which belong to the descriptive report genre. Each author of the texts individualizes their own purpose in consistence with the general purpose of the genre, and employs resources at each stratum as strategies to pursue this purpose. In this process, each author uniquifies his identity through his unique ways of coding, and also negotiates his personal identity with the identities of the other two authors into personality types by showing similarities in their coding orientations at various degrees, and then negotiates with other authors of the corporate websites into a master identity of the IT industry and finally into a culture.

6. Analytic tools and application procedures: The specific telos-conditioned genre operationalization process preconditions semiotic resources at the register and discourse semantic strata, which are adopted as tools for the analysis of specific genres. A register is a configuration of field, tenor and mode variables. Field refers to the sets of potential activity sequences oriented to some global institutional purpose. It can be analyzed along several dimensions: the degree of sharing among members of a culture, the degree of specialization, the nature of socialization, and the type of knowledge structure. Tenor is the negotiation of social relationships among participants, and can be analyzed along the dimensions of social status, social contact and affect. Mode refers to the role of a modality in realizing social action, and can be analyzed along the dimensions of monologue/dialogue and

action/reflection. Semiotic resources at the discourse semantic stratum are grouped into several systems. The appraisal, involvement and negotiation systems deal with interpersonal meanings, the ideation system and the external part of the conjunction system deal with ideational meanings, while the internal part of the conjunction system, the identification system and the periodicity system deal with textual meanings.

The analysis of a specific genre should be carried out along the dimensions of realization, instantiation, and individuation simultaneously, though the focus can be on any one of them. It can proceed either in the top-down or bottom-up order along the stratification hierarchy of a semiotic based on the principle of metaredundancy. The basic method is to work out the semiotic configurations at one stratum based on that of the adjacent stratum. Such an analysis should be telos-oriented, with the pursuit of the general purpose of the specific genre as the key factor conditioning the semiotic configuration at each stratum. Likewise, the analysis of a macro-genre should also be telos-oriented, and should work out the basic logico-semantic relations that help organize the elementary genres into a unity and help pursue the most general purpose of the macro-genre.

## 7.2 Significance of the Research

The establishment of a telos-oriented model of genre analysis paves a new way for the development of both genre theory and genre analysis. Specifically, the significance of the research is shown in the following aspects:

First, the definition of genre as typification of telos-oriented social actions makes it possible to introduce a teleological perspective to genre, and thus bringing a new approach to genre study. The definition also makes it possible to integrate theories of teleology and sociology with the genre theories of SFL. In the research, Smith's teleological theory, Russian activity theory, Giddens's structuration theory, Schutz

& Luckmann's typification theory, Bakhtin's theory of addressivity, and Bernstein's theory of sociology are integrated with SFL's theory of connotative and denotative semiotics to develop a new model of genre analysis. The diversity of theoretical sources helps improve the theoretical soundness of the new model, and also paves the way for genre study in the future.

Second, a telos-oriented model of genre is a social semiotic theory of genre. Genres are purpose-oriented social actions, while all meaning-making actions are social actions. As a result, the model is applicable not only to the study of genres realized by language, but also to genres realized by other modalities and multimodalities, as is partly illustrated by the study of website homepage and content-page genres. This will be conducive to the development of social semiotics in general.

Third, the development of a telos-oriented genre system provides a paradigmatic perspective to the genre theory. Most of the genre work in SFL focuses on the discussion of generic or schematic structure, with little attention to the system side of the phenomenon. This is inconsistent with SFL's principle of priority of system over structure. The research provides an approach to the study of the systemic side of genre, from which generic structure can be derived. This will be conducive to the development of the genre theory in SFL.

Fourth, genre has been explored along three dimensions of semantic variation simultaneously: realization, instantiation, and individuation. Genre realization has been discussed before in SFL, but is more explicitly illustrated with specific texts in this study. As the exploration of instantiation and individuation is still at the infant stage, the study of genre instantiation and individuation in close relation to genre realization provides new insights for the study of genre and the study of instantiation and individuation in general.

Fifth, the research provides an appliable approach to the study of text structure. It is generally accepted that a text is not simply a combination of sentences or clauses. It has its inherent structure that is different from the grammatical structure of sentences. However, the exact nature of text structure is still not clear. In this study, three macro-structure units are suggested: genre, stage, and message. When a genre is instantiated into a specific text, these structural units are actually the basic semantic structural units of the text (note that since a text is an instance of the corresponding genre, the text structure is also an instance of the corresponding generic structure). In addition, as message is considered as realized by ranking clauses, it bridges the gap between textual units and grammatical units.

Finally, tools for genre analysis are provided at the register and discourse semantic strata in addition to the genre strata. The methods and specific procedures for the application of the model are specified. This provides readers with specific ways for genre analysis. In addition, the application of the model to the study of corporate website genres provides a new way for the genre-based study of websites and for the study of hyper-texts in general.

## 7.3 Limitations and Suggestions for Future Work

Due to restrictions in both theory and practice, the study has some limitations. Theoretically, the underdevelopment of teleology restricts the available teleological theories that form a part of the base of the current study, and thus inevitably exert negative influence on the establishment of a telos-oriented genre model, while the underdevelopment of linguistic theories (especially theories of text and context) exerts negative influence on the adequacy of the analytic tools and of the specific data analysis. It seems that inspirations can be derived from Russian activity theory, but more work is still required for an in-depth exploration.

Practically, due to the heuristic nature of this study, the operationalization of the telos-oriented model of genre is tested with examples from a small corpus consisting of 16 corporate websites in IT industry rather than proved against large-scale corpora. A quantitative study based on a larger corpus covering more genres is in need to better prove the applicability of such a new model.

# Appendix Data Samples

## 1. Example 1 of the Operating Procedure Genre: Job Search of Lenovo

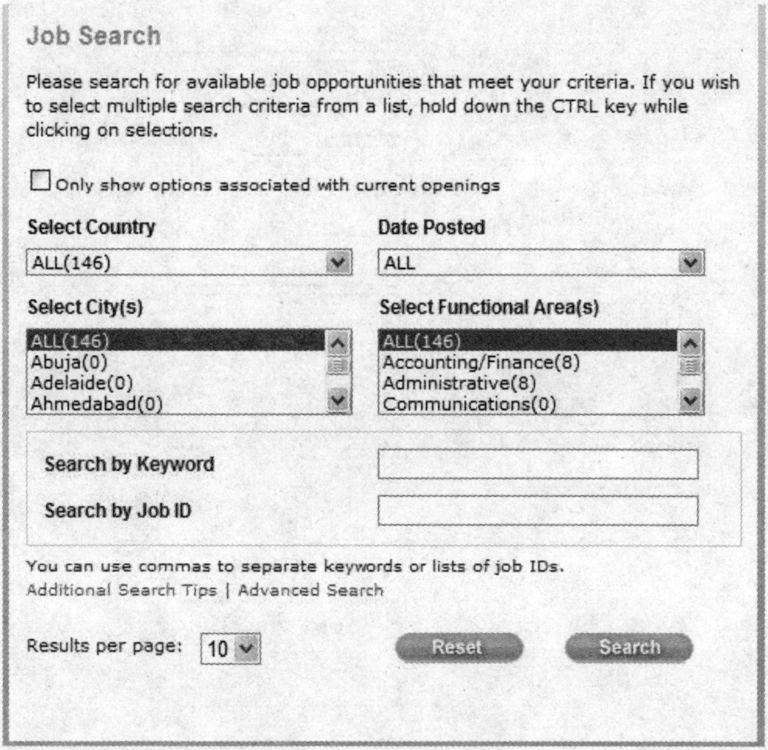


(http://www. lenovocareers. com/JobSearch. aspx, accessed on October 28, 2010)

## 2. Example 2 of the Operating Procedure Genre: Create an Apple ID

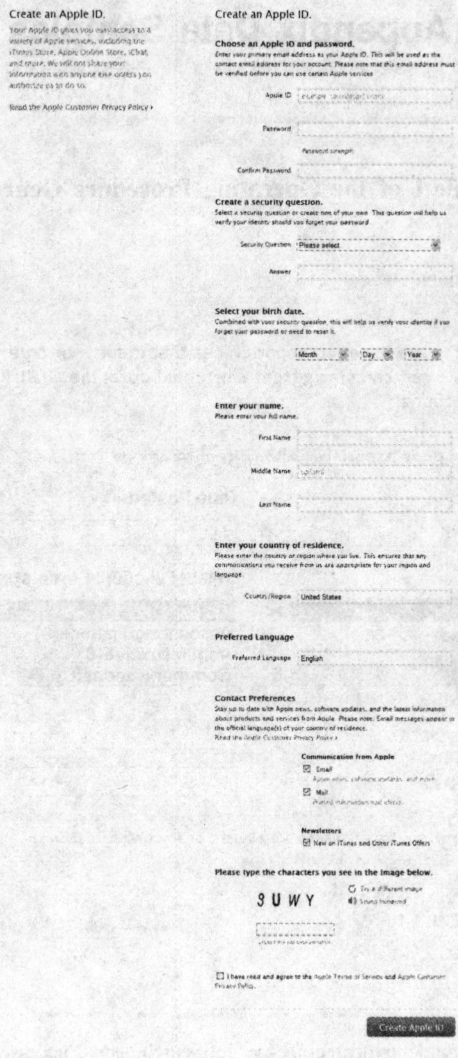


( https://appleid. apple. com/cgi-bin/WebObjects/MyAppleId. woa/wa/createAppleId? createacctype = lite&userid = jobs&localang = en_US&returnURL = http://www. apple. com/jobs/signin/us-corp. html, accessed on October 28, 2010)

### 3. Example 3 of the Operating Procedure Genre: Build a Customer Version of Motolora's Corporate Responsibility Report

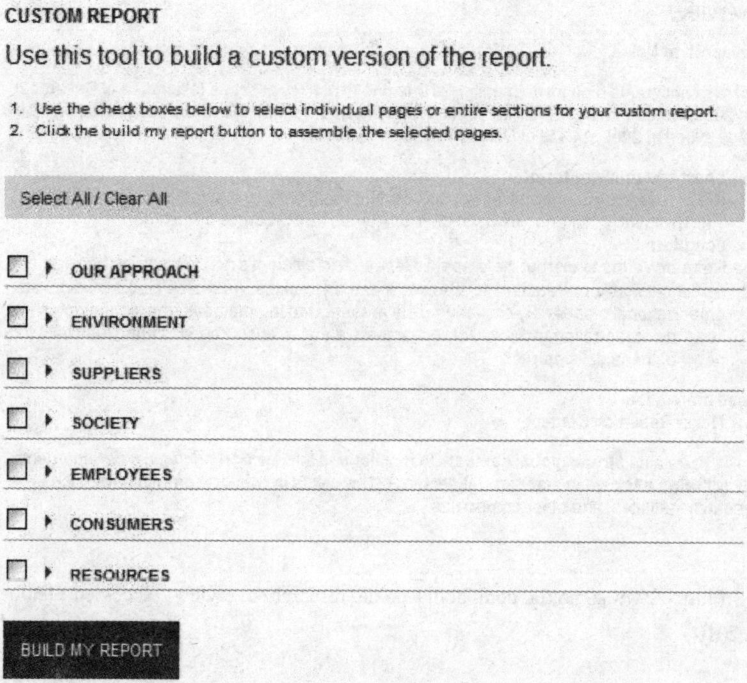

CUSTOM REPORT

Use this tool to build a custom version of the report.

1. Use the check boxes below to select individual pages or entire sections for your custom report.
2. Click the build my report button to assemble the selected pages.

Select All / Clear All

- OUR APPROACH
- ENVIRONMENT
- SUPPLIERS
- SOCIETY
- EMPLOYEES
- CONSUMERS
- RESOURCES

BUILD MY REPORT

(http://responsibility. motorola. com/index. php/custom_report, accessed on October 28, 2010)

## 4. Example 1 of the Descriptive Report Genre: Nokia Research Overview

### Overview

**Research at Nokia**

Nokia's continuous high investment in R&D is one of our key success factors. As of December 31, 2009, we employed 17,196 in research and development with R&D expenses totalling EUR 5.909 billion in 2009, 14.4% of Nokia's net sales in 2009.

- **Short and medium term.**
  Nokia researchers support the product development units to master key technologies and their evolution. This enables us to develop competitive products efficiently.
- **Long-term.**
  Research aims to disrupt the present. Research in different sciences with global participation is a prerequisite for creating these disruptions. Research also serves as an organizational pioneer. By challenging the present working methods and technologies we keep the organization moving. Our researchers are also encouraged to bring forth ideas for new business development.

Read more about
- Nokia Research Center

Nokia maintains **strong global contacts** to monitor and influence technological developments. We actively participate in standardization and R&D projects in cooperation with universities, research institutes, and other companies.

(http://www.nokia.com/about-nokia/research/overview, accessed October 26, 2010)

## 5. Example 2 of the Descriptive Report Genre: Vision 2020 of Samsung

**Vision 2020**

As stated in its new motto, Samsung Electronics' vision for the new decade is, "Inspire the World, Create the Future."

This new vision reflects Samsung Electronics' commitment to inspiring its communities by leveraging Samsung's three key strengths: "New Technology," "Innovative Products," and "Creative Solutions." -- and to promoting new value for Samsung's core networks -- Industry, Partners, and Employees. Through these efforts, Samsung hopes to contribute to a better world and a richer experience for all.

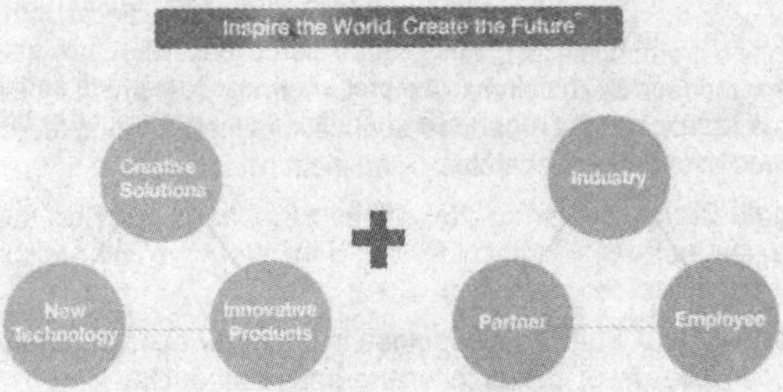


As part of this vision, Samsung has mapped out a specific plan of reaching $400 billion in revenue and becoming one of the world's top five brands by 2020. To this end, Samsung has also established three strategic approaches in its management: "Creativity," "Partnership," and "Talent."

Samsung is excited about the future. As we build on our previous accomplishments, we look forward to exploring new territories, including health, medicine, and biotechnology. Samsung is committed to being a creative leader in new markets and becoming a truly No. 1 business going forward.

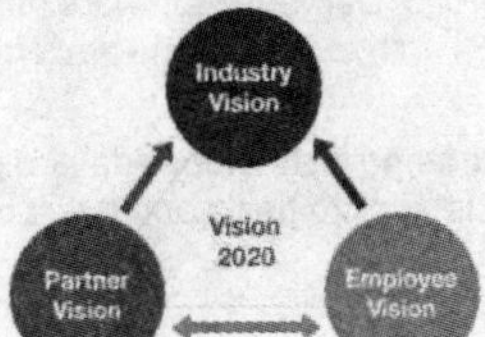


(http://www.samsung.com/us/aboutsamsung/corporateprofile/vision.html, accessed on October 28, 2010)

## 6. Example 1 of the Compositional Report Genre: The Company Organization of Intel

### Company Organization

At the end of 2009, we reorganized our business to better align our major product groups around the core competencies of Intel ® architecture and our manufacturing operations. After the reorganization, we have nine operating segments:

- *PC Client Group.* Delivering a high-quality computing and Internet experience through Intel architecture-based products and platforms, primarily for notebooks, netbooks, and desktops.
- *Data Center Group.* Delivering server, storage, and workstation platforms for small, medium, and large enterprises.
- Embedded and Communications Group. Delivering Intel architecture-based products as solutions for embedded applications through long life-cycle support, software and architectural scalability, and platform integration.
- *Digital Home Group.* Delivering Intel architecture-based products for next-generation consumer electronics devices with interactive Internet content and traditional broadcast programming.
- *Ultra-Mobility Group.* Building a business in the next-generation handheld market segment with low-power Intel architecture-based products.
- *NAND Solutions Group.* Delivering advanced NAND flash memory products for use in a variety of devices.
- *Wind River Software Group.* A wholly owned subsidiary delivering device software optimization products to the embedded and handheld market segments, serving a variety of hardware architectures.
- *Software and Services Group.* Delivering software products and services, in addition to promoting Intel architecture as the platform of choice for software development.
- *Digital Health Group.* Delivering technology-enabled products that are designed to reduce healthcare costs and connect people and information to improve patient care and safety.

(http://www.intc.com/corpInfo.cfm, accessed on October 26, 2010)

## 7. Example 2 of the Compositional Report Genre: The Company Structure of Nokia

### Structure

July 1, 2010

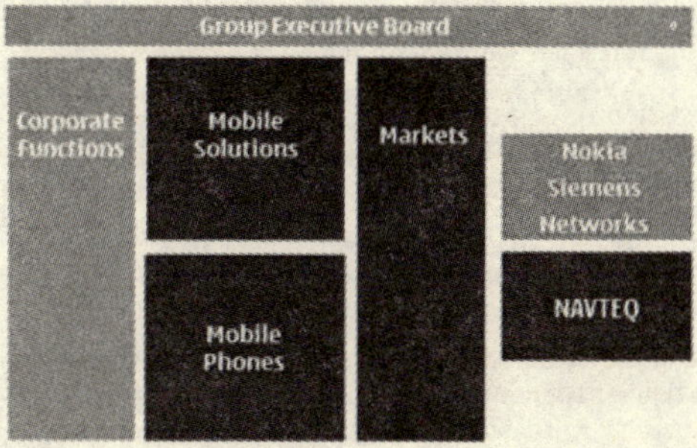


Our organizational structure is designed to position us for a world where the mobile device, the Internet and the computer are fusing together.

***Mobile Solutions*** is responsible for developing and managing our portfolio of smartphones and mobile computers. The team is also busy developing a world-class suite of internet services under the Ovi brand, with a strong focus on maps and navigation, music, messaging and media. ***Mobile Phones*** is responsible for developing and managing our portfolio of affordable mobile phones, as well as a range of services that people can access with them. ***Markets*** manages our supply chains, sales channels, brand and marketing activities, and is responsible for delivering our mobile solutions and mobile phones to the market.

***Nokia Siemens Networks***, jointly owned by Nokia and Siemens, provides wireless and fixed network infrastructure, communications and networks service platforms, as well as professional services to operators and service providers.

***NAVTEQ*** is a leading provider of comprehensive digital map data and related location-based content and services for automotive navigation systems, mobile navigation devices, Internet-based mapping applications, and government and business solutions.

(http://www. nokia. com/about-nokia/company/structure, accessed on October 26, 2010)

## 8. Example 3 of the Compositional Report Genre: Sony's Outline of Principle Operations

**Outline of Principal Operations**

Select a Section

**Sony Corporation of America**

- Howard Stringer, Chairman, Chief Executive Officer and President, Sony Corporation; Chairman and CEO, Sony Corporation of America
- Headquartered in New York, NY
- U.S. subsidiary of Sony Corporation, Japan (Sales for fiscal year ended March 31, 2010: approximately $78 billion)

**Sony Entertainment Inc.**

- Howard Stringer, President
- Robert Wiesenthal, Executive Vice President and Chief Strategy Officer
- The umbrella holding company dedicated to maximizing the value of Sony's entertainment assets, including Sony Pictures Entertainment, Sony Music Entertainment, and the joint venture Sony/ATV Music Publishing

**Sony Network Entertainment**

- Sony Network Entertainment exists to drive vision, strategy and service delivery for network services across the entire Sony Group, with a goal of offering consumers compelling, connected entertainment experiences across a variety of Sony devices.

**Gracenote**

- Gracenote®, a wholly-owned subsidiary of Sony Corporation of America, is a single source provider of advanced media identification, management, discovery and enrichment solutions.

**Sony Card℠**

- Sony Card℠, issued by Capital One® is a versatile credit card that gives consumers numerous opportunities, through everyday purchases, to earn points redeemable for Sony products and services
- The Sony Card has an attractive point structure and enables cardholders to earn rewards fast.

5 points per $1 spent on Sony purchases at Sony stores, Sony.com and Sony authorized retailers
3 points per $1 spent on all restaurants meals and movies, including online movie rentals
1 point per $1 spent on everyday purchases, like groceries and gasoline

- Additionally, Sony Card customers will benefit from PointsPlus, a program exclusive to Sony Rewards members. This program enables customers to earn extra points when they shop at specific retailers, including AMC Theaters, Old Navy, K-mart, Hotels.com, Drugstore.com, GameStop, Best Buy and Sears, among others. The complete list of retailers is available at www.sonyrewards.com.
- For additional information about the Sony Card, visit **www.sonyrewards.com/sonycard** or call 877-717-SONY (7669).

**Sony Plaza Public Arcade & Sony Wonder Technology Lab**

- Operates in Sony's U.S. headquarters at 550 Madison Avenue in New York, NY
- Sony Wonder Technology Lab, Sony Corporation of America's free interactive technology and entertainment museum for all ages, opened May 25, 1994
- The 14,000-square foot facility occupies four floors and is located adjacent to the Sony Plaza Atrium
- The third and fourth floors (redesigned in October 2008) feature 14 interactive exhibits focused on signals processing and transmission, nanotechnology, robotics, virtual surgery, the evolution of devices, animation and HDTV. The third floor also boasts a 72-seat High Definition theater.
- The second floor (redesigned August 2003) features interactive exhibits that allow visitors to design their own video games, create their own movie trailers, and learn to play musical instruments as backup to Sony artists.
- Sony Wonder Technology Lab has welcomed over 3.3 million guests since it opened in 1994.
- For additional information about the Sony Wonder Technology Lab, visit **www.sonywondertechlab.com**.

(http://www.sony.com/SCA/outline/corporation.shtml, accessed on October 26, 2010)

## 9. Example 1 of the News Story Genre: IBM Board Approves Quarterly Cash Dividend

Press room > Press releases >

**IBM Board Approves Quarterly Cash Dividend**

- Press release
- Contact(s) information
- Related XML feeds

**ARMONK, N.Y. - 26 Oct 2010:** The IBM (NYSE: IBM) board of directors today declared a regular quarterly cash dividend of $0.65 per common share, payable December 10, 2010 to stockholders of record November 10, 2010.

With the payment of the December 10 dividend, IBM will have paid consecutive quarterly dividends every year since 1916.

The board today also authorized $10 billion in additional funds for use in the company's stock repurchase program. IBM said it will repurchase shares on the open market or in private transactions from time to time, depending on market conditions.

This amount is in addition to approximately $2.3 billion remaining at the end of September 2010 from a prior authorization. With this new authorization, IBM will have approximately $12.3 billion for its stock repurchase program. IBM expects to request additional share repurchase authorization at the April 2011 board meeting.

Samuel J. Palmisano, IBM chairman, president and chief executive officer said "IBM's higher value, higher margin business strategy has enabled the return of $91 billion since 2003 to our shareholders through share repurchases and dividends. We've done this while investing to bring new products and services to market, and expanding IBM's business into new, emerging markets."

(http://www-03. ibm. com/press/us/en/pressrelease/32868. wss, accessed on October 28, 2010)

## 10. Example 2 of the News Story Genre: Intel's New Specification Simplifies Digital Signage Development

### Intel's New Specification Simplifies Digital Signage Development

Posted by IntelPR Oct 8, 2010

**Taiwan Digital Signage Special Interest Group, Microsoft and NEC Support Spec Addressing Fragmented Market**

**NEWS HIGHLIGHTS**

- Intel's Open Pluggable Specification allows for easier installation, use and maintenance of digital signs.
- Microsoft, NEC and others support Intel's digital signage Open Pluggable Specification.
- The specification will address the fragmented market to make digital signs more intelligent and connected.

---

DIGITAL SIGNAGE EXPO 2010 INDUSTRY FORUM, San Diego, Oct. 8, 2010 – During a keynote today, Intel Corporation announced a specification that will help standardize the design and development of digital signs, a form of communication using digital display screens such as LCD, touch screens or projectors in public venues, and pluggable media players.

The Open Pluggable Specification (OPS) is supported by industry leaders in digital signage, including Microsoft*, NEC Display Solutions* and the Taiwan Digital Signage Special Interest Group*.

"The Open Pluggable Specification was created by Intel to address fragmentation in the digital signage market and simplify device installation, use, maintenance and upgrades," said Jose Avalos, director of retail and digital signage, Embedded and Communications Group, Intel. "With the specification, digital signage manufacturers will be able to deploy interchangeable systems faster and in higher volumes, while lowering costs for development and implementation."

A prototype demonstration design for the OPS was developed based on an Intel® Core™ processor running Microsoft Windows Embedded Standard 7*. The first fanless and compact pluggable solution for digital signage applications, the OPS features Intel® vPro™ Technology with Keyboard-Video-Mouse redirection capabilities that allow an IT administrator to run diagnostic tests, install upgrades and view and control the digital display content remotely.

Installing digital signage equipment based on Intel® architecture, such as the prototype demonstration, creates scalable digital signage applications that can easily network with other equipment for interoperability or upgrade to fit each customer's digital signage requirements, future-proofing technology investments.

The Open Pluggable Specification is available today at http://edc.intel.com/Applications/Digital-Signage/OPS.

(http://newsroom.intel.com/community/intel_newsroom/blog/2010/10, accessed on October 28, 2010)

## 11. Example 3 of the News Story Genre: HP Completes Acquisition of ArcSight

**HP Completes Acquisition of Arc Sight**

Company takes new approach to help customers secure applications and services from build through deployment

PALO ALTO, Calif., Oct. 22, 2010

---

HP today announced that it has completed the acquisition of ArcSight, a leading security and compliance management company, for $43.50 per share, or an enterprise value of $1.5 billion.

Integrating ArcSight's security portfolio with HP's IT operations management portfolio will allow organizations to converge millions of events across IT operations and security, providing deeper context than either platform alone. This represents a new security approach that will help businesses understand risk by making visible everything from activity to configuration state, role rights and past history.

By aligning IT assets with business objectives, chief information officers will have a common context and consolidated view of all IT risk and compliance issues for business services and applications. Customers will be able to monitor real-time events and activities, assess the risk and impact to their business operations, and quickly respond to and correct potential threats.

Further details on the ArcSight product integration into the HP Software and Solutions portfolio as HP expands into the security information event management (SIEM) market will be announced at a later date.

Upon the closing of the acquisition, all remaining outstanding shares of ArcSight common stock, other than those held by stockholders who properly perfect appraisal rights under Delaware law, were converted into the right to receive $43.50 per share in cash. As a result of the transaction, ArcSight has become a subsidiary of HP.

( http://www. hp. com/hpinfo/newsroom/press/2010/101022a. html, accessed on October 28, 2010)

## 12. Example 1 of the Homepage Genre: Nokia's Homepage

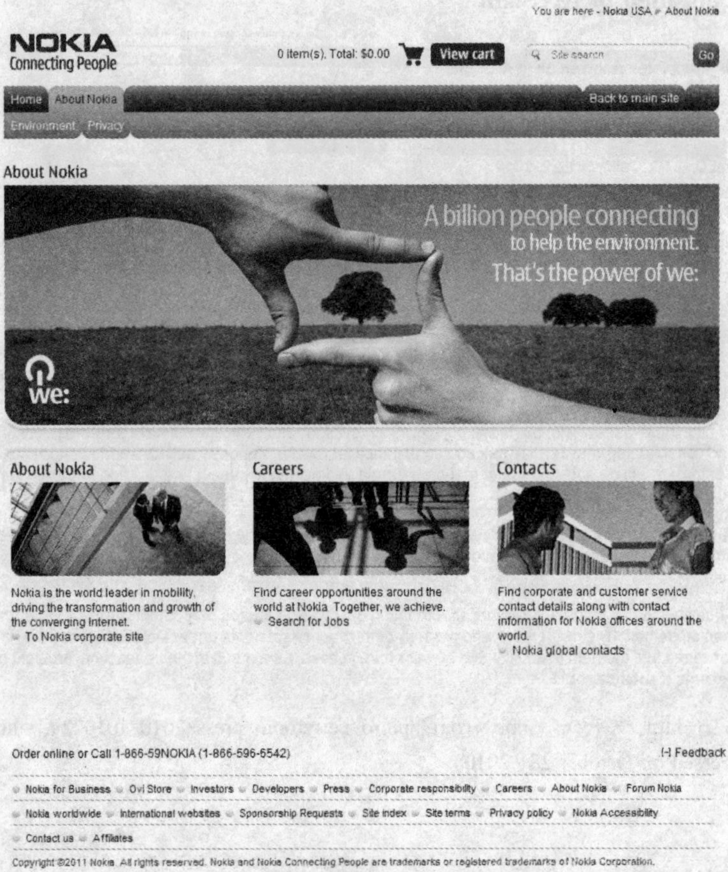


(http://www. nokia. com/, accessed on October 26, 2010

## 13. Example 2 of the Homepage Genre: Compaq's Homepage

(http://www. compaq. com/country/index. html, accessed on October 26, 2010)

## 14. Example 1 of the Content Page Genre: Acer's Social Responsibility

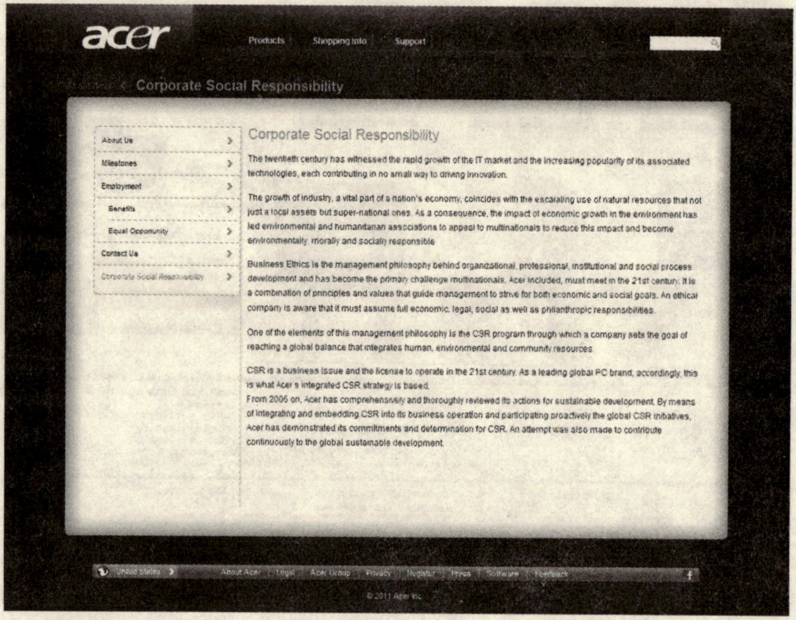


(http://us. acer. com/ac/en/US/content/csr, accessed on October 26, 2010)

**15. Example 2 of the Content Page Genre: The Partner Collaboration of Samsung**

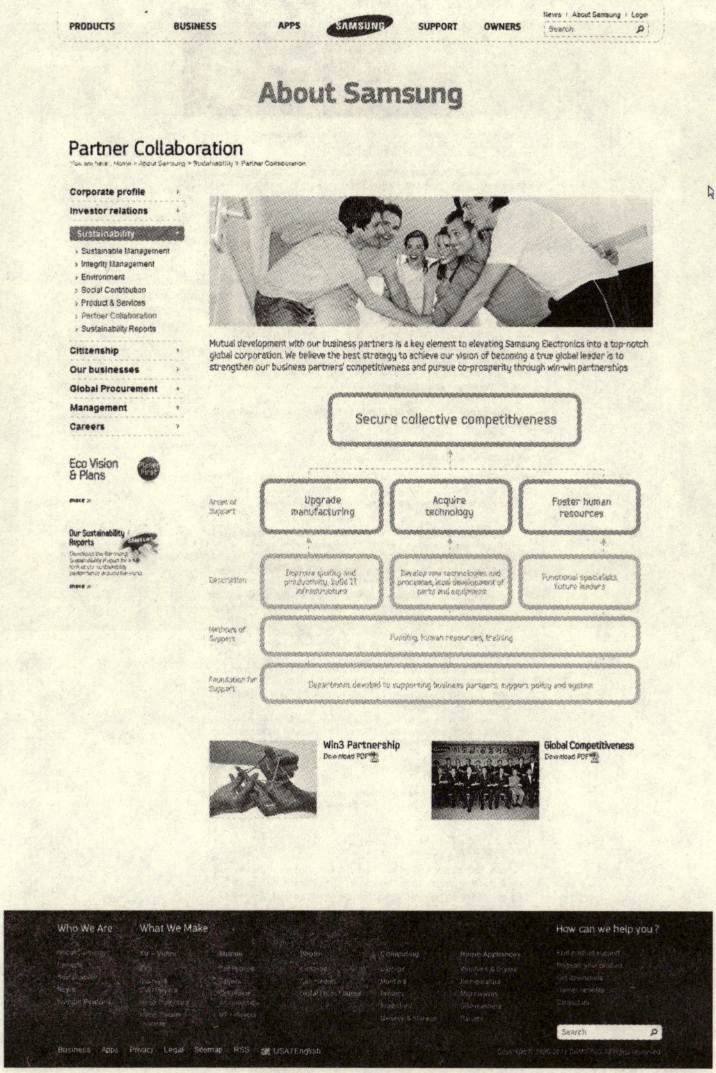


(http://www. samsung. com/us/aboutsamsung/sustainability/partnercollaboration/partnercollaboration. html, accessed on October 26, 2010)

## 16. Example 1 of Macro-Genres: Intel Corporate Information

Home > About intel > Investor Relations > Corporate Information

At Intel, we strive for transparency in how we do business and interact with our stakeholders. This section of the website is intended to provide content and links to key corporate information including a corporate profile, strategy, general corporate documents including board committee charters, and links to corporate governance & ethics, corporate responsibility, and executive biographies.

We are the world's largest semiconductor chip maker, based on revenue. We develop advanced integrated digital technology products, primarily integrated circuits, for industries such as computing and communications. Integrated circuits are semiconductor chips etched with interconnected electronic switches. We also develop platforms, which we define as integrated suites of digital computing technologies that are designed and configured to work together to provide an optimized user computing solution compared to components that are used separately. Our goal is to be the preeminent provider of semiconductor chips and platforms for the worldwide digital economy

Intel Corporation was incorporated in California in 1968 and reincorporated in Delaware in 1989.

### Company Organization

At the end of 2009, we reorganized our business to better align our major product groups around the core competencies of Intel ® architecture and our manufacturing operations. After the reorganization, we have nine operating segments:

- *PC Client Group.* Delivering a high-quality computing and Internet experience through Intel architecture-based products and platforms, primarily for notebooks, netbooks, and desktops.
- *Data Center Group.* Delivering server, storage, and workstation platforms for small, medium, and large enterprises.
- Embedded and Communications Group. Delivering Intel architecture-based products as solutions for embedded applications through long life-cycle support, software and architectural scalability, and platform integration.
- *Digital Home Group.* Delivering Intel architecture-based products for next-generation consumer electronics devices with interactive Internet content and traditional broadcast programming.
- *Ultra-Mobility Group.* Building a business in the next-generation handheld market segment with low-power Intel architecture-based products.
- *NAND Solutions Group.* Delivering advanced NAND flash memory products for use in a variety of devices.
- *Wind River Software Group.* A wholly owned subsidiary delivering device software optimization products to the embedded and handheld market segments, serving a variety of hardware architectures.
- *Software and Services Group.* Delivering software products and services, in addition to promoting Intel architecture as the platform of choice for software development.
- *Digital Health Group.* Delivering technology-enabled products that are designed to reduce healthcare costs and connect people and information to improve patient care and safety.

### Products

We design and manufacture computing and communications components, such as microprocessors, chipsets, motherboards, and wireless and wired connectivity products, as well as platforms that incorporate these components. We strive to optimize the overall performance improvements of our products by balancing increased performance capabilities with improved energy efficiency. Increased performance can include faster processing performance and other improved capabilities, such as multithreading and multitasking. Performance can also be improved through enhanced connectivity, storage, security, manageability, utilization, reliability, ease of use, and interoperability among devices. Improved energy efficiency is achieved by lowering power consumption in relation to performance capabilities, which may extend utilization time for battery-powered form factors and reduce system heat output, thereby providing power savings and reducing the total cost of ownership.

We offer products at various levels of integration, to allow our customers flexibility in creating computing and communications systems. The substantial majority of our revenue is from the sale of microprocessors and chipsets.

(http://www.intc.com/corpInfo.cfm, accessed on October 28, 2010)

# Bibliography

[1] Aristotle. 1942. *The Poetics of Aristotle* [M]. Translated by P. H. Ebbs. Chapel Hill: the University of North Carolina Press.

[2] Aristotle. 1974. *The Poetics of Aristotle* [M]. Translated by S. H. Butcher. New York: Dover.

[3] Aristotle. 1987. *Poetics with Tractatus Coislinianus, Reconstruction of Poetics II and the Fragments of the On Poets.* Translated by R. Janko. Cambridge: Hackett.

[4] Askehave, I. and A. E. Nielsen. 2005. What are the characteristics of digital genres? -genre theory from a multi-modal perspective [A]. In *Proceedings of the* 38$^{th}$ *Hawaii International Conference on System Sciences*. Washington DC: IEEE Computer Society.

[5] Askehave, I. and J. Swales. 2001. Genre identification and communicative purpose: a problem and a possible solution [J]. *Applied Linguistics*, 22/2: 195-212.

[6] Bakhtin, M. 1973. *Marxism and the Philosophy of Language* (M). L. Matejka and I. R. Titunik (trans.). New York: Seminar Press.

[7] Bakhtin, M. 1981. *The Dialogical Imagination* [C]. Translated by C. Emerson and M. Holquist. Austin: University of Texas Press.

[8] Bakhtin, M. 1985. *The Formal Method in Literary Scholarship: A Critical Introduction to Sociological Poetics* [M]. Cambridge: Harvard University Press.

[9] Bakhtin, M. 1986. The problem of speech genres [A]. In C. Emerson and M. Holquist (eds.). *Speech Genres and Other Late Essays* [C]. 60-101. Austin: University of Texas Press.

[10] Baldry, A. 2000. ESP in a visual society: Comparative and historical dimensions in multimodality and multimediality [A]. In A. Baldry (Ed.). *Multimodality and multimediality in the distance learning age: Papers in English linguistics*. 41-89. Campobasso: Palladino Editore.

[11] Baldry, A. and P. J. Thibault. 2006. *Multimodal Transcription and Text Analysis: A Multimedia Toolkit and Coursebook* [M]. London: Equinox.

[12] Barthes, R. 1966. Introduction to the structural analysis of narratives [J]. *Communications*, 8.

[13] Barthes, R. 1977. *Image, Music, Text* [M]. London: Paladin.

[14] Bateman, J. A. 2008. *Multimodality and Genre: A Foundation for the Systematic Analysis of Multimodal Documents* [M]. New York: Palgrave.

[15] Bazerman, C. 1988. *Shaping Written Knowledge: The Genre and Activity of the Experimental Article in Science* [M]. Madison: University of Wisconsin Press.

[16] Bednarek, M. 2010. Corpus linguistics and systemic functional linguistics: interpersonal meaning, identity and bonding in popular culture [A]. In Bednarek, M. and J. R. Martin (eds.). *New Discourse on Language: Functional Perspectives on Multimodality, Identity, and Affiliation* [C]. London and New York: Continuum.

[17] Benson, J. D. and W. S. Greaves. 1981. Field of discourse: theory and application [J]. *Applied Linguistics*, 2 (1): 45-55.

[18] Bernstein, B. 1990. *The Structuring of Pedagogic Discourse: Class, Codes and Control IV* [M]. London: Routledge and Kegan Paul.

[19] Bernstein, B. 1999. Vertical and horizontal discourse: an essay [J]. *British Journal of Sociology of Education*, 20 (2): 157-173.

[20] Bernstein, B. 2000. *Pedagogy, Symbolic Control and Identity: Theory, Research, Critique* [M]. London: Taylor and Francis.

[21] Berry, M. 1981a. Systemic linguistics and discourse analysis: a multilayered approach to exchange structure [A]. In Coulthard and Montgomery (eds.). *Studies in Discourse Analysis* [C]. 120-145. London: Routeledge and Kegan Paul.

[22] Berry, M. 1981b. Towards layers of exchange structure for directive exchanges [J]. *Network*, 2: 23-32.

[23] Bhatia, V. K. 1993: *Analysing genre — language use in professional settings* [M]. London: Longman.

[24] Bhatia, V. K. 1997a. Applied genre analysis and ESP [A]. In T. Miller (ed). *Functional approach to written text: classroom applications* [C]. Washington D. C.: United States Information Agency.

[25] Bhatia, V. K. 1997b. Introduction: genre analysis and world englishes [J].

*World Englishes*, 16: 313-319.

[26] Bhatia, V. K. 1999. Analysing genre: an applied linguistic perspective [C]. A keynote address given at the 12th World Congress of Applied Linguistics in Tokyo (1-6 August, 1999).

[27] Campbell, K. K. and K. H. Jamieson. 1978. Form and genre in rhetorical criticism: an introduction [A]. In Campbell and Jamieson (eds.). *Form and Genre: Shaping Rhetorical Actions* [C]. Falls Church, Va: The Speech Communication Association.

[28] Caple, H. 2006. Nuclearity in the news story - the genesis of image-nuclear news stories [A]. In C. Anyanwu (ed.). *Empowerment, Creativity and Innovation: Challenging Media and Communication in the 21st century* [C]. Adelaide: Australia and New Zealand Communication Association and the University of Adelaide.

[29] Caple, H. 2008. Intermodal relations in image-nuclear news stories [A]. In L. Unsworth (ed.). *Multimodal Semiotics: Functional Analysis in Contexts of Education* [C]. 125 - 138. London: Continuum

[30] Caple, H. 2009. *Playing with Words and Pictures: Intersemiosis in a New Genre of News Reportage* [D]. Unpublished PhD Thesis. Sydney: the University of Sydney.

[31] Cloran, C. 1989. Learning through language: the social construction of gender [A]. In R. Hasan and J. R. Martin (eds.). *Language Development: Learning Language, Learning Culture* [C]. 111 - 151. New York: Ablex.

[32] Cloran, C. 1999. Contexts for learning [A]. In F. Christie (ed.). *Pedagogy and the Shaping of Consciousness* [C]. 31 - 65. London: Cassell.

[33] Cloran, C. 2000. Socio-semantic variation: different wordings, different meanings [A]. In L. Unsworth (ed.). *Researching Language in Schools and Communities: Functional Linguistic Perspectives* [C]. 152 - 183. London: Cassell.

[34] Crowston, K. and M. Williams. 1997. Reproduced and emergent genres of communication on the World-Wide Web [A]. In *Proceedings of the 30th Annual Hawaii International Conference on System Sciences*. Vol. VI. Los Alamitos, CA: IEEE Computer Society Press.

[35] Crowston, K. and M. Williams. 1999. The effects of linking on genres of web documents [A]. In *Proceedings of the 32nd Annual Hawaii International Conference on System Sciences*. Los Alamitos, CA: IEEE Computer Society

Press.

[36] Crowston, K. and M. Williams. 2000. Reproduced and emergent genres of communication on the World-Wide Web [J]. *The Information Society*, 16 (3): 201 - 215.

[37] Devitt, A. J. 1991. Intertextuality in tax accounting: generic, referential, and functional [A]. In C. Bazerman and J. Paradis (eds.). *Textual Dynamics of the Professions*. Madison: University of Wisconsin Press. 336-357.

[38] Eggins, S. and J. R. Martin. 1997. Genres and registers of discourse [A]. In T. A. van Dijk (ed.). *Discourse as Structure and Process* [C]. London: SAGE Publications.

[39] Engeström, Y. 1987. *Learning by Expanding: An Activity-theoretical Approach to Developmental Research* [M]. Helsinki: Orienta-Konsulit.

[40] Fawcett, R. P., A. van der Mije & C. van Wissen. 1988. Towards a systemic flowchart mode for discourse structure [A]. In R. P. Fawcett, and D. Yang (eds.). *New Developments in Systemic Linguistics Volume 2: Theory and Application* [C]. London: Frances Pinter.

[41] Freedman, A. and P. Medway. 1994. *Genre and the New Rhetoric* [C]. London: Taylor & Francis.

[42] Frentz, T. S. and T. B. Farrell. 1976. Language-action: a paradigm for communication [J]. *Quarterly Journal of Speech*, 62: 333-349.

[43] Garver, E. 1994. *Aristotle's Rhetoric: An Art of Character* [M]. Chicago and London: The University of Chicago Press.

[44] Genette, G. 2000. The architext [A]. In D. Duff (ed.). *Modern Genre Theory* [C]. Essex: Pearson Education Limited.

[45] Giddens, A. 1984. *The Constitution of Society* [M]. Berkeley: University of California Press.

[46] Gregory, M. 1967. Aspects of varieties differentiation [J]. *Journal of Linguistics*, 3: 177-198.

[47] Gregory, M. 1988. Generic situation and register: a functional view of communication [A]. In J. D. Benson, M. J. Cummings & W. S. Greaves (eds.). *Linguistics in a Systemic Perspective* [C]. Amsterdam: John Benjamins.

[48] Gregory, M. and S. Carroll. 1978. *Language and Situation: Language Varieties and Their Social Contexts* [M]. London: Routledge and Kegan Paul.

[49] Halliday, M. A. K. 1961. Categories of the theory of grammar [J]. *Word*,

17 (3): 242-92.
[50] Halliday, M. A. K. 1965. Speech and situation [J]. *Bulletin of the National Association for the Teaching of English: Some Aspects of Oracy*, 2 (2): 14-17.
[51] Halliday, M. A. K. 1966a. Some notes on 'deep' grammar [J]. *Journal of Linguistics*, 2 (1): 57-67.
[52] Halliday, M. A. K. 1966b. The concept of rank: a reply [J]. *Journal of Linguistics*, 2 (1): 110-118.
[53] Halliday, M. A. K. 1973. *Explorations in the Functions of Language* [M]. London: Edward Arnold.
[54] Halliday, M. A. K. 1978. *Language as Social Semiotic: the Social Interpretation of Meaning* [M]. London: Edward Arnold.
[55] Halliday, M. A. K. 1979. Modes of meaning and modes of expression: types of grammatical structure, and their determination by different semantic functions [A]. In D. J. Allerton, E. Carney & D. Holcroft (eds.). *Function and Context in Linguistics Analysis: Essays Offered to Wiliam Haas* [C]. 57-79. Cambridge: Cambridge University Press.
[56] Halliday, M. A. K. 1992. How do you mean? [A]. In M. Davies and L. Ravelli (eds.). *Advances in Systemic Linguistics: Recent Theory and Practice* [C]. 20-35. London: Pinter.
[57] Halliday, M. A. K. 1994. An Introduction to Functional Grammar [M]. London: Edward Arnold.
[58] Halliday, M. A. K. 1999. The notion of context in language education [A]. In M. Ghadessy (ed.). *Text and Context in Functional Linguistics* [M]. Amsterdam: John Benjamins.
[59] Halliday, M. A. K. 2003. Introduction: on the "architecture" of human language [A]. In J. Webster (ed.). *On Language and Linguistics* [C]. London and New York: Continumm.
[60] Halliday, M. A. K. 2005. *Computational and Quantitative Studies* (edited by J. J. Webster) [C]. London: Continumm.
[61] Halliday, M. A. K. and C. Matthessien. 2004. *An introduction to Functional Grammar* [M]. London: Hodder Arnold.
[62] Halliday, M. A. K. and R. Hasan. 1976. *Cohesion in English* [M]. London: Longmans.
[63] Halliday, M. A. K. and R. Hasan. 1985. *Language, Text and Context: As-*

*pects of Language in a Social Semiotic Perspective* [M]. Geelong: Deakin University Press.

[64] Halliday, M. A. K., A. Mcintonsh, & P. Strevens. 1964. *The Linguistics Sciences and Language Teaching* [M]. London: Longmans.

[65] Harrel, J. and W. A. Linkugel. 1978. On rhetorical genre: an organizing perspective [J]. *Philosophy and Rhetoric*, 11: 261-281.

[66] Hasan R. 1985b. The identity of a text [A]. In M. A. K. Halliday and R. Hasan *Language, Text, and Context: Aspects of Language in a Socio-semiotic Perspective* [M]. 97-119. Geelong, Vic.: Deaking University Press.

[67] Hasan, R, 1977. Text in systemic-functional model [A]. In W. Dressler (ed.). *Current Trends in Text Linguistics* [C]. 228-246. Berlin: Walter de Gruyter.

[68] Hasan, R. 1985a. The structure of a text [A]. In M. A. K. Halliday and R. Hasan *Language, Text, and Context: Aspects of Language in a Socio-semiotic Perspective* [M]. 52-69. Geelong, Vic.: Deaking University Press.

[69] Hasan, R. 1995. The conception of context in text [A]. In P. H. Fries and M. Gregory (eds.). *Discourse in Society: Systemic Functional Perspectives* [C]. Norwood, New Jersey: Ablex.

[70] Hasan, R. 1996a. Speech, semiotic mediation and the development of higher mental functions [A]. In C. Colarn, D. Butt, & G. Williams (eds.). *Ways of Saying: Ways of Meaning: Selected Papers of Ruqaiya Hasan* [C]. London: Cassell.

[71] Hasan, R. 1996b. The nursery tale as a genre [A]. In C. Colarn, D. Butt & G. Williams (eds.). *Ways of Saying: Ways of Meaning: Selected Papers of Ruqaiya Hasan* [C]. London: Cassell.

[72] Hasan, R. 1999. Speaking with reference to context [A]. In M. Ghadessy (ed.). *Text and Context in Functional Linguistics* [C]. Amsterdam: John Benjamins.

[73] Hasan, R. and C. Cloran. 1990. A sociolinguistic interpretation of everyday talk between mothers and children [A]. In M. A. K. Halliday, J. Gibbons & H. Nicholas (eds.). *Learning, Keeping and Using Language: Selected Papers from the Eighth World Congress of Applied Linguistics* [C]. 16-21. Philadelphia: John Benjamins.

[74] Hood, S. 2008. . Summary writing in academic contexts: implicating meaning in processes of change [J]. *Linguistics and Education*, 19: 351 - 365.

[75] Hyon, S. 1996. Genre in three traditions: implications for ESL [J]. *TESOL Quarterly*, 30 (4): 693-722.

[76] Iedema, R. 1997. The history of the accident news story [J]. *Australian Review of Applied Linguistics*, 20 (2): 95-119.

[77] Iedema, R., S. Feez, and P. White. 1994. *Stage two: Media literacy. A report for the Write it Right Literacy in Industry Research Project by the Disadvantaged Schools Program* [R]. N. S. W. Department of School Education.

[78] Kennedy, G. A. 2007. *Aristotle on Rhetoric: A Theory of Civic Discourse* [M]. Oxford: University of Oxford Press.

[79] Kinneavy, J. L. 1971. *A Theory of Discourse: the Aims of Discourse* [M]. Englewood Cliffs, New Jersey: Prentice-Hall International.

[80] Knight, N. K. 2010. Wrinkling complexity: concepts of identity and affiliation [A]. In M. Bednarek and J. R. Martin (eds.). *New Discourse on Language: Functional Perspectives on Multimodality, Identity, and Affiliation* [C]. London and New York: Continuum.

[81] Knox, J. S. 2009. *Multimodal Discourse on Online Newspaper Homepages: A social-semiotic perspective* [D]. Unpublished PhD Thesis. Macquarie University.

[82] Kok, K. C. A. 2004. Multisemiotic mediation in hypertext [A]. In K. L. O'Halloran (ed.). *Multimodal Discourse Analysis: Systemic Functional Perspectives* [C]. 131-162. London and New York: Continuum.

[83] Kress, G and T. van Leeuwen. 1996/2006. *Reading Images: The Grammar of Visual Design* [M]. London: Routledge.

[84] Kress, G. and T. van Leeuwen. 2000. Color as a semiotic mode: notes for a grammar of colour [J]. *Visual Communication*, 1 (3): 343 - 368.

[85] Kress, G. and T. van Leeuwen. 2001. *Multimodal Dscourse: the Modes and Media of Contemporary Communication* [M]. London: Arnold.

[86] Kress, G. R. 1976. *Halliday: System and Function in Language* [C]. Oxford: Oxford University Press.

[87] Lemke, J. L. 1984. *Semiotics and Education* [R]. Toronto: Toronto Semiotic Circle.

[88] Lemke, J. L. 1987. The topology of genre: text structures and text types. Manuscript. University of Sydney.

[89] Lemke, J. L. 1995. *Textual Politics: discourse and social dynamics* [M].

London and Bristol, PA: Taylor and Francis.

[90] Leontjev, A. N. 1977. Activity and consciousness [A]. In P. N. Fedoseyev et al. (eds.). *Philosophy in the USSR: Problems of Dialectical Materialism* [C]. Moscow: Progress Publishers.

[91] Leontjev, A. N. 1978. *Activity, Consciousness and Personality* [M]. Englewood Cliffs, N. J.: Prentice-Hall.

[92] Leontjev, A. N. 1979. On vygotsky's creative development (Preface to Volume 3 of *The Collected Works of L. S. Vygotsky* in English). Berlin: Springer.

[93] Leontjev, A. N. 1981. *Problems of the Development of the Mind* [M]. Moscow: Progress Publishers.

[94] Martin, J. R. 1984. Language, register, and genre [A]. In F. Christie (ed.). *Children Writing: Reading*. 21-29. Geelong, Vic.: Deakin University Press.

[95] Martin, J. R. 1985. Process and text: two aspects of human semiosis [A]. In J. D. Benson and W. S. Greaves (eds.). *Systemic Perspectives on Discourse: Selected Theoretical Papers from the 9th International Systemic Workshop* (*Advances in Discourse processes* 15) [C]. 248-274. Norwood, N. J.: Ablex.

[96] Martin, J. R. 1991. Intrinsic functionality: implications for contextual theory [J]. *Social Semiotics*, 1 (1): 99-162.

[97] Martin, J. R. 1992. *English Text: System and Structure* [M]. Philadelphia: John Benjamins.

[98] Martin, J. R. 1993. Genre and literacy-modelling context in educational linguistics [J]. *Annual Review of Applied Linguistics*, 13: 141-172.

[99] Martin, J. R. 1994. Macro-genres: the ecology of the page [J]. *Network*, 21: 29-52.

[100] Martin, J. R. 1995. Text and clause: fractal resonance [J]. *Text*, 15 (1): 5-42.

[101] Martin, J. R. 1996. Types of structure: deconstructing notions of constituency in clause and text [A]. In E. H. Hovy and D. R. Scott (eds.). *Computational and Conversational Discourse: Burning Issues-an Interdisciplinary Account* [C]. 39-66. Heidelberg: Springer.

[102] Martin, J. R. 1997. Analysing genre: functional parameters [A]. In F. Christie and J. R. Martin (eds.). *Genre and Institutions: Social Processes in*

*the Workplace and School* [C]. 3-39. London: Cassell.

[103] Martin, J. R. 1999a. Mentoring semogenesis: genre-based literacy pedagogy [A]. In F Christie (ed.). *Pedagogy and the Shaping of Consciousness: Linguistic and Social Processes* (*Open Linguistics Series*) [C]. 123-155. London: Cassell.

[104] Martin, J. R. 1999b. Modelling context: a crooked path of progress in contextual linguistics [A]. In M. Ghadessy (ed.). *Text and Context in Functional Linguistics* [C]. 25-61. Amsterdam: John Benjamins

[105] Martin, J. R. 2000. Factoring out exchange: types of structure [A]. In M. Coulthard, J. Cotterill & F. Rock (eds.). *Working with Dialogue* [C]. Tubingen: Niemeyer.

[106] Martin, J. R. 2001a. A context for genre: modelling social processes in functional linguistics [A]. In J. Devilliers and R. Stainton (eds.). *Communication in Linguistics: Papers in Honour of Michael Gregory* [C]. 287-328. Toronto: GREF.

[107] Martin, J. R. 2001b. Language, register and genre [A]. In A. Burns and C. Coffin (eds.). *Analysing English in a Global Context* [C]. London: Routledge.

[108] Martin, J. R. 2001c. Fair trade: negotiating meaning in multimodal texts [A]. In P. Coppock (ed.). *The Semiotics of Writing: Transdisciplinary Perspectives on the Technology of Writing* (*Semiotic and Cognitive Studies X*) [C]. 311-338. Turnhout, Belgium: Brepols.

[109] Martin, J. R. 2006. Genre, ideology, and intertextuality: a systemic functional perspective [J]. *Linguistics and the Human Sciences*, 2.2: 275-298.

[110] Martin, J. R. 2007a. Genre and field: social processes and knowledge structures in systemic functional semiotics [A]. In L. Barbara and T. B. Sardinha (eds.). *Proceedings of the 33rd International Systemic Functional Congress* [C]. 1-35. São Paulo: PUCSP.

[111] Martin, J. R. 2007b. Construing knowledge: a functional perspective [A]. In F Christie and J. R. Martin (eds.). *Language, Knowledge and Pedagogy: Functional Linguistic and Sociological Perspectives*. 34-64. London: Continuum.

[112] Martin, J. R. 2008a. Innocence: realization, instantiation and individuation in a Botswanan town [A]. In A. Mahboob and N. K. Knight (eds.). *Questioning Linguistics* [C]. 32 - 76. Newcastle: Cambridge Scholars Pub-

lishing.

[113] Martin, J. R. 2008b. Tenderness: realization and instantiation in a Botswanan town [A]. In N. Norgaard (eds.). *Systemic Functional Linguistics in Use* [C]. Odense: Odense Working Papers in Language and Communication, 29: 31 - 62.

[114] Martin, J. R. 2008c. Intermodal reconciliation: mates in arms [A]. In L Unsworth (ed.). *New Literacies and the English Curriculum: Multimodal Perspectives* [C]. London: Continuum.

[115] Martin, J. R. 2009. Boomer dreaming: the texture of recolonisation in a lifestyle magazine [A]. In G. Forey and G. Thompson (eds.). *Text-type and Texture* [C]. 250 - 283. London: Equinox.

[116] Martin, J. R. 2010a. Semantic variation: modelling realization, instantiation and individuation in social semiosis [A]. In M. Bednarek. and J. R. Martin (eds.). *New Discourse on Language: Functional Perspectives on Multimodality, Identity, and Affiliation* [C]. London/New York: Continuum.

[117] Martin, J. R. 2010b. Preface to *Genres on the Web: Computational Models and Empirical Studies* [A]. In A. Mehler, S. Sharoff & M. Santini (eds.). *Genres on the Web: Computational Models and Empirical Studies* [C]. Springer.

[118] Martin, J. R. and C. Matthiessen. 1991. Systemic typology and topology [A]. In F. Christie (ed.). *Literacy in Social Processes: papers from the inaugural Australian Systemic Linguistics Conference* [C]. 345-383. Darwin: Centre for Studies in Language in Education, Northern Territory University.

[119] Martin, J. R. and D. Rose. 2003. *Working with Discourse: Meaning Beyond the Clause* [M]. London: Continuum.

[120] Martin, J. R. and D. Rose. 2007. *Working with Discourse: Meaning beyond the Clause* (2nd *edition*) [M]. London: Continuum

[121] Martin, J. R. and D. Rose. 2008. *Genre Relations: Mapping Culture* [M]. London: Equinox.

[122] Martin, J. R. and M. Stenglin. 2007. Materialising reconciliation: negotiating difference in a post-colonial exhibition [A]. In T. Royce and W. Bowcher (eds.). *New Directions in the Analysis of Multimodal Discourse* [C]. 215 - 238. Mahwah, New Jersey: Lawrence Erlbaum Associates.

[123] Martin, J. R. and P. R. R. White. 2005. *The Language of Evaluation*:

*Appraisal in English* [M]. London: Palgrave.

[124] Martinec, R. 1998. Cohesion in action [J]. *Semiotica*, 120 (1/2): 161-180.

[125] Martinec, R. 2000a. Rhythm in multimodal texts [J]. *Leonardo*, 33 (4): 289-297.

[126] Martinec, R. and T. van Leeuwen. 2008. *The Language of New Media Design* [M]. London: Routledge.

[127] Martinec. R. 2000b. Types of processes in action [J]. *Semiotica*, 130 (3/4): 243-68.

[128] Matthiessen, C. 1995. *Lexicogrammatical Cartography: English Systems* [M]. Tokyo: International Language Sciences Publishers.

[129] Matthiessen, C. 2007. The 'architecture' of language according to systemic functional theory: developments since the 1970s [A]. In R. Hasan, C. Matthiessen & J. Webster (eds.). *Continuing Discourse on Language: a functional perspective Volume* 2 [C]. 506-562. London: Equinox.

[130] Mehler, A., S. Sharo, & M. Santini. 2010. *Genres on the Web: Computational Models and Empirical Studies* [C]. Heidelberg: Springer.

[131] Miller, C. R. 1984. Genre as social action [J]. *Quarterly Journal of Speech*, Volume 70: 151-167.

[132] Miller. C. R. 1994. Rhetorical community: the cultural basis of genre [A]. In A. Freedman & P. Medway (eds.). *Genre and the New Rhetoric* [C]. London: Taylor & Francis.

[133] Morris, P. 1994. *The Bakhtin Reader: Selected Writings of Bakhtin, Mdevedev and Voloshinov* [C]. London: Edward Arnold.

[134] Muller, J. 2000. *Reclaiming Knowledge: Social Theory, Curriculum and Education Policy* [M]. London: Routledge.

[135] Nielsen, J. and M. Tahir. 2002. *Homepage Usability: 50 Websites Deconstructed* [M]. Indianapolis: New Riders.

[136] O'Toole, M. 1994. *The Language of Displayed Art* [M]. London: Leicester University Press.

[137] Painter, C. and J. R. Martin. 1986. Introduction [A]. In C Painter & J R Martin [Eds.] *Writing to mean: teaching genres across the curriculum* [C]. Applied Linguistics Association of Australia (Occasional Papers 9): 1-10.

[138] Pearce, W. B. and F. Conklin. 1979. A model of hierarchical meanings in coherent conversation and a study of indirect responses [J]. *Communication*

*Monographs*, 46: 76-87.

[139]Poynton, C. 1984. Names as vocatives: forms and functions [J]. *Nottingham Linguistic Circular*, 13: 1-34.

[140]Poynton, C. 1985. *Language and Gender: Making the Difference* [M]. Geelong, Vic.: Deakin University Press.

[141]Poynton, C. 1990a. The privileging of representation and the marginalising of the interpersonal: a metaphor (and more) for contemporary gender relations [A]. In T. Threadgold and A. Cranny-Fancis (eds.). *Feminine/Masculine and Representation* [C]. 231-255. Sydney: Allen and Unwin.

[142]Poynton, C. 1990b. *Address and the Semiotics of Social Relations: a Systemic-functional Account of Address Forms and Practices in Australian English* [D]. Unpublished PhD thesis. Department of Linguistics, University of Sydney.

[143]Riggenbach, H. 1999. *Discourse Analysis in the Language Classroom Volume* 1: *The Spoken Language* [M]. Ann Arbor: The University of Michigan Press.

[144]Schryer, C. F. 1993. Records as genre [J]. *Written Communication*, 10: 200-234.

[145]Schryer, C. F. 1994. The lab vs. the clinic: Sites of competing genres [A]. In A. Freedman and P. Medway (eds.). *Genre and the New Rhetoric* [C]. 105-124. London: Taylor and Francis.

[146]Schutz, A. and T. Luckmann. 1973. *The Structure of the Life World* [M]. Translated by R. M. Zaner and H. T. Engelhardt. Evanston, IL: Northwestern University Press.

[147]Scott, J. and G. Marshall. 2005. Teleology. *A Dictionary of Sociology* [Z]. Oxford: OUPOxford.

[148]Shepherd, M. and C. Watters. 1998. The evolution of cybergenres [A]. In *Proceedings of the* 31*st Annual Hawaii International Conference on System Science* [C], Vol. 2: 97 - 109. Los Alamitos, CA: IEEE Computer Society Press.

[149]Shepherd, M. and C. Watters. 1999. The functionality attribute of cybergenres [A]. In *Proceedings of the* 32*nd Hawaii International Conference on System Science*. Big Island, Hawaii: IEEE.

[150]Smart, G. 1992. Exploring the social dimension of a workplace genre, and the implications for teaching [J]. *Carleton Papers in Applied Language Stud-*

*ies*, 9: 33-40.

[151] Smart, G. 1993. Genre as community invention: a central bank's response to its executive's expectations as readers [A]. In R. Spilka (ed.). *Writing in the Workplace: New Research Perspectives*. 124-140. Carbondale: Southern Illinois University Press.

[152] Smith, Q. 1981. Four teleological orders of human action [J]. *Philosophical Topics*, 12 (3): 312-335.

[153] Swales, J. M. 1981. *Aspects of Article Introductions* (Aston ESP Research Report 1) [R]. Birmingham, England: University of Aston in Birmingham, Language Studies Unit.

[154] Swales, J. M. 1986. A genre-based approach to language across the curriculum [A]. In M. L. Tickoo (ed.). *Language across the Curriculum* [C]. 10-22. Singapore: Regional English Language Center.

[155] Swales, J. M. 1990. *Genre analysis: English in academic and research settings* [M]. Cambridge: Cambridge University Press.

[156] Thompson, S. 1994. Frameworks and contexts: a genre-based approach to analysing lecture introductions [J]. *English for Specific Purposes*, 13: 171-186.

[157] Thurstun, J. 2004. Teaching and learning the reading of homepages [J]. *Prospect*, 19(2).

[158] Ure, J. and J. Ellis. 1977. Register in descriptive linguistics and linguistic sociology [A]. In O. Uribe-Villas (ed.). *Issues in Sociolinguistics* [C]. 197-243. The Hague: Mouton.

[159] Van Huyssteen, W. 2003. Teleology. *Encyclopedia of Science and Religion* [Z]. New York: Macmillan Reference USA.

[160] Van Leeuwen, T. 1999. *Speech, Music, Sound* [M]. London: Macmillan.

[161] Van Leeuwen, T. 2005. *Introducing Social Semiotics: An Introductory Book* [M]. London: Routledge.

[162] Ventola, E. 1987. *The Structure of Social Interaction: A Systemic Approach to the Semiotics of Service Encounters* [M]. London: Frances Printer.

[163] Voloshinov, V. N. 1986. *Marxism and the Philosophy of Language* [M]. Translated by L. Matejka and I. R. Titunik. Massachusetts: Harvard University Press.

[164] Vygotsky, L. 1978. *Mind in Society* [M]. Cambridge, MA: Harvard Uni-

versity Press.

[165] Vygotsky, L. 1997a. Consciousness as a problem for the psychology of behavior [A]. In R. W. Rieber and J. Wollock (eds.). *The collected works of L. S. Vygotsky: Vol. 3. Problems of the theory and history of psychology.* 63 - 80. New York: Plenum Press.

[166] Vygotsky, L. 1997b. The problem of consciousness [A]. In R. W. Rieber and J. Wollock (eds.). *The collected works of L. S. Vygotsky: Vol. 3. Problems of the theory and history of psychology.* 129 - 138. New York: Plenum Press.

[167] Warrington, J. 1963. *Aristotle's Poetics* [M]. London: J. M. Dent and Sons Ltd.

[168] Wells, G. 1999. Dialogic Inquiry: towards a sociocultural practice and theory of education [M]. Cambridge: Cambridge University Press.

[169] White, P. R. R. 1997. Death, disruption and the moral order: the narrative impulse in mass 'hard news' reporting [A]. In F. Christie and J. R. Martin (eds.). *Genres and Institutions: Social Processes in the Workplace and School* [C]. 101-133. London: Cassell.

[170] Williams, G. 2001. Literacy pedagogy prior to schooling: relations between social positioning and semantic variation [A]. In A. Morais, H. Baillie &B. Thomas (eds.). *Towards a Sociology of Pedagogy: The Contribution of Basil Bernstein to Research* [C]. 17 - 45. New York: Peter Lang.

[171] 方琰 (Fang, Y.). 1998. 浅谈语类[J]. 外国语, (1): 17-22.

[172] 方琰 (Fang, Y.). 2002. 语篇语类研究[J]. 清华大学学报(哲学社会科学版), 17 (增1): 17-21.

[173] 胡壮麟 (Hu, Z. L.), 朱永生 (Zhu, Y. S.), 张德禄 (Zhang, D. L.), 李战子 (Li, Z. Z.). 2005. 系统功能语言学概论 [M]. 北京:北京大学出版社.

[174] 胡壮麟 (Hu, Z. L.), 朱永生 (Zhu, Y. S.), 张德禄 (Zhang, D. L.). 1988. 系统功能语法概论 [M]. 长沙: 湖南教育出版社.

[175] 胡壮麟 (Hu, Z. L.). 2007. Powerpoint — 工具, 语篇, 语类, 文体 [J]. 外语教学, 28 (4): 1-5.

[176] 黄国文 (H. G. W.). 2001. 语篇分析的理论与实践 — 广告语篇研究 [M]. 上海: 上海外语教育出版社.

[177] 李美霞 (Li, M. X.). 话语类型研究 (M). 2007. 北京: 科学出版社.

[178] 杨信彰 (Yang, X. Z.). 2006. 英语的情态手段与语篇类型 [J]. 外语

与外语教学，202（1）：1-4.
[179]张德禄（Zhang，D. L.）. 2002. 语类研究概览[J]. 外国语，140（4）：13-22.
[180]张德禄（Zhang，D. L.）. 2002. 语类研究理论框架探索[J]. 外语教学与研究，(5)：339-344.
[181]张德禄（Zhang，D. L.）. 2005. 语言的功能与文体［M]. 北京：高等教育出版社.
[182]朱永生（Zhu，Y. S.），严世清（Yan，S. Q.）. 2001. 系统功能语言学多维思考［M]. 上海：上海外语教育出版社.
[183]朱永生（Zhu，Y. S.）. 语境动态研究（M）. 2005. 北京：北京大学出版社.
[184]http://us. acer. com
[185]http://welcome. hp. com/country/us/en/welcome. html#Product
[186]http://www. apple. com/
[187]http://www. cisco. com/
[188]http://www. compaq. com/country/index. html
[189]http://www. dell. com/
[190]http://www. ibm. com/us/en/
[191]http://www. intel. com/
[192]http://www. lenovo. com/lenovo/US/en/index. html
[193]http://www. linux. com/
[194]http://www. microsoft. com
[195]http://www. motorola. com/us
[196]http://www. nokia. com
[197]http://www. samsung. com/us/
[198]http://www. siemens. com/entry/cc/en/
[199]http://www. sony. com/index. php